T0295857

ROUTLEDGE LIBRARY EDITIONS:
THE ECONOMICS AND BUSINESS OF
TECHNOLOGY

Volume 47

TECHNOLOGY AND EMPLOYMENT PRACTICES IN DEVELOPING COUNTRIES

TECHNOLOGY AND EMPLOYMENT PRACTICES IN DEVELOPING COUNTRIES

HUBERT SCHMITZ

LONDON AND NEW YORK

First published in 1985 by Croom Helm

This edition first published in 2018
by Routledge
2 Park Square, Milton Park, Abingdon, Oxon OX14 4RN

and by Routledge
711 Third Avenue, New York, NY 10017

Routledge is an imprint of the Taylor & Francis Group, an informa business

British Library Cataloguing in Publication Data
A catalogue record for this book is available from the British Library

ISBN: 978-1-138-50336-6 (Set)
ISBN: 978-1-351-06690-7 (Set) (ebk)
ISBN: 978-0-8153-5680-6 (Volume 47) (hbk)
ISBN: 978-1-351-12712-7 (Volume 47) (ebk)

Publisher's Note
The publisher has gone to great lengths to ensure the quality of this reprint but
points out that some imperfections in the original copies may be apparent.

Disclaimer
The publisher has made every effort to trace copyright holders and would welcome
correspondence from those they have been unable to trace.

TECHNOLOGY AND EMPLOYMENT PRACTICES IN DEVELOPING COUNTRIES

HUBERT SCHMITZ

INSTITUTE OF DEVELOPMENT STUDIES
UNIVERSITY OF SUSSEX

CROOM HELM
London • New York • Sydney

© 1985 Hubert Schmitz
Croom Helm Ltd, Provident House, Burrell Row,
Beckenham, Kent, BR3 1AT
Croom Helm Australia, 44-50 Waterloo Road,
North Ryde, 2113, New South Wales
Reprinted 1987

British Library Cataloguing in Publication Data

Schmitz, Hubert
    Technology and employment practices in
    developing countries.
    1. Labor supply—Developing countries—
    Effect of technological innovations on
    I. Title
    331.12'5'091724   HD6331
    ISBN 0-7099-3301-0

Published in the USA by
Croom Helm
in association with Methuen, Inc.
29 West 35th Street
New York, NY 10001

Library of Congress Cataloging in Publication Data

Schmitz, Hubert.
    Technology and employment practices in developing
countries.

    Bibliography: p.
    1. Labor supply—Developing countries—Effect of
technological innovations on. 2. Labor supply—Brazil—
Effect of technological innovations on. I. Title.
HD5852.S34 1985   331.11'422   85-6640
ISBN 0-7099-3301-0

Printed by Antony Rowe Ltd, Chippenham, Wiltshire

CONTENTS

TABLES AND FIGURES

Tables

Tables

Tables

Tables

Annex Tables

Figures

For Anna

ACKNOWLEDGEMENTS

This study was carried out in collaboration with Manfred Bienefeld. I wish to thank him for the support he gave at all stages of the research. Both his general advice and detailed criticism were of great help.

Various friends and colleagues of the Institute of Development Studies and the Science Policy Research Unit at the University of Sussex and of the Institute of Industrial Economics at the University of Rio de Janeiro read the manuscript or parts of it. I thank them for their valuable comments, especially Martin Godfrey, Kate Young, Chris Colclough, Susan Joekes, Raphie Kaplinsky, Kurt Hoffman, Howie Rush, Fabio Erber, Vera Pereira, José Ricardo Tauile and Liliana Acero.

The industry studies which form the centre piece of this book are based on factory visits, interviews with owners/managers of firms and information from trade unions and machinery suppliers. I am very grateful for their generous collaboration without which the research would not have been possible.

Essential backup in some technical questions was provided by the Centro de Tecnologia da Indústria Química e Têxtil in Rio de Janeiro and by the Shirley Institute of Manchester.

Finally, I wish to acknowledge the financial support received. Most of the information was collected while I was on an assignment for the International Labour Organisation in Brazil. The costs for local travel and research assistance were borne by the Instituto de Planejamento Econômico e Social. The Serviço Nacional de Aprendizagem Industrial financed the part of the study which gives a quantitative account of technical change and labour utilisation in the textile industry. A research grant from the Overseas Development Administration (ODA/ESCOR) to the Institute of Development Studies enabled me to write up the data and produce this book. I would like to express my gratitute to all of them.

Special thanks are due to Zoë Mars for copy editing the manuscript, to Marguerite Cooke for efficient secretarial support and to Beverley Harries and Joan Thomas for typing the final version.

Of course the responsibility for everything that is said in the book is mine alone.

INTRODUCTION

The objective of this study is to analyse the extent to which and the way in which technological change determines the utilisation of labour in less developed economies. The interest in this question was triggered by observations made during factory visits and discussions with managers in the Brazilian textile industry. These revealed that the technologically most advanced firms preferred production workers without any previous experience in this industry. This policy seemed particularly puzzling in areas which have a long tradition in textile production and a surplus of labour with practical experience in this industry. At the same time both government and employers continued to refer to lack of education and skills as one of the main bottlenecks to industrialisation and the absorption of modern technology.

The research compares firms which are technologically very advanced with firms which use less sophisticated machinery and equipment, and analyses how technology shapes their demand for labour. The study is concerned with the impact of technological change on the utilisation of labour in terms of number of jobs, recruitment, training, skill requirements, labour turnover, wages and internal mobility; it also investigates the impact on the utilisation of external labour in the form of subcontracting of small producers and employment of outworkers.

The work is divided into three parts. Part 1 reviews the literature. On the question of how technological change affects the utilisation of labour only one thing seems clear: it is labour saving; the innovation generally reduces the number of workers per unit of output in the branch where it is applied. When it comes to the question of how technological change affects the type of employment, one is confronted with contradictory views.

The scenarios found in the literature range from:

a) the 'post-industrial society', in which sophisticated technology absorbs all routine activities into the machines and requires high degrees of skill,

1

commitment, and autonomy from a stable, well-paid workforce, to

b)   theses about the continuing degradation of work in the twentieth century world, in which a major concern in the devising of technological innovations is to de-skill the jobs and turn them into calculable and standardisable routines, so that labour becomes more easily replaceable and cheaper.

Of course these scenarios only represent the extremes in the employment literature. Between them are various theories which posit a segmentation of labour markets as a result of technological development or of management's attempt to achieve control over the production process.

Our main problem is that there is a wealth of studies on the advanced countries, but little which deals explicitly with technology related patterns of employment in developing countries. The problem, however, is not just one of lack of attention. The debate in the advanced countries always centres on the impact of new technologies upon an existing situation. In less developed countries, the technology is often the same, but the existing situation rarely is. This difference gives rise to new questions. It also explains why modern technology in developing countries is generally associated (at 'least implicitly) with a privileged workforce, i.e. higher skill requirements, better wages and greater stability.

In Part 2 these issues are examined empirically, starting from the assumption that the impact of technology on labour varies between different categories of labour and different industries. Four industries are investigated which are thought to represent different stages of technological development: 1. the production of chemical fibres; 2. cotton spinning and weaving; 3. clothing manufacture; and 4. the production of hammocks. These industries are examined on the basis of factory visits, interviews with owners/managers of firms, and information from their personnel departments, as well as from trade unions, machinery suppliers and secondary sources.

While the empirical focus is on four specific Brazilian industries, the implications are thought to be of interest to developing countries in general. This is why Part 3 begins by exploring possibilities of classifying technologies according to the type of labour utilisation they are likely to produce. The remainder of Part 3 draws out lessons from the case studies; these also trigger some wider thoughts which go beyond immediate conclusions. For instance, on the question of skills the study reveals that technical change has led to a reduction in necessary training time; this process has been accompanied by a concentration of technical knowledge in a small group of managerial and technical workers. Such a tendency is well known from studies carried out in advanced countries. This book suggests however that both the processes of destruction of old skills and creation of new skills are often different in developing countries. The former is different, because their industrial base is younger; as modern industry is often newly implanted in developing countries (in the course of import substitution), certain skills never existed within their labour force; hence it does not always make sense to talk about de-skilling. The latter is different, because the creation of new skills is most pronounced in those industries which develop and produce the new technologies and these are generally not located within less developed countries.

As regards the impact of technical change on wages, the study shows two directions which run contrary to each other. On the one hand the limited training required under modern technical conditions makes the worker more easily replaceable and thus exerts a downward pressure on wages in some industries. On the other hand, in certain kinds of modern industry, the employers' main concern is a stable and reliable workforce. Costs of interruption, particularly in continuous process production, are high and workers' incorrect or negligent work can cause severe damage. High wages and internal promotion schemes are used here to ensure stability and dependable work performance. Thus, wages and employment conditions come to be determined primarily by factors endogenous to the firm and less by labour market conditions. Since technologies which induce this 'reliability wage' are probably becoming more dominant, the book draws attention to some potentially wide-ranging theoretical and political implications.

The concern of employers with control over the labour process surfaces in a number of circumstances as a decisive factor in explaining their policies towards labour. However, it is suggested that the control aspect of technology has in developing countries three dimensions which make it different from that in the advanced countries: 1. technology is generally imported; 2. the labour surplus is greater; and 3. trade union power and labour resistance at shop-floor level is weaker.

These are some of the themes elaborated in the book. Amongst the other questions included are: what impact can micro-electronics be expected to have on labour utilisation in developing countries, in what kind of labour processes is the employment of outworkers likely to continue, and what kind of policy implications can be derived in the areas of employment, training, wages and industrial project evaluation?

Finally it should be stressed that the concentration on technology in this study does not express an a priori view of technological determinism, in the sense that the blind operation of technological forces determines the utilisation of labour. The main concern of the research has been to understand how technology intervenes in employers' policies of recruitment, training, wages, turnover and promotion of internal workers, and in their policies towards the utilisation of an external labour force. An attempt has been made to isolate the specific influence of technology on labour use, without however excluding from the analysis the product markets, the labour supply, labour legislation and the general political conditions. We have avoided, hopefully, the danger of transforming the opportunities of technology into the imperatives of technology.

Part One

TECHNOLOGICAL CHANGE AND LABOUR UTILISATION IN
MANUFACTURING INDUSTRY: A REVIEW OF THE LITERATURE

Chapter 1

THE LABOUR PROCESS IN THE HISTORY OF ECONOMIC THOUGHT

The objective in this first part of the study is to review the
main propositions put forward in the literature on how
technology shapes the demand for labour. This is done in two
stages: first we examine how the subject has been treated in
the history of economic thought (this chapter); we then assess
the views which have been expressed specifically in relation to
developing countries (chapter 2). Throughout, the emphasis is
on the impact which technological change has on skill
requirements and on wages.

CLASSICAL POLITICAL ECONOMY

The labour process as the combination of the material
instruments of production and the social organisation
of labour is a classical theme for economists. To those who
venture into the 'real world' to run industrial enterprises it is a
daily concern. This has probably never been clearer than at
present. The current crisis with its intensified competition shows
relentlessly that lasting success in industry depends on rapid
technical change and an efficient organisation of labour.1/
    Those economists who remain in academia are inescapably
reminded by Adam Smith in the first chapter of his great work
that the wealth of nations is based on advances in the labour
process. The progress begins with the division of labour, the
main advantages of which were first spelt out by Smith (1776)
as follows:

    This great increase of the quantity of work which, in
    consequence of the division of labour, the same number of
    people are capable of performing, is owing to three
    different circumstances: first to the increase of
    dexterity in every particular workman; secondly, to

the saving of the time which is commonly lost in passing from one species of work to another; and lastly, to the invention of a great number of machines which facilitate and abridge labour, and enable one man to do the work of many. (p. 112)

Smith occupied himself primarily with the advances made in labour productivity. It was Charles Babbage in his work On the Economy of Machinery and Manufacture (1832) who expounded the advantages which employers gained in the utilisation of labour, particularly in the training and remuneration of workers:

Of the time required for learning. It will readily be admitted that the portion of time occupied in the acquisition of any art will depend on the difficulty of its execution; and that the greater the number of distinct processes, the longer will be the time which the apprentice must employ in acquiring it. Five or seven years have been adopted, in a great many trades, as the time considered requisite for a lad to acquire a sufficient knowledge of his art, and to repay by his labour, during the latter portion of his time, the expense incurred by his master at its commencement. If, however, instead of learning all the different processes...his attention be confined to ' one operation, a very small portion of his time will be consumed unprofitably at the commencement, and the whole of the rest of it will be beneficial to his master. (p.132)

Apart from shortening the time of training, the division of labour enables the employer to hire cheaper workers. Babbage pinpointed

that the master manufacturer, by dividing the work to be executed into different processes, each requiring different degrees of skill and force, can purchase exactly that precise quantity of both which is necessary for each process: whereas, if the whole work were executed by one workman, that person must possess sufficient skill to perform the most difficult, and sufficient strength to execute the most laborious, of the operations into which the art is divided. (pp. 137-8)

This is what later writers, for example Marshall and Braverman, called the Babbage principle: labour power capable of performing a certain process may be bought more cheaply as dissociated elements than as capacity integrated in a single worker.

Andrew Ure saw clearly that the division of labour was only the beginning. In his Philosophy of Manufactures (1835) he hails the breakthrough which the application of machinery brings to the politics of production. By decomposing a process into its constituents, and embodying each part in an automatic machine, a person of common care and capacity may be entrusted with any of the said elementary parts after a short probation, and may be transferred from one to another, on any emergency, at the discretion of the master. Such translations are utterly at variance with the old practice of the division of labour, which fixed one man to shaping the head of a pin, and another to sharpening its point...(p.22)

Ure was particularly fascinated by the potential of machinery 'in training human beings to renounce their desultory habits of work and to identify themselves with the unvarying regularity of the complex automaton' (p.15). The prospect of reducing the contribution of labour to one of merely minding the machines made him plead for science to be brought more systematically into the factory. 'The principle of the factory system then is to substitute mechanical science for hand skill ...'(p.20). This was central to Ure not just in order to reduce the necessary training time, but also to enhance the employer's control of the work process:

By the infirmity of human nature it happens that, the more skilful the workman, the more self-willed and intractable he is apt to become...The grand object therefore of the modern manufacturer is, through the union of capital and science, to reduce the task of his work-people to the exercise of vigilance and dexterity...(pp.20-1, emphasis added)

Karl Marx (1867) could not have agreed more, except that he looked at the same question from the point of view of labour:

The implementation of labour, in the form of machinery, necessitates the substitution of natural forces for human force, and the conscious application of science, instead of rule of thumb. In manufacture, the organisation of the social labour process is purely subjective; it is a combination of detail labourers; in its machinery system, modern industry has a productive organism that is purely objective, in which the labourer becomes a mere appendage to an already existing material condition of production. (p. 364)

This relationship between technology and labour was most vividly depicted by Charles Chaplin in the film 'Modern Times'. It shows how the labour process is designed around the performance of the machine and how the worker has to perform in accordance with its needs rather than vice versa. Marx (1933) calls it the real subordination of labour to capital. This is distinguished from the merely formal subordination of labour,

9

where labour works for capital but where the labour process itself is still under the control of the worker. The clearest example of the latter is the outworker or small subcontractor. In the first volume of Capital, Marx analyses the stages of the development towards real subordination from simple cooperation (chapter 13) through manufacture (chapter 14) to machinofacture (chapter 15). The introduction of machinery is a culmination of this development because it allows capital to break the limits within which it can effect a real command over the labour process.

It is within this context of the subordination of labour to capital that Marx analyses what is of central concern to us: the relationship between technological change and labour requirements. Under machinofacture, capital can design and organise the labour process without reference to the traditional skills and craft. With the division of labour in manufacture the skill requirements are already reduced, but each worker still has some degree of control over content and intensity of work. In machinofacture, the porosity and room for judgment is further reduced. 'There the movements of the instrument of labour proceed from him, here it is the movements of the machine that he must follow' (1867, p.398) The skill implications are drawn out by Marx as follows:

> Along with the tool, the skill of the workman in handling it passes over to the machine. The capabilities of the tool are emancipated from the restraints that are inseparable from human labour-power...in the place of the hierarchy of specialised workmen that characterises manufacture, there [is], in the automatic factory, a tendency to equalise and reduce to one and the same level every kind of work that has to be done by the machine minders...

> So far as division of labour reappears in the factory, it is primarily a distribution of the workmen among the specialised machines...The essential division is into workmen who are actually employed on the machines...and into mere attendants of these workmen. Among the attendants are reckoned more or less all 'feeders' who supply the machines with the material to be worked. In addition to these two principal classes, there is a numerically unimportant class of persons, whose occupation it is to look after the whole of the machinery and repair it from time to time; such as engineers, mechanics, joiners, etc. This is a superior class of workmen, some of them scientifically educated, others brought up to a trade ...(p. 396)

In as far as machinery dispenses with skills and muscular power, it becomes a means of drawing on a wider range of workers, putting downward pressure on the levels of remuneration. This is one relationship between technological advance and wages drawn out by Marx. A second is more indirect: technical change results in the displacement of workers, constantly replenishing the reserve army of labour with the effect of holding wages down.

Without doubt Marx provides a powerful framework within which to understand technological change and the resulting utilisation of labour. This must be recognised even though the homogenisation of labour into a mass of de-skilled low-paid workers has never been as pervasive and sweeping as his analysis implies. De-skilling is a tendency which constantly reasserts itself, but it is accompanied by the creation of new skills. Technological innovations provide capital with the means of reasserting control in the workplace, but at the same time give some groups of workers increased leverage to fight for better pay and conditions of work. These are issues to which we will return later.

Even though Marx laid the foundation for an analysis of the labour process, the subject virtually disappeared from the agenda of economic theorists, both in the Marxist and neo-classical line of thought. Let us first deal with the latter. Alfred Marshall, one of its founding fathers, still displayed wide knowledge of technology and the organisation of labour, and devoted considerable attention to the labour process, as much in his Principles of Economics (1920) as elsewhere. His followers, however, increasingly abandoned the subject and indeed the modern standard text books of neo-classical economics largely ignore it.

The problem is not just one of inadequate attention, but an inherent difficulty in dealing with the labour process. To start with, technical change is awkward ground for neo-classical economics, because of its central concern with the production function, an essentially static concept.2/ The production function relates inputs used to output obtained at a given technological level, that is, technology is an exogenous variable. The very same problem extends to the neo-classical explanation of labour demand because it is an application of production function theory: the hiring and payment of workers is seen as determined by marginal productivity. Thus the two poles of our investigation, namely technical change and labour utilisation, never meet. Moreover, the political dimension of production, namely control, entirely escapes the neo-classical framework.

TAYLORISM AND MANAGEMENT STUDIES

This charge cannot be levied against another branch of 'bourgeois' economics: management studies. The scientific management movement was initiated by F. W. Taylor in his works

Shop Management (1903) and Principles of Scientific Management (1911). His main concern was not so much the development of a new technology but the elaboration of new management methods and the reorganisation of work at any technological level. He starts from a critique of conventional management; its main problem, he believes, is that most of the specific expertise about how best to perform a job and how quickly it can be done resides in the worker. In his view this is the obstacle to increasing efficiency and greater prosperity for both employer and employee. He therefore suggests that 'managers assume... the burden of gathering together all the traditional knowledge which in the past has been possessed by the workmen and then of classifying, tabulating and reducing this knowledge to rules, laws and formulae...(1911 p.36). To discover the most efficent way of working, Taylor and his followers proposed time, and later, motion studies. The aim is to plan ahead each worker's task and specify 'not only what is to be done but how it is to be done and the exact time allowed for doing it' (1911, p.39).

The principle behind Taylor's thinking is central for our discussion of skills. In simple terms, what he advocates, is the division of head and hand: it is management that thinks, the worker merely executes minutely specified tasks. 'As far as possible the workmen, as well as the gang bosses and foremen, should be entirely relieved of the work of planning ...All possible brain work should be removed from the shop and centred in the planning or laying-out department...'(1903, pp.98-9). Through a system of functional foremanship the plan would then be put into practice, that is the organisation and control of the work would be carried out by a number of specialised officers. Consequently the cost and time of training could be reduced for foremen as well as for the workmen themselves. The more a job is planned, organised and controlled in all its details from above, the less room there is for judgment and initiative and the less skill is required to carry it out. Indeed Taylor believed that the full potential of his ideas would not be realised

> until almost all of the machines in the shop are run by men who are of smaller calibre and attainments, and who are therefore cheaper than those required under the old system. The adoption of standard tools, appliances, and methods throughout the shop, the planning done in the planning room and the detailed instructions sent from this department... permit the use of comparatively cheap men even on complicated work. (1903, p.105)

Thus Taylor clearly realises that adopting his system would enable employers to pay lower wages. At the same time, running through his work is the ideological assertion that the greatly enhanced efficiency makes 'ample room for a large increase in wages for the workmen and an equally great increase in profits for the manufacturer' (1911, p.30).

Taylorist principles were taken a step further by Henry Ford, though with a new method: the moving assembly line. Probably no single other device symbolises more clearly the division of head and hand in industry. The moving conveyor resolves technologically some of the central problems in the organisation of work. It is a means of 'taking the work to the men instead of the men to the work' (Ford 1922, p.80); it provides unambiguous direction as to what operation each worker has to perform; it sets the pace at which the work is to be done. 'The net result is the reduction of the necessity for thought on the part of the worker and the reduction of his movements to a minimum' (p. 80).

There is no doubt as to the implications of assembly-line based mass production for training and skills. For the majority of workers, training only takes a few days.3/ What it does to wages is less clear. Ford's policy of paying high wages was seen as a consequence of very high labour turnover which in turn resulted from dissatisfaction with work on the assembly line. Certainly high wages helped Ford to bring down turnover, but this has not developed in the literature to a general proposition that high wages are required to deal with workers who are discontented with the nature of their work.4/

There was, however, increasing concern in the management literature that in striving for efficiency in production, all sight of the human factor was lost. Thus management studies began to draw on the work of industrial psychologists and 'human relations experts' (for example, Mayo 1933). Job satisfaction and workers' motivation became a concern of research, culminating in proposals for job rotation, job enlargement or job enrichment (for example, Walker and Guest 1952; McGregor 1960; Herzberg 1966). The objective is to make work more varied and interesting. Essentially, however, these ideas are measures which merely reorganise pre-planned and de-skilled jobs in order to increase efficiency at a given technological level.

A more recent trend in management studies emphasises that technical change itself has solved many of the problems of strenuous repetitive work. The machines themselves now perform this work so that '...in many settings of modern technology, man has ceased to be an extension of the machine and has become its supervisor instead' (Davis and Taylor 1972, p.11). Changes are seen as leading to a new era in technology and labour requirements:

> One of the forces driving the transition into the post-industrial era is the growing application of automated computer aided production systems. This development is bringing about crucial changes in the relationship between technology and the social organisation of production -

changes of such magnitude that the displacement of men and skills by computers is reduced to the status of a relatively minor effect.

The most striking characteristic of sophisticated automated technology is that it absorbs routine activities into the machines, creating a new relationship between the technology and its embedded social system; the humans in automated systems are interdependent components required to respond to stochastic, not deterministic conditions - i.e. they operate in an environment whose 'important events' are randomly occurring and unpredictable. Sophisticated skills must be maintained, though they may be called into use only very occasionally...

Still further, the new technology requires a high degree of commitment and autonomy on the part of the workers in the automated production processes. (Davis 1971a, p. 419)

In fact, the requirements of skill and commitment are thought to be of such fundamental importance that where necessary the 'technological system' should be adapted to the 'social system' in order to achieve the workers' full cooperation. Thus, a central theme of this strand of management studies, which conceptualises the factory as a socio-technical system, is that technology should not be taken as given in the design of jobs. On the basis of a number of empirical studies the joint optimisation of the technological and social system is advocated. 'Socio-technical systems analysis is felt to offer one of the best approaches to meeting the post-industrial challenge' (Davis 1971a, p.425). 'An extrapolation of the post-industrial trends suggests that the social and technological environments of organisations will hasten the widespread use of various forms of self-sufficient, autonomous work groups' (Davis 1971b, p. 171).5/

Socio-technical systems analysis is one framework in which the thesis of upgrading of industrial work in the course of technological progress has been developed. A very similar picture emerges from some strands of industrial sociology. Blauner (1964) is the most notable exponent of the view that the degradation of work is being progressively overcome.6/ His work concentrates on the relationship between technology and alienation at work, but since alienation is closely associated with loss of skill and control, his theory of the long-range trends of industrial work is of interest:

Alienation has travelled a course that could be charted on a graph by means of an inverted U. In the early period, dominated by craft industry, alienation is at its lowest level and the worker's freedom at a maximum. Freedom declines and the curve of alienation...rises sharply in the period of machine industry. The alienation curve continues upward to its highest point in the assembly-line industries of the twentieth century...But with automated industry there is a counter trend, one that we can fortunately expect to become even more important in the future. The case of the continuous process industries, particularly the chemical industry, shows that automation increases the worker's control over his work process and checks the further division of labour...the result is meaningful work in a more cohesive, integrated industrial climate. The alienation curve begins to decline from its previous height as employees in automated industries gain a new dignity from responsibility and a sense of individual function – thus the inverted U. (p. 182)

THE LABOUR PROCESS IN RECENT MARXIST THOUGHT

All this is in complete contrast to the recent Marxist literature on the labour process. It rejects the theory that modern work, as a result of new technologies and automation, requires higher levels of training and greater exercise of intelligence and mental effort. Instead it sees a continuing degradation of work in the twentieth century and increased concentration of production know-how in management. New forms of organisation of work, such as semi-autonomous work groups are not seen as a break from this tendency, but merely as a move from individual to collective control, facilitated by new computer-based information and control systems.

It is only since the seventies that the labour process has again become of central concern to Marxist analysis after a century of almost complete neglect. This is difficult to explain given the fast pace at which technology has developed since Marx.7/ The most thorough and comprehensive attempt at filling this gap has been provided by Braverman in Labour and Monopoly Capital (1974). Although widely debated and criticised even by those who share his general framework (for example, Elger 1979), his book is already a classic on the labour process and has inspired a new wave of studies (for example, Zimbalist 1979; Politics and Society 1978).

The central theme of his book is the degradation of work, resulting from the separation of conception and execution of work, which is used by capital as a means of achieving effective control. For Braverman the division of labour brought about by scientific management epitomises the separation of conception from execution. The introduction of more advanced forms of machinery brought about by harnessing science to the labour process both compounds and complements scientific management in separating conception from execution. Thus, the tendencies of the labour process under the guiding principle of managerial control are towards the de-skilling of work on the one hand and the creation of an apparatus of

15

conception on the other. The process does not stop here. Braverman proceeds to show that conception is itself a labour process and therefore subject to the same separation of head and hand. Hence along with the small number of managers and engineers required to master the science and technology there appear armies of auxiliary 'white collar' workers.

The part of Braverman's work which is of most direct interest to us is that dealing with the effects on skill requirements of advances in automation. For empirical evidence he refers to detailed studies by Bright, whose main conclusion is that 'the upgrading effect had not occurred to anywhere near the extent that is often assumed. On the contrary, there was more evidence that automation has reduced the skill requirements of the operating workforce, and occasionally of the entire factory force, including the maintenance organisation' (p. 220).

Braverman also rebuffs those who suggest that continuous flow production, as found in the chemical industry, reverses this trend:

> The chemical operator is singled out, time and again, as the outstanding beneficiary of 'automation', and the praises of this job are sung in countless variations. The work of the chemical operator is generally clean, and it has to do with 'reading instruments' and 'keeping charts'. These characteristics already endear him to all middle class observers, who readily confuse them with skill, technical knowledge etc. Yet few have stopped to think whether it is harder to learn to read a dial than to tell time. (p.224)

Hence he believes that the chemical operator is unlikely to escape low wages. Another new technology, numerically controlled machines, is viewed similarly: its operator must have the training and intelligence required to perform several rather straightforward prescribed routines, but he does not possess the technical skills of the experienced machinist. 'The intelligence corresponding to these latter skills is on the tape in numerical control' (p. 202). (Producing the tapes can in itself be turned into fragmented, de-skilled work). Braverman is careful to add that this does not mean that the pay of the machinists is immediately reduced to operator levels the moment numerical control is introduced. In unionised situations management is often forced to be content to wait until the historical process of devaluation of the worker's skill takes effect and the relative pay scale falls to its expected level.

Braverman's thesis of the progressive polarisation of skills comes out most clearly in his critique of the conventional view that technical change tends to raise the average skill required:

Since, with the development of technology and the application to it of the fundamental sciences, the labour processes of society have come to embody a greater amount of scientific knowledge, clearly the 'average' scientific, technical, and in this sense 'skill' content of these labour processes is much greater now than in the past. But this is nothing but a tautology. The question is precisely whether the scientific and 'educated' content of labour tends towards <u>averaging</u>, or, on the contrary <u>polarisation</u>. If the latter is the case, to then say that the 'average' skill has been raised is to adopt the logic of the statistician who, with one foot in the fire and the other in ice water, will tell you that 'on the average', he is perfectly comfortable. The mass of workers gain nothing from the fact that the decline in their command over the labour process is more than compensated for by the increasing command on the part of the managers and engineers. On the contrary, not only does their skill fall in an absolute sense (in that they lose craft and traditional abilities without gaining new abilities adequate to compensate the loss), but it falls even more in a relative sense. The more science is incorporated into the labour process, the less the worker understands the process; the more sophisticated an intellectual product the machine becomes, the less control and comprehension of the machine the worker has. (p. 425)

COMPLEXITY AND SEGMENTATION

Thus the scenarios emerging from this review of how technology influences skills and wages differ widely. It should be added that this review, by virtue of being short, cannot adequately reflect the wealth of material on the subject; in particular it is biased towards economic and against sociological writers. Nevertheless, it is believed that the views cited are the ones which dominate the discussion and which need to be addressed. They were formulated with the advanced industrial countries in mind and the question arises of the extent to which they 'live up to the facts'. Again, in the context of this study we cannot survey the case material on the industrialised countries.8/ One general lesson from the available empirical work should, however, be emphasised, because it is particularly pertinent for our subsequent analysis of technology related employment patterns in developing countries.

This major point which comes out of a reading of the case material is that, in attempting to assess the long run tendencies, the complexities of the real world often get lost. This complexity arises in the first instance from the uneven nature of technological progress. Even in the most advanced countries the mechanisation and automation of industrial

17

production is incomplete. Often this is because satisfactory technical solutions do not exist. But even if they do exist, their application depends on the pressure which the industry or firm is under. These pressures are basically twofold: they either arise from competition with other producers or from conflict with labour. Government policies and managerial outlook are further determinants of the diffusion of new technologies.

How then does one cope with the many different kinds of labour processes existing in reality? Clearly there is a need to group processes with similar characteristics. Indeed typologies of production processes are suggested in the literature (for example, Marx 1867; Bright 1958; Touraine 1962; Woodward 1965;) and we shall discuss their usefulness at a later stage (chapter 9).

A further complication arises from the fact that within industries, mechanisation or automation is sometimes only applicable to parts of the production process and even where applied may have differing impacts on different sections of the workforce. Hence empirical investigation requires a categorisation of the workforce which can capture these differences and is applicable across industries for purposes of comparison.

Authors such as Braverman are not unaware that the real subordination of labour is an ideal realised by capital only within certain limits and unevenly among industries. Yet at the same time his analysis points persistently towards the creation of a homogeneous mass of de-skilled low-paid workers. It seems that this is not quite what has actually happened. Partly because technology developed unevenly, partly for other reasons, a segmented labour market came into being. For the United States, for instance, it has been suggested that there are three segments with different degrees of skill requirements, wage levels and stability.9/

For developing countries one would expect such segmentation to be more pronounced, since most modern technology is imported from countries which have different labour supply conditions. In the next step of our study we will examine the literature which deals specifically with developing countries.

NOTES

1. See for example the reports in Fortune, 15 June 1981, 'Working smarter', and in Business Week, 3 August 1981, 'The speed up in automation'.
2. As remarked by Heertje in Economics and Technical Change (1977), 'As the importance of the production function increased, so the question of technical change receded into the background' (p. 94).

3. Ford reports on his own plant: 'The length of time required to become proficient in the various occupations is about as follows: 43 per cent of all the jobs require not over one day of training; 36 per cent require from one day to one week; 6 per cent require from one to two weeks; 14 per cent require from one month to one year; 1 per cent require from one to six years' (1922, p. 110).

4. Presumably because even Ford was a high wage employer for only a few years; see Beynon (1973, ch.1).

5. The collection of articles in Design of Jobs edited by Davis and Taylor (1972) provides a comprehensive account of how modern management studies approach the question of technological modernisation and labour utilisation.

6. For a more sceptical view from the realm of industrial sociology see Goldthorpe et al. (1969).

7. For a discussion of the reasons for and consequences of abandoning the labour process in Marxist studies, see the introduction to Braverman (1974); see also Harvey (1982, ch. 4).

8. Some of the most interesting case material includes Bright (1958, 1966); Forslin et al. (1981); Gerstenberger (1975); ILO (1981a); Nichols and Beynon (1977); Rothwell and Zegveld (1979); Stone (1975); Wilkinson (1983). Further studies are listed in an annotated bibliography by Whiston, Senker and Macdonald (1980). Another useful bibliography is contained in Zimbalist (1979).

9. For a theory and a review of empirical evidence of labour market segmentation, see Edwards (1979, ch. 9); see also Friedman (1977).

Chapter 2

TECHNOLOGY RELATED PATTERNS OF LABOUR UTILISATION IN
DEVELOPING COUNTRIES

The wealth of both theoretical and empirical material on the
labour process in the advanced countries contrasts with the
dearth of literature relating to developing countries. At
first sight this seems surprising. After all, there is an
extensive body of literature on both technology and labour
markets in developing countries. Indeed, over the last decade
there has been much effort to bring technology into
socio-economic analysis of developing countries, but this
effort has mainly been directed at questions of technological
choice and transfer of technology (for instance Bhalla 1975;
Stewart 1978; Vaitsos 1974). While considerable advance has
been achieved in these two relatively new areas of
investigation, the much more traditional area of technological
change and its impact on labour utilisation has been neglected.
Similarly in the literature on labour markets in developing
countries there has been an extensive debate distinguishing
between subsistence and capitalist sectors (Lewis 1954),
traditional and modern sectors (Fei and Ranis 1964), upper and
lower circuits (Santos 1975), hegemonic and marginal poles (Nun
1969; Quijano 1974), or formal and informal sectors (ILO 1972).
While these theories incorporate ideas of the impact of
technology on labour, they tend to be based on abstract
assumptions rather than studies of the labour process.

THE RELEVANCE OF CONTEXT

The problem, however, is not just one of lack of attention.
There is an underlying reason why technology related patterns
of employment have not appeared as a focus of study and have
surfaced at best in the context of other concerns. The debate

in the advanced countries is always about the impact of technological change upon an existing situation. In developing countries the technology is often the same (since it is imported from advanced countries), but the existing situation rarely is. It tends to be different in that the industrial sector is incomplete, often still in its infancy, and many entrants into the industrial labour force come from the non-industrial sector. This difference gives rise to different questions and concerns. Let us elaborate.

Many new technologies introduced in the advanced countries clearly have a de-skilling effect in the sense that the previous technology required greater skills from the worker. In the context of less developed countries with less of an industrial tradition, the skill implications are often very different. This is clearest where new lines of production are introduced which do not replace previous ones. Most import substitution falls into this category. De-skilling arising from the introduction of new technologies is not an issue here. On the contrary, if new techniques simplify the work and make certain skills of workers unnecessary, this may be considered progress in that more unskilled people are made employable; ease of skill acquisition may be a positive asset. The same with wages. A new technology in advanced countries often enables the employers to have recourse to cheaper workers i.e. workers who earn wages which are lower than those paid to workers employed on the old machinery or equipment. The same technology in less developed countries may give rise to relatively high wages if workers with the required skills (even though limited) are difficult to find.

Of course, with the growth of industry in developing countries and with advances in import substitution in their economies, the above argument becomes increasingly suspect. Thus it might hold better for Tanzania or Papua New Guinea than for India or Brazil. Still, the above considerations help us to understand why modern technology in developing countries is generally associated with higher skill requirements, better wages and greater stability.

Heavy emphasis on investment in education and training, for example, was partly nurtured by the belief that technological modernisation requires greater skills. Indeed, the majority of developing countries have devoted a rising proportion of their GNP to the education sector over the last two decades. To the extent that investment went into primary schooling, this seems to have paid off. There is now ample evidence that primary schooling makes people more productive at work (Colclough 1982). In relation to secondary and higher education, there are doubts. Economic and social returns to investment in this form of education are lower than for primary schooling (Colclough 1982). Further doubts come from studies which show that secondary and higher education often bear little relationship to job functions. Nevertheless, employers' demands for formal qualifications are escalating. Faced with an over-supply of labour, they use educational certificates as a way of screening or sieving the job applicants, giving preference to those with higher educational credentials (Dore 1976; Oxenham 1980).

In assessing the divergence between what is taught and what is required at work, most attention has been given to the quality of education, in particular the curricula and examination systems. They have been found to be geared too much to academic achievement and passing examinations. However, the other side of the equation, namely the job functions, has remained largely unexplored. At least as far as industrial work is concerned, there has been little detailed study of what skills are actually required and how they are likely to change with technological modernisation. Studies which do examine such questions are generally limited to the manpower needs at the managerial and technical level, leaving out the bulk of the industrial work force engaged on the shop floor.1/

Thus there is little in the literature on education in developing countries2/ which is of direct concern to the pursuit of this study, save one argument: that the schooling system is important in the formation of industrial workers by providing non-cognitive or social skills (Bowles 1978). Behaviour patterns (discipline etc.) are taught at school which are desirable at the place of work. This moulding effect is thought to be particularly important for workers who do not come from an urban industrial background:

> [Schooling] can be a means of training those coming from an agricultural milieu, characterised by the reproduction of parental roles within production, into the new set of social attitudes required from a wage worker: time consciousness, adjustment to supervision, routine, fragmented tasks etc. Further formal technical training can reinforce this transmission. (Acero 1980, p.380)

These social skills acquired at school are thought to be directly functional to the world of work, particularly in the modern industrial sector.

As already indicated, there is little explicit treatment of technology related patterns of employment in the literature on industrialisation and labour markets. What we do find is the implicit view that the modern sector labour force is privileged in terms of skills, wages and stability. Take for example the formal-informal sector debate. This debate arose from the recognition in the early seventies that despite high rates of growth the modern or formal sector was unable to employ the available labour force productively. A considerable part of the urban population made its living in the informal sector about which very little was known, except that it was characterised - amongst other features - by small-scale, simple technology, ease of entry, severe competition and low earnings. Unskilled migrants were thought to have their best chance of work in the informal sector. Conversely, the formal sector was characterised by large enterprises, foreign ownership, sophisticated technology, high wage rates, low labour turnover and formally acquired skills (ILO 1972; Nigam and Singer 1974; Sethuraman 1976).3/

A similar scenario emerges from the Latin American dependency literature. Nun (1969) and Quijano (1974) are the authors of this school who have most explicitly dealt with the implications of dependent industrialisation for labour markets. In their view the growth of a hegemonic industrial sector leads to the marginalisation of a large part of the labour force, because this sector is grafted onto, but not integrated with, the Latin American production matrix. Employment in the hegemonic sector itself does not provide an outlet, because the advanced technologies employed only require a small, stable, sophisticated workforce which is paid high wages. Thus, the manpower available in the market is marginalised and 'no longer constitutes a "reserve" for those hegemonic levels of industrial production but an excluded labour force, which, as changes in the technical composition of capital progress, loses in a permanent and not a transitory way the possibility of being absorbed into those hegemonic levels of production' (Quijano 1974, p.418). This theory has been widely debated in Latin America, but the assumptions about the technology and labour employed in the hegemonic sector have not been subjected to much empirical investigation.

What would one expect from such an investigation? Clearly the main questions are what technologies are actually used in the formal or hegemonic sector, and how the employment practices in the technologically advanced firms differ from those which are less advanced. One might even have to disaggregate within firms in order to distinguish between core processes and ancillary operations. This type of study, however, which analyses employment according to technological level, is hard to find. What we do have are proxies.

For example, there is a body of literature which compares the labour practices of multinational and local firms. It is generally recognised that the subsidiaries of multinationals use more capital-intensive techniques than those employed by local manufacturing firms (Meller and Mizola 1982).4/ Workers employed by international firms seem to be better off. An ILO study in 1976 concluded that:

> The average level of earnings of employees in multinational enterprises far exceeds those of their counterparts in all national firms...To a large measure these differences in wages and salaries are related to the exceptional economic characteristics of multinationals in

23

these countries. They typically have much larger plant sizes, higher ratios of capital to labour, higher labour productivity...In the more detailed comparisons, generally restricted to the large national employers in developing countries, the differences in pay between the two types of firms were found to be much less pronounced than indicated by the global averages...However, in almost all the cases the multinationals had pay levels at least in line with those of the better paying national employers, and some multinationals...appeared to have pay levels substantially above even the better paying national employers. (pp.49-50)

Since 'multinationality' is associated with high capital intensity, can we conclude that the workforce in technologically advanced firms tends to be employed on privileged terms? This would be a hazardous step to take, since the explanation for the higher wages could also be sought in two other factors. The first is locus of ownership; multinational enterprises may prefer to pay high wages to avoid the hostility of unions or governments, or they may feel the need to maintain some semblance of parity with wages paid to expatriate staff. The second factor is to do with market structures. Multinationals often operate in protected internal markets or cartellised international markets. This may allow them to absorb higher wages easily.

As regards the skill requirements and training practices of multinational firms, a more recent ILO study (1981b) concludes that:

a major emphasis in practically all of the enterprises surveyed (in terms of training resources used) is on training programmes for higher and medium-level managerial staff and for technical 'cadres' considered to be the key personnel for the optimal functioning of the enterprise. The training for manual workers (especially un- and semi-skilled) is usually less developed, although in terms of numbers it represents the bulk of multinational enterprise training efforts.

Most of this training for these production workers seems to be geared towards complementing existing skills as required for the immediate performance of a specific production-line function in the enterprise ensuring a short-run return on the training investment. Such training is often brief and mainly on the job. It is usually more specific than in local enterprises and sometimes of limited use in the wider national labour market...The training of skilled workers, which is normally provided only for a small portion of the labour force, appears to be generally of high calibre and also of considerable value in the national labour market. (p. 126)

These findings throw some doubt on the earlier mentioned ideas that firms with advanced technology have skill requirements which are difficult to meet with local workers. While such firms have problems at the managerial and technical levels, for the bulk of the workforce the required skills can be taught in a very short time. Unfortunately the available studies deal with either questions of skill requirements and training, or with wages and working conditions, but rarely bring the different aspects of labour utilisation together. Thus it is difficult to obtain a comprehensive picture of the pattern of labour utilisation associated with multinational/advanced technology firms.

The view that the workforce employed by modern industry is in any way privileged, is most severely challenged by those studies which focus on export manufacturing in developing countries. Massive increases in industrial production for exports resulted to some extent from the shifting of production from the centre to the periphery, a move which was facilitated by the installation of export processing zones. The employment thus created proved to be unstable, training received was very limited, and wages were low (Fröbel et al. 1977; NACLA 1975; Elson and Pearson 1981):

> The employment structure in free production zones and world market factories is extremely unbalanced. Given a virtually unlimited supply of unemployed labour, world market factories at the free production zones, or other sites, select one specific type of worker, chiefly women from the younger age groups. The criteria used for the selection of workers are unambiguous: the labour which is employed is that which demands the least remuneration, provides the maximum amount of energy (i.e. fresh labour which can be expected to work at a high intensity) and which is predominantly unskilled or semi-skilled. (Fröbel et al., p. 37)

INFERENCES FROM THE EVIDENCE

The problem is how to interpret these experiences in our pursuit of technology related employment patterns. Certainly there is not much of an upgrading of the local labour force occurring in this production for the world market. But can we conclude from this that modern technology in the periphery has a degrading effect on labour (low skill content, low wages etc.)? Not really. It has to be recognised that the technology employed in export manufacturing is not always very

advanced.   Export   processing   typically   occurs   in   those
processes   where   automation   proves   difficult,   for   example,   in
the   production   of   clothes   and   shoes,   or   in   the   labour   intensive
parts   of   electronics   and   photographic   equipment.5/   Then   there
is   the   factor   of   competition   and   its   impact   on   labour.   The
competitive   pressure   in   production   for   exports   is   much   more
severe   than   in   import   substituting   industries,   and   this
probably   goes   some   way   towards   explaining   the   harsh   employment
conditions in export industries.

       This   latter   point   raises   a   more   general   question.
Technology   is   a   major   factor   in   explaining   the   utilisation   of
labour,   but   of   course   there   is   no   mechanical   relationship
between   the   two.   Employment   practices   are   also   influenced   by
competition,   size   of   firm,   labour   legislation,   trade   unions
etc.   Thus   it   is   only   ever   possible   to   assess   the   relative
importance   of   technology.   The   difficulty   in   achieving   this   is
clearly   evidenced   in   one   of   the   few   studies   which   focus   on
technology   and   employment   practices   in   developing   countries.   A
comparison   of   ten   cotton   spinning   plants   in   five   Asian   countries
showed   on   the   one   hand   common   features   in   training   schemes;   'on
the   other   hand,   in   spite   of   technological   similarities   at   the
factory   level,   considerable   differences   in   the   internal   wage
and   allocative   structure   were   found'   between   the   various
countries   (Nihei   et   al.   1979,   p.134).   The   authors   were   finally
driven   to   the   conclusion   that   these   differences   'are   a   function
of   the   general   level   of   industrial   development   of   a   given
society   rather   than   the   direct   result   of   the   impact   of
technology' (p. 134).

       This   idea   is   also   at   the   centre   of   Ron   Dore's   'late
development   effect'.   He   suggests   that   the   fact   that   in   certain
countries   industrialisation   started   late   accounts   for
similarities   in   employment   relations   amongst   them,   and   major
differences   from   the   early   industrialisers.   Empirical
investigation   of   his   hypotheses   in   various   countries   did   indeed
reveal   some   recurring   features,   but   often   for   differing   reasons
(Dore   1974,   1975;   Mackintosh   1975a,   1975b;   Sanchez   Padron
1975).

       This   is   not   surprising.   Trying   to   identify   and   explain
patterns   of   employment   across   countries   is   a   complex   task   which
demands   research   in   a   contentious   field,   where   technological,
economic,   political   and   probably   even   cultural   factors
intervene.   The   best   one   can   hope   to   do   is   to   push   back   the
frontiers   of   uncertainty   a   little   and   provide   the   rationale   for
what   one   observes.   In   this   study   we   have   chosen   to   focus   on
technology   and   to   push   back   the   frontiers   a   little   from   this
end.   More   precisely,   we   want   to   explore   to   what   extent   and   in
which   way   technology   determines   the   utilisation   of   labour.   To
simplify   our   task,   the   investigation   is   limited   to   one   country,
namely   Brazil,   which   has   however   considerable   internal
differences   in   terms   of   industrialisation   and   labour   markets.
In   essence,   the   study   consists   of   comparisons   of   firms   which

are at different stages of technological development and are located in different regions of the country. The case material is presented in Part 2, which begins with a methodological section. In Part 3 the lessons which can be drawn from these case studies are discussed; it also draws on some results of other micro-economic studies which could not be conveniently reviewed in this short survey of the main strands of the literature.

A SIDE ISSUE : TECHNOLOGY AND OUTWORK

However, before we delve into the case material, a further dimension of labour utilisation should be discussed: that is, the utilisation of external labour in the form of the subcontracting of small firms and the employment of outworkers. This is an alternative or complementary way of organising a firm's labour process. The question we wish to pursue – as a side issue of the project – is how this form of labour utilisation develops under different technological conditions.

Marx (1867, 1886) and Dobb (1946) analysed the role of the putting out system in the industrialisation of Britain and Western Europe and saw it as very much a transitory form which was soon to make room for the direct subordination of labour in capitalist production; technological progress above all was to put an end to decentralised production and employment. This view can also be found in Lenin's writings (1898, 1899). He examined the question in great detail because in his country outworkers constituted a large part of the industrial labour force:

> It would not be amiss to make a detailed study of its actual organisation, a study of the conditions which make it preferable for manufacturers to give out work to be done in the home. The manufacturers undoubtedly find it more profitable, and we shall understand why if we bear in mind the low earnings of the handicraft men in general... By giving out material to be worked up at home, the employers pay lower wages, economise on premises, partly on implements, and on supervision...get workers who are more scattered, disunited, and less capable of self defence, and also unpaid task masters for these workers ...in the shape of those handicraftsmen they employ and who, in their turn, employ wage-workers...these wage-workers receive the lowest wages of all. And this is not surprising, for they are subjected to double exploitation: exploitation by their own employer who squeezes his 'own little profit' out of the workers, and exploitation by the manufacturer who gives out material to the small masters. We know that these small middlemen, who are well familiar with local conditions and with the

> personal characteristics of the workers, are particularly
> prolific in inventing different forms of extortion. (1898,
> p. 428)

Lenin emphasises that these relations of production and
employment escape official surveys and that the widespread
existence of small manufacturers must not be mistaken for the
existence of a promising small-scale industry. Indeed he
launches a vigorous attack on those 'petty bourgeois theorists'
who devise policies for the support of small-scale producers.
In his view such measures would preserve conditions of work and
remuneration far worse than those of the workers directly
employed by capitalist firms, and would retard the development
of industry and fully fledged capitalism. 'The Narodniks
contrive to cling to their intention of retarding contemporary
economic development, of preventing the progress of
capitalism, and of supporting small production, which is being
bled white in the struggle against large-scale production'
(Lenin 1898, p. 448).

Historically it is true that large-scale production with
the direct employment of labour has progressed by taking over
branches which were formerly characterised by the putting out
system.6/ But this process has been very uneven, as pointed
out by Schmukler (1977) in a study which stresses the
heterogeneity of forms of production found in Argentinian
industry. She concludes that in some branches the
subcontracting of small firms and employment of outworkers 'do
not constitute transitional forms towards more mature
capitalist relations of production nor do they become an
obstacle to the development of capitalism in the branch'
(p.16). One should add that in the wake of technological
development, conditions for small-scale production and for
subcontracting are continuously recreated. The latest example
is the introduction of micro-electronics in many branches of
manufacturing, as a consequence of which the optimal scale of
output may be lowered significantly (Kaplinsky 1980); it is
conceivable that this may lead to decentralisation of
production under subcontracting or outwork arrangements.

The view that this utilisation of external labour becomes
anachronistic is most clearly belied by the Japanese
experience. In Japan, industrial subcontracting has played and
is still playing an important role in the economy's rapid
industrialisation. Watanabe (1971) stresses that what is
peculiar to Japanese manufacturing is not only the great extent
of subcontracting but even more 'the efficient use of small
enterprises in a wide range of modern industries through
subcontracting' (p.52).

In relation to developing countries, very little is known
about subcontracting and outwork. There is not even a clear
picture of the extent of their existence. Tokman (1978) in a
review article on the relationships between the formal and

informal sectors, concludes that subcontracting is not very important and mostly limited to the clothing industry. Clothing production is indeed a prime example of subcontracting and outwork worldwide but the question of its significance in other industrial branches of developing countries should be left open. While it seems clear that it is shallow in comparison to Japan (Watanabe 1978), its real importance remains unknown largely because research on this question is very difficult. Small subcontractors and outworkers are often not registered and therefore do not appear in official statistics. Their true extent and functioning is even difficult to assess in informal sector surveys unless these are combined with detailed branch specific studies.7/

In the course of the following case studies, the patterns of labour utilisation are examined for industries at different technological levels. While the primary focus is on internal labour, it is proposed to include the utilisation of external labour as a secondary line of investigation. To this end we ask what type of labour processes are farmed out and how technical change affects this practice. Other factors which have a bearing on this question, such as wage differentials between workers in parent firms and subcontracted firms or fluctuations in demand, are also discussed but the focus is on technology which provides the necessary (though not sufficient) condition for the utilisation of external labour to take place.

NOTES

1. Also manpower planning in developing countries is concerned primarily with the demand for 'educated manpower', giving only limited attention to wage employment in general (Jolly 1975).

2. Some incisive reflections on the (non-)relationship between school and work can be found in Salm (1980).

3. For a critical examination of this debate, see Schmitz (1982).

4. There is some evidence that the subsidiaries of multinational firms in less developed countries do adapt their technologies to local conditions and that automation is not always carried as far as it is in their subsidiaries in the central economies (White 1978). Nevertheless their techniques are generally more advanced than those of locally owned firms.

5. In fact the present wave of automation based on the application of micro-electronics might lead to a relocation of production back to the central economies or at least slow down the further growth of exports from the peripheral to the central economies (Kaplinsky 1982).

6. For a good summary of the history of outwork, see Abreu (1980, chapter 1).

7. For a more extensive discussion of this issue, see Schmitz (1982).

Part Two

TECHNOLOGY AND LABOUR IN BRAZILIAN INDUSTRY

Chapter 3

THE APPROACH

The objective of this part of the study is to analyse the extent to which and the way in which technology determines the utilisation of labour in the manufacturing industry in Brazil.1/ We start from the assumption that the impact of technology varies between different categories of labour and different industries. Hence the investigation is carried out by using a case study approach, covering a number of industries which are thought to represent different stages of technological development.

The notion of a 'stage of technological development' implies the existence of some sort of yardstick; this will be sought in the history of industrialisation and technology. As this research is not concerned with technology as such, but the implications of technological change on the utilisation of labour, it would seem useful very briefly to recapitulate the history of how the industrial labour process developed under capitalism. The labour process is understood to be the combination of the material instruments of production (technology) and the social organisation of labour.

The historical tendency has been to:

a)   bring large numbers of workers into one organisation either in the form of the putting out system or by actually joining them under one roof, without altering the existing technology (stage 1);

b)   the next stage was to divide the tasks and develop special instruments for each operation (stage 2);

c)   this was followed by the development of machinery and the subordination of the workers to the machine; the significance of this step is that 'labour serves the machine and no longer does the machine serve labour'(stage 3);

    d)   finally the stage at which the transformation of material, the handling, and the control are automated, leading to a continuous production process in which the worker's main task is to monitor the machines (stage 4).

These four stages will be used as an initial classification of labour processes nowadays, but its adequacy will have to be examined in the course of this study, particularly in relation to less developed economies. The classification in no way implies that all industries go through all of these stages. Also, industrial labour processes in reality rarely conform entirely to any one of these stages as there are often core and ancillary operations with different labour processes.

For this work four Brazilian industries were chosen. While they are all related to the textile sector, they were selected with a view to providing a wide spectrum of different labour processes. In fact, they are thought to represent cases which approximate to the four types of labour processes discussed above, but the extent to which this is the case needs to be examined in the course of this work. The characteristics of the four types are as follows:

a) In the production of hammocks technology virtually stagnated and most of its operations are to this day done manually. Its labour utilisation is characterised by: non-registration of part of the internal workforce, subcontracting of non-registered domestic workshops, and extensive use of outworkers.

b) The clothing industry has seen a considerable increase in the efficiency of machines, but is only just beginning to be able to break the basic unit of one operator per machine. Due to the labour intensity of clothing manufacture and the limited technological advance employers resorted to the fragmentation of jobs, complemented by the application of principles of Taylorism, in particular time and motion studies. Thus productivity increases have been achieved mainly through a combination of increasing the internal division of labour and the development of specialised equipment for each operation.

c) In cotton spinning and weaving, technological change has been very rapid over the recent decades and increases in labour productivity have been among the highest in manufacturing industry as a whole. The improvement and the fast rise in the number of machines which can be attended by one person have made it an increasingly capital intensive industry. For the time being the main job on the shop floor remains that of the machine operator. Despite the rapid progress the production process is still basically discontinuous.

d) The production of synthetic fibres is fully automated. They can be produced in a continuous flow from the feeding in of the raw materials to the finished product. The production workers' main job is to monitor the machines either by means of electronic instruments or by direct observation, and make, if necessary, small adjustments, or when great irregularities occur, call on their supervisors.

Enterprises of these four industries are neither in conception nor reality homogeneous in their technological conditions or other characteristics. Thus the four case studies provide comparisons between industries and between firms within an industry.

The study is based primarily on information obtained from firms of the four selected industries. Most of the information was collected in 1978 and 1979; some supplementary information was gathered in 1980. The fieldwork covered 25 spinning and weaving mills, 25 clothing manufacturers, 16 hammock producers and only four, albeit very large, synthetic fibre plants. The selection of firms was made from stratified non-random samples. Initial stratification was by size of firm, and selection within each sub-sample was by technological level. Some of the hammock and clothing firms were clandestine and hence did not appear in any register; their inclusion in the research was made possible by access gained through informal contacts.

The production facilities of all investigated enterprises were visited in order to gain first hand knowledge of the labour processes involved. Interviews were held with their managers or owners in free conversational form, but following a previously worked out interview schedule. The interview covered aspects of the firm's autonomy, size, technological 'outfit', relationship to machinery supplier, product market, local labour market, labour legislation and its policy with regard to recruitment, training, wages, internal promotion, labour turnover, and utilisation of external labour. Aspects of internal labour utilisation were discussed separately for the following categories: production managers, maintenance workers, foremen, machine operators and auxiliary workers. Administrative personnel were excluded. Detailed quantitative information was requested from firms' personnel departments on labour force composition, turnover and wages. Complementary information was collected from trade unions, machinery suppliers and secondary sources.

The analysis of the four industries, each representing a different stage of technological development, constitutes the main body of the research. This takes the form of inter-industry and intra-industry comparisons. The comparison of enterprises within industries is richer for the case of cotton spinning and weaving and the clothing industry, as differences in these industries are much more pronounced than in the production of hammocks and synthetic fibres.

In addition the impact of technological change over time within one of the industries is examined. This is done for the cotton spinning and weaving industry covering the period 1950-1980. The investigation is three pronged, using information from an analysis based on hypothetical firms, from

35

macro sources and factory visits and interviews, each casting light on the technological development in a different way.

To trace the implications of technological change on employment over time through the study of real firms is very difficult for a number of reasons: in the first place technological innovations are often introduced piecemeal, most notably in the spinning and weaving industry; in the second place there are other factors which influence the utilisation of labour, such as changes in management, in labour legislation or product markets. In order to overcome these difficulties the research on this industry includes a study based on hypothetical factories for the years 1950, 1960, 1970 and 1980. These factories which are only 'created' for illustrative purposes are assumed to use the most modern machinery available in the respective years, but all produce the same type of cotton yarn and cloth. Thus the changes in labour productivity, efficiency of machines, capital-labour ratio, capital-output ratio, number of spindles or looms per worker, labour force composition and skill requirements can be calculated. The labour force is broken down into five categories; managerial and technical staff, foremen, machine operators, auxiliary workers and maintenance workers.

The selection and specification of machinery and the elaboration of the above indicators and manpower requirements for each of the factories are based on information from machinery suppliers, spinning and weaving mills and the technical literature. This part of the work was carried out in conjunction with a team of textile engineers from the Centro de Tecnologia da Indústria Química e Têxtil in Rio de Janeiro, on the basis of a jointly worked out research programme and methodology (IPEA/PNUD 1979).

The main purpose of this study is to lay down in quantitative terms the potential impact of technological change and to gain a clear idea of the tendency one could expect to occur in the real world. Thus the exercise can only provide 'relative information' which has to be contrasted with what actually happened in the Brazilian economy. On the basis of surveys undertaken by the UN Economic Commission for Latin America, UNIDO and the Brazilian Government, a rough picture can be built up of the diffusion of technological innovations in the country's textile industry. Data from the Industrial Census is used to calculate how total employment, labour productivity and capital intensity developed in reality in the spinning and weaving industry as a whole, over the period 1950-1975.

This is complemented by information on the utilisation of labour, which comes from the factory visits and interviews (described above). The sample of the cotton spinning and weaving firms includes firms using different vintages of technology but in most cases there is no clear match with the model factories. Still, having gained a clear idea of the technological tendencies through the analysis of the hypothetical firms, it becomes more feasible to examine the differences in the utilisation of labour in relation to technical change and to assess the relative importance of other influences.

NOTES

1. As mentioned in the Introduction, there is a danger that the focus of the study pushes us into technological determinism. We have tried to avoid this by taking into account the other factors which influence the utilisation of labour. Moreover, we are aware that the technology in itself is not an independent variable, but is shaped by the social relations of production. The case studies presented in this book do not go into this (generally under-explored) issue. However, the question of its general relevance in developing countries is explicitly raised in chapter 9.

Chapter 4

THE COTTON SPINNING AND WEAVING INDUSTRY

We begin with cotton spinning and weaving1/ which is the country's oldest and most important industry. Of the four industries covered in this work, it is the one which was studied in greatest detail. It received the fullest treatment in that changes in technology and labour were analysed on the basis of project engineering data, macro economic data, and information from factory visits and interviews. Thus, while it is not at the top (or bottom) end of our labour process classification, it serves as a reference point for the subsequent industries.

THE PRODUCTION PROCESS OF COTTON YARN AND CLOTH

Traditionally spinning and weaving was considered a labour intensive line of production. From the 1950s onwards, however, rapid technological change turned it into a highly capital intensive industry in the advanced industrial countries. With some delay it has followed the same path in less developed countries. Technically the production process is as follows:

Spinning: the mill receives the raw material in a compressed form in bales, containing a certain amount of dirt. The bales are broken up and the cotton is partially cleaned by a machine with rapidly revolving cylinders, and also often by some form of blowing operation, to remove stray particles. In the next operation, 'carding', the cotton is further opened, thinned and cleaned and the fibres are brought more in line with one another. A carding engine consists of a number of revolving cylinders covered with spikes; the fibres are brushed by the cylinder spikes until they are lying more or less in the same direction and form a thin web. The web is then cut up to form a number of separate strands, the slivers, which are slightly twisted and collected in large cans. The cans are moved to the next machine, the 'drawframe', where several slivers are put together and pulled out into one new sliver. This process tends to further straighten and align the fibres. In the next stage they are simultaneously pulled and twisted to form a 'roving' which is like a very soft thick string. The rovings are then put on a 'spinning frame'; this machine alternates the roving and twists it to form a thread, and winds the thread onto spools. Finally a winding machine transfers the thread from the spools onto a larger package, the 'cone'.

Weaving: in order to produce a cloth it is necessary to prepare the 'warp' (threads which run across the cloth) and 'weft' (those which run the length of the cloth). The warp threads are wound from the cones on to the beam, an extra large reel. This is then 'sized' by immersing it in a chemical solution which makes the threads stiffer and more able to withstand the strain of weaving. The beam is placed in the loom and the warp ends are attached so that the woven cloth is wound round another large reel. The thread required for the weft is first wound from the cone onto a spool, called 'pirn', which is placed inside the shuttle; this is propelled from side to side weaving in and out of the warp threads and thus forming the cloth. In some modern looms alternative ways of carrying the weft thread across have been applied, dispensing entirely with the shuttle.

This is a resumé of the spinning and weaving process.2/ Even though the basic principles of the process have changed little, increases in labour productivity (or possibilities for them) are among the highest in manufacturing industry. Many operations which used to be carried out by the worker are now performed by the machine, in the transformation of material and in control. The reduction of manual intervention meant that the number of machines per worker could be raised. At the same time the operating speed of equipment increased, raising the production capacity per machine. Finally, attempts have been made to automate the handling of intermediate products and link up the separate processes more closely. The piling up of intermediate products is costly; it means working capital is bound up for longer, more space is occupied, etc. A more continuous process has been a constant preoccupation in textile R & D, but any advance has been limited to the first stages in spinning. Overall the transformation of raw cotton into cloth remains a discontinuous process.

TECHNOLOGICAL CHANGE AND EMPLOYMENT 1950-80: THE ENGINEER'S ACCOUNT

Documenting the technological development and its implications for labour through a study of mills in operation presents many difficulties. Technology is rarely the only determining factor nor the only one that changes. In the real world, management, product markets, legislation and unions do not stand still to allow the researcher to isolate the impact of changing technology on labour. For this reason we have drawn on a team of engineers and asked them the following question: What would have been the up-to-date technological 'outfit' of a textile mill in 1950 which produces x amount of product y. The same question was asked in relation to 1960, 1970 and 1980. The outcome provided four comparable mills, producing the same type of yarn and cloth, but with a different set of machines; these represent the most modern and workable equipment (i.e. not in an experimental stage) available in the four reference years. The rationale of this exercise within the overall study has already been referred to in the previous methodological section. The method applied and the limits of the exercise are further detailed in the course of this section.

A similar study, even though with somewhat different objectives, was carried out in the sixties by L. Spreafico on behalf of the UN Economic Commission for Latin America (ECLA 1966). With some adaptations, the specifications of the 1950 and 1960 mills were taken from this work. For 1970 and 1980 new factories had to be 'constructed'. The information for this was collected from machinery suppliers, spinning and weaving firms, technical journals and staff members of the Centro de Tecnologia da Indústria Química e Têxtil. A detailed account of the research procedure and the technical details are contained in CETIQT (1980). Unless indicated otherwise, the data presented in this section and the corresponding tables in the Annex are quoted from this report.3/

As mentioned before, for the purpose of this investigation, the type of product is kept constant; its technical specifications are detailed in Table A1 of the Annex. In brief, it is a fabric, made of 18 count yarn with 20 threads per square cm (both warp and weft). What changes is the technological 'outfit'of the 1950, 1960, 1970 and 1980 plants; Tables A2 and A3 in the Annex describe the machinery used in the respective years; Tables A4, A5, A6 and A7 give the corresponding production plans and numbers of machines; Table A8 contains details of the cost of the machinery. Finally, Table A9 lists all the workers required to operate the mills, by department and by occupation. These detailed technical tables in the Annex provide the backbone of this study and will be of interest to the textile specialist. Here, in the main text, however, we will discuss the changes in technology and labour using summary tables (derived from those in the Annex) and categories which do not require specific knowledge of the textile industry. Technological change will be assessed first in terms of labour productivity, machine performance, capital-labour ratio and capital-output ratio. Subsequently the implications for labour are analysed in terms of numbers of workers per department and per occupational category and changing skill requirements within each category.

Since technological progress in spinning and weaving did not proceed at the same pace, the two stages will initially be dealt with separately. Table 4.1 gives the main characteristics of the spinning mills. It shows, for example, that the 1950 mill could produce 7,538 kg of yarn per day with 250 workers on three shifts and with 139 machines which cost close to US$2 million. Unfortunately we could not keep the output entirely constant for the following years because machine capacity increased. Nevertheless some trends immediately become apparent: employment is dramatically reduced, the number of machines also decreases, but investment in machinery rises.

Table 4.1: Production, Employment and Investment in Spinning 1950-80

	1950	1960	1970	1980
Output (kg/day of 23 hours)	7,538.48	8,774.96	9,605.26	10,594.09
Number of machines	139	110	82	65
Investment in machinery (US$,1980)	1,963,249	2,652,362	5,487,275	9,950,780
Number of workers on 3 shifts*	250	133	86	48

*Three managerial posts in spinning are not included.
Source: see Annex, Tables A4 to A9.

The evolution of the technological development emerges more clearly from the indicators in Table 4.2, which are derived from the basic data in Table 4.1. Comparisons are further facilitated in Table 4.3, in which the indicators are translated into index numbers. The most startling result is the sixfold increase in output per worker, which required, however, an even greater increase in investment in machinery per worker. In comparison the output per machine increased little.   Clearly R & D in textile machinery was geared primarily towards a reduction of the labour content.

All indicators in Table 4.3 show the most substantial increase for the decade of the seventies.   This is due to the introduction of the so called 'open-end. spinning' technology in the 1980 plant.   This new technology not only increased the output per worker in the spinning operation itself, but also eliminated two stages in the production process: first, by feeding the spinner directly from the drawing frame, the roving frame operation is done away with; second, by producing bigger output packages, the cone-winding is eliminated.

Developments in weaving followed broadly the same trend as those in spinning, but there were some differences.   This is brought out by Tables 4.4, 4.5 and 4.6, which correspond to those presented for spinning.

Table   4.2:   Output   per   Worker,   Output   per   Machine, Capital-output Ratio and Capital-labour Ratio in Spinning 1950-80

	1950	1960	1970	1980
Output per worker (kg/worker/hour)	3.93	8.60	14.57	28.79
Output per machine (kg/machine/hour)	2.36	3.47	5.09	7.09
Capital-output ratio (investment/kg/day in US$)	260.43	302.26	571.28	939.28
Capital-labour ratio (investment/worker in US$)	7,853.00	19,442.57	63,805.52	207,307.91

Source: see Table 4.1.   The indicators are not identical to those calculated in CETIQT (1980), but they are derived from the same basic data.

The capital-output ratio increased in both spinning and weaving at almost the same pace over the three decades. Capital intensity in weaving did not increase quite as fast as in spinning and also labour productivity moved up a little more slowly.   Output per machine developed in both processes at the same pace until 1970, but shot up faster in weaving in the 1980 plant.   This was due to the introduction of a radically new weaving technology, the shuttleless loom.   The use of these looms has three distinct advantages: a) they eliminate the winding machines; b)   they operate at higher speeds than conventional looms; c) they can weave three fabrics simultaneously (multi-phase weaving).

Table 4.3: Output per Worker, Output per Machine, Capital-output Ratio, and Capital-labour Ratio in Spinning 1950-80 (in index numbers)

	1950	1960	1970	1980
Output per worker	100	219	371	732
Output per machine	100	147	216	300
Capital-labour ratio	100	116	219	361
Capital-output ratio	100	254	812	2640

Source: Table 4.2.

Table 4.4: Production, Investment and Employment in Weaving 1950-80

	1950	1960	1970	1980
Output (m/day of 23 hours)	56,374.38	65,826.00	70,324.80	79,620.48
Number of machines	550	538	286	146
Investment in machinery (US$, 1980)	2,190,795	3,222,358	5,717,413	10,197,440
Number of workers (3 shifts)*	330	232	134	90

*Three managerial posts in weaving are not included.
Source: see Annex, Tables A4 to A9.

To sum up, both spinning and weaving experienced a massive increase in capital intensity over the three decades, making production on three shifts more necessary than ever. The higher production rates of the machines and above all the reduction in manpower made possible a sixfold increase in labour productivity in spinning and a fourfold increase in weaving. The productivity indicators emerge from the comparison of factories which were equipped throughout with machinery of the same vintage and which produced only one standardised product. While this is rare in the real world, the factories compared are not from the dream world of engineers. The machinery selected was the most modern at the time, but was also proven in real plants. The performance indicators provided by machinery manufacturers were checked against the information from mills which had bought and operated such machines. Thus the indicators given in the above

43

tables are not based on maximum operating speeds, but on a performance of labour and machines which can be achieved in practice.

Table 4.5: Output per Worker, Output per Machine, Capital-output Ratio and Capital-labour Ratio in Weaving 1950-80

	1950	1960	1970	1980
Output per worker (m/worker/hour)	22.28	37.00	68.46	115.39
Output per machine (m/machine/hour)	4.46	5.32	10.69	23.71
Capital-output ratio (investment/ m/day, in US$)	38.86	48.95	81.30	128.08
Capital-labour ratio (investment/ worker in US$)	6,638.77	13,889.47	42,667.26	113,304.88

Source: Table 4.4.

Table 4.6: Output per Worker, Output per Machine, Capital-output Ratio, and Capital-labour Ratio in Weaving 1950-80 (in index numbers)

	1950	1960	1970	1980
Output per worker	100	166	307	517
Output per machine	100	119	240	532
Capital-output ratio	100	126	209	330
Capital-labour ratio	100	209	643	1707

Source: Table 4.5.

A textile specialist might raise some doubts about how representative the selected product and machines are. Clearly there are variations within the spinning and weaving industry. For example, the spinning technology of the 1980 plant is not suitable for the production of very fine yarns; equally the latest weaving technology is more suited for weaving coarser yarns. Thus a different choice of product would have led in some stages of the production process to a different selection of machinery. However, this would not have affected the trends shown above in any fundamental way. Of course they must be understood as trends made possible by technology available to industry, and not necessarily as outcomes of technology applied across industry. These technological options were potentially available but were not universally taken up.

Despite the considerable improvements in productivity which can be observed in the comparison of the four plants, one must not assume that the most modern is the most economical, be it from a micro or macro economic point of view. Clearly the choice of technology will depend on the relative labour and capital costs in the country concerned. Indeed, the original ECLA study (1966) was primarily concerned with technological choice and shows in quantitative terms that the most modern project is not the most economical for Latin American conditions. The CETIQT study (1980) had different terms of reference, but also raises doubts about the suitability of the most recent technology for Brazil.

A number of textile firms in Brazil, both national and foreign, have however bought such technology; it is widely acknowledged that this is partly due to government incentive policy which tends to reward the use of expensive machinery rather than the employment of labour. While these questions are important for employment policy, they are not the object of this study.4/

The objective here is to document the impact which available technology has on the utilisation of labour. Later we shall extend the analysis and examine the impact of actually applied technologies. In order to investigate the utilisation of labour in detail the many different occupations will be grouped as follows:

1   Managerial and technical staff
2   Foremen and instructors
3   Machine operators
4   Auxiliary workers
5   Maintenance workers

There are some occupations which do not fall neatly into these categories, but for our purpose this simple classification can go a long way towards making the main employment trends more transparent. If there are cases when results depend on debatable categorisation of certain occupations, this will be pointed out.

The basic data for most of the following analysis are contained in Table A9 of the Annex. It presents the occupations of the entire workforce of the mills corresponding to the years 1950, 1960, 1970 and 1980; it also indicates which department they work in. Administrative personnel are excluded. A summary of the data is contained in Tables 4.7 and 4.8, which give the changes in the workforce by occupational category and by department.

Table 4.7: Labour Requirements in Spinning and Weaving by Department 1950-80

Department	1950	1960	1970	1980
Spinning	253	136	89	51
Weaving	333	235	137	93
Maintenance	26	24	30	30
Various	31	31	36	34
Total	643	426	292	208

Source: Table A9 in Annex.

Table 4.8: Labour Requirements in Spinning and Weaving by Occupational Category 1950-80

Occupational category	1950	1960	1970	1980
Managerial and technical staff	14	14	15	15
Foremen/training instructors	16	16	14	14
Machine operators	346	190	120	81
Auxiliary workers	189	145	93	51
Maintenance workers	78	61	50	47
Total	643	426	292	208

Source: Table A9 in Annex.

Since the labour figures (Tables 4.7 and 4.8) relate to mills with differing output, they were adjusted for a uniform daily production of 79,620 m (see Tables 4.9, 4.10 and 4.11). This brings the 1950, 1960 and 1970 plants up to the level of the 1980 mill. Thus one distortion in the comparison due to differences in output is eliminated. At the same time, another distortion is introduced because there is fixed and variable labour. The existence of some jobs, in particular in the managerial and maintenance field, is little affected by output changes, at least not within a certain range. For this reason, we will draw on both the adjusted and unadjusted figures, depending on which are more appropriate.

Table 4.9: Production and Labour Force in Spinning and Weaving 1950-80 (adjusted)

Year	Production (m/day)	Labour force total	Production adjusted	Labour force adjusted
1950	56,374	643	79,620	908
1960	65,826	426	79,620	515
1970	70,325	292	79,620	331
1980	79,620	208	79,620	208

Source: Tables 4.4 and 4.7

Table 4.10: Labour Requirements in Spinning and Weaving by Department 1950-80 (adjusted)

Department	1950	1960	1970	1980
Spinning	357	164	101	51
Weaving	470	284	155	93
Maintenance	37	29	34	30
Various	44	38	41	34
Total	908	515	331	208

Source: Tables 4.7 and 4.9

Table 4.10 shows the full extent of the labour force reduction by department. In spinning it amounted to 85.5 per cent and in weaving to 80.2 per cent. In order to assess the changes in maintenance labour, the breakdown by occupation is more useful than the one by department; a number of maintenance workers do not belong to the maintenance department, but are directly allocated to the three shifts in the spinning and weaving department, (compare Table A9 in Annex). Thus Table 4.11 shows a decline in maintenance workers by 57.3 per cent on the adjusted figures. This is, however, somewhat exaggerated because many maintenance posts are fixed and relatively little affected by output changes. The 39.7 per cent decline on the non-adjusted figures (Table 4.8) is probably more accurate.

Continuing the analysis by occupational category, the most significant change occurred amongst machine operators. Manual intervention on many machines was reduced over time; a number of operating jobs even disappeared and their number was not compensated by the few new jobs which were introduced (compare Table A9 in the Annex). Overall the category decreased by 76.6 per cent (unadjusted, Table 4.8); since most of this labour is variable, the adjusted indicators are more appropriate, showing a decline of 83.4 per cent (Table 4.11). The category of auxiliary workers was almost equally heavily reduced, namely by 73.0 per cent or 80.9 per cent respectively. The number of foremen and instructors did not go down as rapidly. From 1970 onwards there is only one foremen per shift in the pre-spinning, spinning, pre-weaving and weaving section, leaving little room for further reduction. This is reflected in a decline of 'only' 36.4 per cent on the adjusted scale (unadjusted 12.5 per cent).

Table 4.11: Labour Requirements in Spinning and Weaving by Occupational Category 1950-80 (adjusted)

Occupational category	1950	1960	1970	1980
Managerial and technical staff	20	17	17	15
Foremen/instructors	22	19	16	14
Machine operators	489	230	136	81
Auxiliary workers	267	175	105	51
Maintenance workers	110	74	57	47
Total	908	515	331	208

Source: Tables 4.8 and 4.9.

The number of managerial and technical posts remained virtually constant.5/ On the managerial side this is not surprising, because these posts form part of a plant's hierarchy irrespective of the technology applied on the shop floor. The technical side is rarely divorced from the managerial; specialised technical knowledge is necessary to run the production process.

Since the number of workers in each category decreased with differing intensity, there is a marked change in the composition of the workforce (see Table 4.12 and Figure 4.1). The share of shopfloor workers (machine operators and auxiliary workers) decreases from 83.2 per cent to 63.4 per cent. In contrast, the share of managerial, supervisory and technical workers goes up to 14 per cent and the share of maintenance workers rises to almost a quarter of the workforce in the most modern plant. In this sense, the modern technology can be said to require a more sophisticated workforce.

Table 4.12: Labour Force Composition in Spinning and Weaving by Occupational Category 1950-80 (in percentages)

Occupational Category	1950	1960	1970	1980
Managerial and technical staff	2.2	3.3	5.1	7.2
Foremen and instructors	2.5	3.8	4.8	6.8
Machine operators	53.8	44.6	41.1	38.9
Auxiliary workers	29.4	34.0	31.8	24.5
Maintenance workers	12.1	14.3	17.2	22.6
Total	100.0	100.0	100.0	100.0

Source: Tables 4.8 and 4.11

Figure 4.1: Labour Force Composition in Spinning and Weaving by Occupational Category 1950-1980

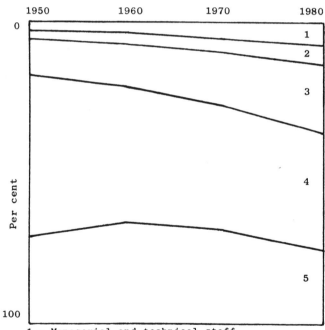

1 = Managerial and technical staff
2 = Foremen and instructors
3 = Maintenance workers
4 = Machine operators
5 = Auxiliary workers

But what about the requirements of skill and knowhow within each occupational category? They developed in different directions and will be explored further, beginning with the machine operators. The latter continue to be the most numerous category, even though they suffered the most severe losses. The job content of machine minders changed significantly over the last three decades. Mechanical and electronic devices have reduced their intervention in the production. Table 4.13 lists a number of tasks which traditionally were all performed by the operative, and shows which of these can nowadays be done by the machines themselves in the various stages of production.

Table 4.13: Automation of Tasks in Spinning and Weaving in 1980

Task \ Machine	Opener/scutcher	Card	Drawing frame	Roving frame	Ring spinning	Open-end spinning	Cone winder	Pirn winder	Warper	Sizing machine	Loom
Feeding in of material	■	■				■					
Removing product (doffing)	■					■					
Stopping machine if fed-in material is broken		■	■		■	■	■	■	■		■
Stopping machine if material breaks in transformation process		■	■		■	■	■	■	■		■
Repairing fault (piecing)					■	■					
Cleaning	■	■	■	■	■	■	■	■			

 = executed automatically by machine

In order to illustrate what operatives actually do, let us take two examples, the operator of the spinning machine and the operator of the loom. Tables 4.14 and 4.15 give the descriptions of a spinner and weaver for 1950 and 1980.

Table 4.14: Job Description of Spinner in 1950 and 1980

Spinner's tasks in 1950	Spinner's tasks in 1980
1. To patrol, constantly, each machine in the complement by turn, in order to attend to the feed, correct sliver defects, and piece broken ends	1. To patrol the complement of machines, following a predetermined schedule (route, time, etc.) and without turning back, and observing quickly the emptying (i.e. state) of the supply cans, sliver breakages, and small faults, and taking preventative action
2. To help the doffers to doff and re-start the machine	
3. To remove by hand the rings of cotton ('laps') formed on the clearer rolls	2. To change the feed cans
4. To replace faulty travellers	3. To substitute the automatic piecing or cleaning system, in the case of defects
5. To collect waste and 'fly'	
6. To take note of mechanical defects and report them to the mechanic or foreman	4. To take note of machine malfunctions and report to the mechanic or foreman
7. To clean and oil his/her machines	

Table 4.15: Job Description of Weaver in 1950 and 1980

Weaver's tasks in 1950	Weaver's tasks in 1980
1. To check the cloth fell when starting the loom so as to avoid the formation of bars	1. To supply the loom with weft cones
2. To box the shuttle correctly each time the loom is set on	2. To patrol the set of looms, following a predetermined schedule and without turning back, and observing quickly in order to locate, directly or indirectly (e.g. signal lights), broken ends, run-out ends, missing ends, drawing-in faults (mis-draws), dirt, and cone faults – taking preventive action with the loom in motion or stopped
3. To re-start the loom from the correct crank position always	
4. To be alert always in order to stop the loom to avoid end breakages or warp run-out	
5. To be alert always in order to stop the loom before the weft runs out	3. To report mechanical defects to the mechanic or foreman
6. To remove the empty pirn package every time a pirn is exhausted	

51

7. To patrol the set of looms,
   carefully observing from
   the front and rear to try
   and detect drawing-in
   faults, dirt and yarn faults
   taking preventive action with the
   loom in motion or stopped
8. To correct weaving defects
   resulting from 'banging-off'
   (unweave, re-draw, and
   re-start the loom)
9. Adjust the warp tension by
   attention to the weights and
   chains
10. To correct weaving defects with
    the aid of scissors, tweezers,
    or small combs
11. To clean the loom
12. To oil the shuttle spindle
13. To report mechanical defects
    to the mechanic or foreman

Clearly the number of _different_ tasks has been considerably reduced; many are now performed by the machines themselves, some have been allocated to other workers. A smaller variety of tasks could mean that the job is easier to learn and carry out. But this is not necessarily the case if the number of machines to be operated by one person has increased. In order to compare the difficulty of the jobs in 1950 and 1980, the tasks can be broken down into their various constituent components:

simple locomotion:	moving on foot from one place to another without carrying loads;
loaded locomotion:	moving on foot from one place to another transporting something;
simple manipulation:	carrying out an operation on a machine which does not require motor coordination;
coordinated manipulation:	carrying out an operation on a machine which necessitates motor coordination;
discriminating:	perceiving differences between two things;
problem solving:	ability to relate symptoms to possible causes and finding the best solution.

The textile engineers who provided the technical backstopping for this study analysed the spinner's and weaver's work in these terms comparing their situation in 1950 and 1980. The

results are contained in Tables 4.16 and 4.17. These tables
reveal clearly that those components which are more complicated
and hence require certain skills are greatly reduced. For both
the spinner and weaver there is considerably less 'coordinated
manipulation' and 'problem solving' to do in 1980, whereas
simple repetitive components increase, namely 'discriminating'
between two things and 'simple manipulation'. At the same time
the machine operator is much more on the move6/ because he
looks after an increasing number of machines and covers a wider
area of the factory. In terms of the job description in Tables
4.14 and 4.15, the patrolling of machines is more dominant than
working on the machines.

Table 4.16: Components of a Spinner's Work During Eight Hours
1950 and 1980

Components	1950	1980
Simple locomotion	10 km	40 km
Loaded locomotion	16 times	2 times
Simple manipulation	212 times	488 times
Coordinated manipulation	198 times	12 times
Discriminating	58 times	164 times
Problem solving	48 times	14 times

Source: CETIQT (1980).

Table 4.17: Components of a Weaver's Work During Eight Hours
1950 and 1980

Components	1950	1980
Simple locomotion	1.5 km	36 km
Loaded locomotion	10 times	4 times
Simple manipulation	362 times	586 times
Coordinated manipulation	282 times	56 times
Discriminating	72 times	212 times
Problem solving	36 times	8 times

Source: CETIQT (1980).

What does this change in the job content mean for the
training of workers, in particular for the length of training
required? The time it takes to train a worker depends on where
and how it is done. Basically there are three possibilities:
a) he could learn the skills as part of a course in a

vocational training institution; b) he could learn in the factory by working alongside practised workers and picking up the necessary skills in the process; c) he could be trained in the factory under the direction and control of an instructor on the machines he is later required to operate.

If we assume that the third method is applied, we can divide the training period into two phases: in the first phase the worker learns all the movements and actions required to operate the machines, without consideration of speed. In the second phase the actions become routinised until he is able to carry them out at a speed which amounts to average labour productivity. Table 4.18 is based on these premises. It shows how long it would take to train a machine operator in 1950 and 1980; the examples taken are again those of the spinner and the weaver. In both cases the training time has decreased by about a third. Assuming a 48 hour week (Brazilian norm), a spinner can now be trained in 6-7 weeks to be fully operative and a weaver in 11-12 weeks. As we shall see later, in the discussion of recruitment and training policies of real firms, these estimates are not just targets but implemented in practice. Moreover, the actual reduction in training time was greater than indicated in Table 4.18, because not only the machines, but also the method of training changed in practice.

Table 4.18: Length of Training of a Spinner and Weaver in 1950 and 1980 (in hours)

Training	Spinner		Weaver	
	1950	1980	1950	1980
Phase 1	120	80	200	150
Phase 2	360	240	600	400
Total	480	320	800	550

Source: CETIQT (1980).

Assessing the impact of technical change on maintenance, supervisory, managerial and technical staff proved much more difficult. This has several reasons. First, the numbers of such workers as well as their tasks are not as directly determined by technology as those of operators. Second, the skills required in such occupations are more complex; they are generally a result of various educational, training and work experiences and thus more difficult to measure (in comparison with the length of training of operators which can be quantified more easily).

Nevertheless, as regards the number of workers in the three categories (managerial and technical staff, foremen and instructors, and maintenance workers), some clear tendencies emerge from Tables 4.8, 4.11 and 4.12. In absolute terms their numbers fall over the 1950-80 period by between 30 and 50 per cent (depending on whether one uses unadjusted or adjusted figures). However, as pointed out before, this decrease is lower than that of machine operators and auxiliary workers. Hence in relative terms their importance increases; in 1950 they account for 17 per cent of the workforce rising to 37 per cent in 1980. In this sense it can be said that the new technologies require a greater number of skilled workers.

At the same time one has to ask how the requirements within these occupations have changed. Unfortunately the research on which much of the previous analysis was based (CETIQT 1980) does not cover this question, but an attempt is made to find some tentative answers by piecing together information collected from various sources.7/

As regards maintenance workers, a reduction in their numbers (in absolute terms) went hand in hand with changes in the type of skills required. An explanation has to take brief recourse to the engineering developments over the last three decades. Increased speed and productivity was partly achieved by improved design and the use of better quality materials in machine building. For instance, the use of nylon flexible couplings helped to eliminate overloading of the gears owing to misalignment and the use of nylon or laminated gears has contributed greatly to the reduction in irregularity arising from worn teeth, poorly fitted gears, loosely fitted studs and other components in the all metal gear trains in machines of 1950 and earlier vintage. Other examples are heavy antifriction bearings with long-life or sealed-for-life lubrication systems (in place of oil impregnated sintered or plain journal bearings), or variable speed drives (in place of pulleys). Such improvements resulted in greater reliability of machinery and a reduction in mechanical maintenance and repair.

The decreasing need for skilled mechanics was accompanied by an increased need for electricians, instruments servicemen and electronics servicemen (Table A10 in the Annex gives the job descriptions of these maintenance workers). In order that the processes could be better controlled, the period between 1950 and 1980 saw a considerable increase in machine instrumentation. Signal lights and audio alarms, added to machines, tell the operator where problems occur and where he needs to intervene. In many instances the signals also provide some guide to the nature of the malfunction.

Thus there has been a shift away from mechanical maintenance to electrical maintenance (also borne out by Table A9 in the Annex). In the large mills, this has been accompanied by a trend towards greater specialisation in the maintenance workforce. Air conditioning provides a good example. In a 1950 mill a maintenance workshop hand was delegated periodically to check the dust transportation fan delivering waste to the settling room. Another hand would check the water sprays - if they were fitted. Manual control was common, the units being switched on and off according to the wishes of the weaver room foreman. By 1980 improvements in the technical performance of control systems had permitted the introduction of central station systems in which the humidification and temperature could be contained within the desired limits. Now an important task for the air-conditioning mechanic is the regular patrolling of the plants to check that sprays are all functioning, water eliminators are clean, compressed air is clean (oil-free for control purposes) and dry, fan driers and speeds are in accordance with specification and refrigeration plants are functioning correctly. To help him he has an array of instruments: site glasses to record water levels, pressure gauges, monometers, schematic control boards equipped with stop/start buttons and associated on/off lights.

Does all this mean that training and skill requirements in maintenance have increased? The suppliers of new technology tend to say no. They point towards the advances made in self-diagnosis through electronic devices and towards the trend to merely replace malfunctioning parts rather than repair them. In contrast, the users of machines often express the view that maintenance has become more complex. How can one explain such divergence of opinions, especially if it occurs in relation to the same machines? Of course one would expect machinery suppliers to emphasise easy maintenance since this is an important sales asset. Conversely the users of the technology may see increased difficulties, because the new technology often requires different maintenance skills, but they forget that others fall away. These aspects are important but unlikely to be the complete explanation.

It seems that whether skill requirements in maintenance increase or not depends also on which phase in the introduction of new technology is being considered. In the initial phase they often increase because of 'teething troubles' which can occur even if the machines were installed by the specialised suppliers. Then later, once well established, the problems are fewer and maintenance work can be routinised and with this the skill requirements tend to decrease until the next round of innovations. This also means that a mill which gradually replaces old with new equipment will need a more skilled maintenance staff than one which starts from scratch with completely new technology and keeps producing without any significant alterations.8/

Generalisations on maintenance skills are further complicated because of the different degrees to which suppliers themselves maintain and repair machines. Practices vary between suppliers. A mill's ability to draw upon maintenance services from outside obviously determines in a direct way the size and skill level of the internal maintenance crew. The introduction of open-end spinning provides a striking example. When these machines first came on the market in the late sixties and early seventies there was a belief that they required a level of maintenance which was too complex to make them suitable for use in developing countries. Hence the machinery makers as well as independent organisations offered to carry out the regular reconditioning of the heads containing the rotors and drafting rollers, thus eliminating an intricate special task from the mill's schedule. Now, however, some mills have their own specialised workers to carry out this task.

Hopefully these considerations bring out the difficulties of deriving a hard and fast conclusion on the changes in maintenance skills. While the de-skilling amongst machine operators can be clearly documented, such a tendency cannot be unequivocally established for maintenance workers. One thing that is beyond doubt, however, is that technological modernisation puts increased demands on the knowhow of the maintenance superintendent. Modern machines embody a greater knowledge than older, simpler machines. The individual maintenance worker can rely on aids (specialised tools, maintenance schedules, etc.) to prevent or repair a breakdown without necessarily understanding the functioning of the machines. The superintendent, however, must have a thorough understanding of all the technical processes involved in order to make effective use of these workers and their specialised instruments. Hence the traditional route for entry to the post of maintenance superintendent, that is artisan training followed by promotion through the workshop and management structure, is increasingly inappropriate unless augmented by a sound engineering education.

The same applies to the superintendents of the spinning and weaving department and production management in general. They do not necessarily need the same grounding in mechanical and electrical engineering, but have to know more about properties of fibres, yarn and cloth and how the desired quality and quantity of output can be achieved. Indeed, in contrast to the past, now most production managers in Brazil (and probably elsewhere) have specialised higher education either to the degree of técnico têxtil (three-year course) or even engenheiro têxtil. This is not an indication of the diploma disease, but reflects the demands on knowhow which production managers have to meet.

To sum up: taking the workforce as a whole, a typical 1980 mill has certainly a greater concentration of knowhow at the

57

top, particularly in the managerial and technical staff, than a 1950 mill. With the simultaneous decrease in training requirements of operators, a certain polarisation of knowhow has occurred. At the same time it is worth recalling that the relative share of the de-skilled segment of the workforce (machine operators and auxiliary workers) has decreased substantially over the last three decades.

THE DIFFUSION OF TECHNOLOGY AND EMPLOYMENT: THE MACRO DATA

In the previous section we analysed what new technologies were available and examined what impact they would have on the utilisation of labour. The objective in this section is to assess what technologies were applied in the Brazilian spinning and weaving industry and what changes they brought about at the macro level.

The diffusion of technology in the Brazilian textile industry has to be seen against its long history. The first Brazilian mills were founded in the middle of last century and by the beginning of this century local capital had begun to supplant imports. From then on until the middle of the twenties was the 'golden age' of the industry. During this period many of today's leading Brazilian firms were established and local production catered for over 95 per cent of internal consumption. After a period of decline in the second half of the twenties, production rose gradually during the thirties. There was a boom during the second world war when Brazil supplied all its own domestic needs and exported to various countries. Since then production has oscillated around a trend of only modest growth, well below average industrial expansion in the country.

Half of the existing equipment in 1945 was installed before 1915, partly because the import of the machinery was prohibited from 1930 to 1937. Then during the second world war machinery was not available from the big industrial economies. After the war, from 1945 to 1953 alone, more money was spent on importation of new equipment than for the whole period 1913 to 1945 (Versiani 1971). However, modernisation was not maintained at this pace for the rest of the fifties and by 1960 the machinery inventory in the cotton sector was as follows - spinning: of the 2.9 million spindles almost all were ring spindles, of which 40 per cent were over 30 years old, and 75 per cent over 10 years old; in the preparation for spinning, the situation was roughly similar with a somewhat higher proportion of machinery of over 30 years of age. Weaving: of 71,000 looms nearly 50,000 were non-automatic, and of these two-thirds were manufactured over 30 years before. The age of the machinery used in the preparation for weaving varied widely. Table A11 in the Annex (based on ECLA 1963) shows a detailed distribution of machinery by age. This was the situation in the South and South-East of the country which accounted for about 80 per cent of the country's spinning and weaving capacity. The remainder was located in the North-East where the machinery was even older, as can be seen from Table A12 in the Annex (based on SUDENE 1961).

During the sixties re-equipment accelerated considerably and by 1970 the average age of machinery was much lower. Table 4.19 shows the extent to which this updating occurred in the case of spindles and looms. Much of this modernisation was aided by government incentives, particularly in the North-East.

In the seventies the modernisation of technology continued. By the end of 1973, approximately 10 per cent of Brazil's weaving capacity already consisted of shuttle-less looms (Tavares and Pereira 1976). Otherwise there is no comprehensive information on the diffusion of new technology, but our fieldwork gave indications of a continued drive to invest in new machinery. At least, this is an impression gained during our factory visits and in interviews with national and foreign machinery suppliers at the International Textile Machinery Exhibition in São Paulo in 1977.9/

Of course, 'new' or 'modern' does not necessarily mean better. In the extensive literature (of the sixties and early seventies) on the Brazilian textile industry there is ample reference to its 'obsolete' machinery park, and a great deal of this judgment is based merely on the age of the machinery. In many cases this is a questionable, if not incorrect, step to take. Since the production process is largely discontinuous a combination of machinery of very different vintages can constitute a very efficient solution, both technically and economically. Moreover, the 'obsoleteness' or not can only be judged against the specific type of yarn or cloth to be produced, and here the differences are often underrated. Thus, the spinning and weaving industry, especially in countries where it has a long tradition, should be expected to have a heterogenous machinery park. This is particularly true in Brazil, because its textile market is very compartmentalised in terms of products, marketing channels and regions. This was certainly the main explanation found by Tavares and Pereira (1976) for the very uneven diffusion of new textile technology in Brazil:

> The success of enterprises in this sector seems to be more associated with their ability in the use of instruments of competition (centred on the product/market) than with an 'aggressive' policy of technological renewal. The latter strategy becomes a priority only when in a determined sub-sector competing enterprises have already exhausted all those possibilities of 'Schumpeterian innovations' which do not involve massive fixed investments. (p. 31)

Table 4.19: Age of Cotton Spinning and Weaving Machinery in 1960 and 1970

Age	1960			1970		
	Ring spindles	Looms non-automatic	Looms automatic	Ring spindles	Looms non-automatic	Looms automatic
Less than 10 years	25.1	5.4	49.6	34.0	6.0	66.0
From 10 to 20 years	35.3			38.0		
From 10 to 30 years		31.3	39.7		62.0	24.0
More than 20 years	39.6			28.0		
More than 30 years		63.3	10.7		32.0	10.0

Source: ECLA (1963) and UNIDO (1973).

Note: Unfortunately the source for the 1970 data does not give absolute numbers, so to what extent the relative importance of automatic versus non-automatic looms increased cannot be documented.

The Cotton Spinning and Weaving Industry

In spite of the unevenness, the trends in labour productivity and labour intensity (derived from the Industrial Census) confirm the major waves of technological modernisation outlined above. As we can see from Table 4.20, labour productivity increased but very little and the share of wages in value added even increased slightly[10] during the fifties, when little technological renewal took place. In contrast, the characterisation of the sixties as a decade of substantial re-equipment is supported by a more than doubling of labour productivity and a fall in the share of wages in value added from almost 40 to 28 per cent suggesting a considerable increase in capital intensity.[11] Finally, the continued diffusion of new technology in the seventies is confirmed by the further decrease in labour content and rise in labour productivity from 1970 to 1975.

Table 4.20: Employment, Productivity and Labour Content in Spinning and Weaving, 1950-75

	1950	1960	1970	1975
No. of enterprises	1153	1285	1813	2306
No. of workers	264,606	231,664	207,725	209,857
Value of output (Cr$1.000)	7,488,112	7,603,495	14,957,405	29,420,503
Value added (Cr$1.000)	4,032,193	3,714,825	7,506,847	10,246,937
Wage bill (Cr$1.000)	1,497,561	1,483,725	2,132,487	2,487,490
Labour productivity (Cr$1.000)	15.24	16.04	36.14	48.82
Labour content (%)	37.14	39.94	28.40	24.27

Source: IBGE, Censo Industrial. For Deflator: Conjuntura Econômica, March 1976, p.114, 'Indice geral de preços, Média do ano'
Notes: All values are expressed in 1975 prices. The indicators used above correspond to the following Census categories:

1 No. of workers = Pessoal occupado - Total
2 Value of output = Valor da produção
3 Value added = Valor da transformação
4 Wage bill = Salários - Total
5 Labour productivity = (3) divided by (1)
6 Labour content = Share of (4) in (3)

Over the entire period (1950-1975), labour productivity rose by 220 per cent. Thus, even though the production of the industry increased substantially (value added rose by 154 per cent), the number of workers suffered an absolute decline of 21 per cent. For one region an attempt was made to study this change in employment in some detail. We chose to do this for the North-East, where the updating of technology was particularly dramatic. As already stated, the spinning and weaving industry in this region was, at the end of the fifties, the country's most backward in technological terms (SUDENE 1961; ECLA 1963); today many of the mills are amongst its most advanced. The decisive decade was that of the sixties when the government, through the regional planning authority SUDENE, initiated a massive re-equipment programme. According to the Industrial Census, employment in the spinning and weaving industry was cut by almost half (46 per cent) over this decade. SUDENE (1971) itself carried out a survey to assess the impact of its policy and reached the conclusion that the net employment effect was a decline of only 4 per cent, that is, employment had hardly changed.

Provoked by this substantial difference, we examined both sources in great detail (Schmitz 1979a), which confirmed that both did in fact cover the same universe. However, no conclusion could be reached as to which result reflected what really happened, not even in discussions with those who had been responsible for the data collection on this industry. Also, both sources are quoted in the literature, giving rise to very different conclusions.12/ What is worse, the data examined and the inconsistencies refer to medium and large-scale enterprises for which one would not expect such discrepancies. The order of magnitude of the data difference certainly calls for great caution in the use of studies which assess the changes in the textile industry exclusively on the basis of one of these sources.

THE UTILISATION OF LABOUR IN PRACTICE: CASE STUDIES

The objective in the previous sections was first to establish the technological tendencies by examining the impact which available technology has on labour; second, to assess to what extent new technology was actually introduced. It was shown that machinery suppliers brought many innovations on to the market which substantially reduce the labour content in textiles. The introduction of new machinery, however, has been very uneven, giving some indication of the heterogeneity of the textile industry. The aim in this section is to show how the labour utilisation works out in practice, how it differs amongst various segments of the industry, and to what extent it is technologically determined.13/

Even though spinning and weaving is a relatively well documented industry, there is little to be found on the pattern of labour utilisation. What follows is mainly based on primary data collected from spinning and weaving firms in the Centre-South and North-East of Brazil. The research procedure was described in the methodological chapter above. Mention should be made, however, of the problems encountered in the categorisation of labour. It was found that when it came to classifying occupations, no two firms were alike. Different firms used different names for the same jobs. In order to make the information comparable, the following procedure was adopted. In the interview we did not start by using our own occupational categories. The respondent was asked to provide the hierarchy and composition of the workforce in the terms used by the firm itself; the job descriptions were discussed in those cases where the terms were unclear. Then the interview and the collection of quantitative information from the personnel department was conducted by using the firm's own occupational terminology, but grouping the occupations according to our own categories. While this did not provide entirely clear distinctions in all cases, it brought us reasonably close to making the data of different firms comparable.

A further problem of comparability arises over wage levels, since the data were collected at different points in time and in different regions. For this reason the remuneration of labour is expressed throughout in multiples of the regional government decreed minimum wage valid at the time. To make this yardstick meaningful it should be explained what one minimum wage stands for. If one considers the basic needs of food, housing, clothing, hygiene and transport of a working class family in Brazil, the minimum wage is at best sufficient to cover the expenses of workers themselves, but totally inadequate to guarantee the subsistence of their families (Calsing 1978). The inadequacy of the minimum wage and the difficulties in access to housing and sanitation are widely acknowledged.

A Case Study from the Centre-South

Our first case study deals with the spinning and weaving industry of Americana in the state of São Paulo. The state of São Paulo accounts for more than half of Brazil's textile production and Americana is the largest textile centre in the interior of the state. One of its major characteristics is its large number of small subcontractors (see Table 4.21) weaving cloth for larger firms of Americana or the capital city of São Paulo. This subcontracting system was investigated in detail in a previous study on the role of small firms in manufacturing (Schmitz 1982), and its main technological aspects are drawn out in chapter 8 below.

Table 4.21: Independent and Subcontracted Firms in the Spinning and Weaving Industry of Americana According to Size of Firm, 1975

Type of firm	Size of firm according to number of workers							Total
	0-4	5-9	10-49	50-99	100-199	200-499	500+	
Independent	10	14	40	10	13	9	6	102
Subcontracted	281	93	80	5	0	0	0	459
Part-independent/ part-subcontracted	2	3	20	3	3	0	0	31
Total	293	110	140	18	16	9	6	592

Source: Universidade Estadual de Campinas, Cadastro Industrial da Sub-Região de Campinas 1975-76, Vol 1

Note: A firm is called 'independent' as opposed to subcontracted if it buys its own raw materials and sells its product on the market.

The main conclusion on this point is that technological change is bringing about a gradual decline in the subcontracting system and that it is being replaced with production from inside the large firms. In other words there is a move from the use of external to internal labour. As can be seen from Table 4.22, the latter makes up approximately three-quarters of textile employment in the town. This workforce is our main object in this section.

Most of the information comes from trade union representatives and from six enterprises: three had between 500 and 1000 workers; they will be called 'large' firms. The other three had more than 100 but less than 500 workers and they will be called 'medium sized' firms. Of the first three, two were subsidiaries of multinational companies and one belonged to a national group which is among the most powerful in the Brazilian textile industry. The three medium sized firms were owned by industrialists from Americana.14/

Labour Supply. At the time this study was carried out (early 1979), there was a glut of cloth on the market. This forced several firms to cut their subcontracted production and/or cut a shift of their internal workforce. The resulting labour surplus was further increased by migration of workers to Americana. The town had gained a reputation for having a particularly booming industry and offering good job opportunities. This was related to the establishment of subsidiaries of several multinational firms of the textile and other industries in Americana. The clearest indication of the labour surplus were the queues of jobseekers which one could observe in front of the factory gates and which were mentioned by employers and trade unionists during the interviews.

Table 4.22: Workers in Independent and Subcontracted Firms in the Spinning and Weaving Industry of Americana According to Size of Firm, 1975

Type of firm	Size of firm according to number of workers							
	0-4	5-9	10-49	50-99	100-199	200-499	500+	Total
Independent	9	94	119	704	1833	2791	4943	11293
Subcontracted	458	609	1238	296	-	-	-	2601
Part-independent/ part-subcontracted	5	22	543	118	437	-	-	1235
Total		472	725	2600	1228	2270	2791	4943	15129

Source: Universidade   Estadual   de   Campinas,   _Cadastro Industrial da Sub-Região de Campinas, 1975-76_, Vol 1

Note: The 'internal labour' referred to in the text corresponds to the workforce of independent enterprises, the 'external labour' corresponds to the workforce of subcontracted enterprises.

Recruitment and Training. In a situation of general labour surplus none of the investigated firms saw any need to communicate by radio or newspaper vacancies for machine operators or auxiliary workers. A sign at the factory gate was sufficient. Apart from that, the people already working in the factory told friends, neighbours and relatives of any vacancies, providing the firms with a constant stream of applicants. All firms listed the job seekers' names and addresses and then called them for interview whenever they needed new machine operators or auxiliary workers. For the other categories higher up the scale recruitment policy was different and will be dealt with later.

The most striking finding on recruitment practices is that the three largest firms preferred production workers <u>without</u> previous experience in the industry. This is particularly puzzling as there was not just a surplus of labour, but that surplus included many people who had previously worked in textile production. It is believed that the reason for this recruitment policy is connected with the technology of the firms. Interviews carried out in Americana confirmed the earlier finding that the skill requirements for machine operators diminished in the course of technological modernisation.

As in the study of hypothetical firms above, the skill requirements were measured by the necessary training time, defined in terms of the time a lay person takes to attain average productivity. Employers were asked to specify the training time, thus defined, for weaving, the most common occupation in Americana.15/ Their replies indicated that within two or three months a person can be trained to produce with average productivity. For most machine operating jobs in spinning or in the preparation for weaving, the training takes only a month; on some machines it is a matter of days. Training tends to be shortest in the case of auxiliary workers.

Once the time and cost of training are reduced to such an extent, the preference for workers who are young and without previous experience becomes a viable proposition for a number of reasons: (a) firms can recruit at very low wage levels; (b) it is not necessary to eliminate work and behaviour patterns picked up in previous textile employment and considered undesirable by the new employers; and (c) closely related to that, the new worker can be more easily moulded to the requirements of discipline, control and hierarchy in the factory. The latter two points were very much stressed by managers and given as the main reason for preferring workers without previous experience in the textile industry. One personnel manager went as far as saying that he preferred persons without any industrial experience at all, as they gave fewest problems in accepting the norms of discipline laid down by management. In this case the potential new employees had to undergo a very careful selection procedure and if accepted were given several days of orientation and instruction with the purpose of adapting them to, and 'raising their consciousness' about, the norms and rules of the factory. In virtually all cases the training for the work itself was given on the job by foremen or special instructors and only took a short time.

In the case of the three medium sized firms the recruitment and training policy was somewhat different. Whenever they could find workers with previous experience they hired these rather than taking on the training of entirely unskilled workers. In the past, many of their new recruits used to come from the subcontractors by whom they had been trained. Since, however, the independent firms introduced new technology, whereas most subcontractors still work with older machinery, this transfer of skills embodied in workers has become less important.

The reason for the difference in recruitment policy between the three large and the three medium enterprises seems to be linked to size of firm. Larger firms can afford to have employees whose sole or main task is selecting and instructing new recruits. There are economies of scale in establishing a special recruitment and training apparatus. In the case of the two multinationals, the general guidelines for recruitment and training came from headquarters. The three medium sized firms dealt with recruitment and training much more on an ad hoc basis and seemed to cope with this very well, possibly because they were managed by the owners; in all three firms the tasks of management were divided among members of the owning family. The reason for the recruitment of experienced workers by these firms cannot be found in technology, as they had very modern machinery in most sections. It seems important to point this out in order to show that the use of the modern technology does not necessarily lead to a preference for unskilled workers; technology provides management with this opportunity, but it is only likely to be taken up if the gains in control and discipline outweigh the costs of training.

All firms recruit the foremen from within their workforce, from among the machine operators. The reasons for this are very simple: the foremen have to be familiar with the specific types of machines which are used in their section and if they have worked on these machines before, they will need only a little extra training. For the additional training needed they are in some cases sent to the SENAI for short courses (SENAI is the government financed vocational training scheme). The second reason is that if there is some room for internal mobility an incentive for workers to improve their performance is provided.

Higher up the hierarchy the picture is more blurred. For the second layer of supervisors (with responsibility for complete stages of production, such as preparation for weaving) both internal and external recruitment can be found. One of the multinationals had established an entry point precisely at this level; they recruited graduates of technical schools, who were trained inside the firm in order later to occupy these positions and subsequently higher posts. The other multinational stuck to its principle of internal recruitment, but 'internal' in this case was not limited to this factory but included other plants of the company. The third large firm also recruited for these posts from inside; its plants manager stressed that his problem in manning these supervisory posts was not one of finding workers with sufficient skill and qualification, but finding workers who are able to command, finding 'men with a loud voice'. The three medium sized firms had no predetermined policy for the position of supervisors, mainly because they did not have many posts of this kind and generally they were occupied by the same person for a long time.

The same holds true for the production manager of the three medium sized firms. These positions were occupied by persons who were trained textile engineers (two years' full-time course) with a very long service record and/or who were members of the owning family. Also in the three large firms the production managers were trained textile engineers. One of the firms selected the manager from amongst the supervisors, given that the newly graduated engineers entered the firm at supervisory level. The second recruited for this post from within the company (not necessarily from within the same plant). The production manager of the third firm had come from outside.

For maintenance all firms preferred skilled workers (mechanics, electricians) who had been trained either in other firms or in vocational training schools (SENAI). As regards SENAI it has an important function in the formation of maintenance workers as the skill and knowhow provided can be used in most types of manufacturing industry. In contrast, for the training of machine operators it is of no importance, as the firms themselves can provide the training more efficiently on the job.

To summarise: the training time of machine operators and auxiliary workers is very brief, between one day and two months. For machine operators skill requirements tend to diminish with technological modernisation. Large firms even prefer young unskilled workers for these jobs, as their training costs are outweighed by advantages in achieving discipline and control. All firms recruit at two distinct levels: a) machine operators and auxiliary workers; and b) production managers or high supervisory level. Recruitment for most foremen is done from within the firm. Training on the job is dominant. Training provided by vocational schools is of importance only in the case of maintenance workers and textile engineers who generally assume high supervisory posts or the position of production manager.

Wages. The first important feature of the wage level in the textile industry of Americana is that the large majority of workers in medium and large-sized firms earn more than the minimum wage. As we shall see later, this is in startling contrast to the North-Eastern textile industry where auxiliary workers only earn the minimum wage and machine operators around one and a half minimum wages. Table 4.23 shows the monthly wages for the different categories of labour.

Table 4.23:   Monthly Wages in the Spinning and Weaving Industry of Americana by Occupational Category (in multiples of minimum wage)

Category of labour	Wage range	Most common wage
Managers	20+	-
Supervisors (mestre)	6.4 - 14.1	7.7
Foremen (contramestre)	4.9 - 9.0	5.8
Machine operators	2.7 - 4.9	3.5
Auxiliary workers	1.1 - 2.2	1.8
Maintenance		
Electrician/mechanic	4.2 - 5.4	-
Assistant	2.1 - 2.6	-

Source: Interviews with management and personnel departments.

Managers and supervisors receive a fixed monthly salary. All others earn by the hour, except the weavers who are on piece rates or in some cases a combination of hourly and piece wages. The working day is eight hours long, the working week 48 hours.

The data indicate a surprisingly wide range of wages for the same occupations. It is possible that in reality these differences are somewhat smaller than appears from the data. The difficulties in comparing categories of labour across firms have already been mentioned and could account for that. Still, there are firms which pay significantly worse or better than others for certain categories of labour and this was confirmed by the trade union representatives.

Weavers earn more in the medium sized firms than in the large firms. This would seem connected to the different recruitment policies; as already shown, the large firms recruit unskilled workers, whereas the medium sized firms go for experienced weavers. Otherwise no clear overall pattern emerges for differences between national and foreign firms. One multinational pays on the whole more than the four national firms (except for weavers), while the other multinational pays generally less than the national firms (again, with some exceptions).

Within firms the wage differences between auxiliary workers (lowest paid) and supervisors (highest paid, leaving out the production managers) are in the order of one to five. Otherwise it is difficult to establish a pattern for wage differentials within firms. There are many variations; for example the firm that pays by far the highest wages to operators of looms (weavers) pays amongst the lowest wages to operators of winding machines. Another firm shows high wage differences within the category of weavers. Those who weave silk earn about 4.5 minimum wages and those who work with other fibres (cotton, polyester, acetate) only 2.9 minimum wages. Because silk is a very costly raw material, the firm is prepared to pay more in order to achieve greater care and responsibility from the silk weavers.

One aspect which comes out relatively clearly is discrimination in the payment of female labour, especially in low-skilled work. For instance, one of the multinationals calls the unskilled male worker 'servente' and pays him 2.2 minimum wages and the unskilled female worker 'adjudante' and pays her 1.8 minimum wages. The worst paid machine operating job is pirn winding, partly because it requires very little skill (can be learnt in one day), but also probably because it is exclusively staffed by women. Weaving is an occupation done by both men and women, but between them no differences in wages are apparent. A very sharp difference emerges when it comes to promotion to foremen. Not a single 'forewoman' was found in any of the investigated factories, let alone a woman supervisor or manager.

Labour Turnover. In the view of the president of the textile workers union of Americana, the most worrying aspect of labour relations was the high labour turnover in the industry. In fact, much of his and his staff's work was occupied with 'administering' this turnover. Once a worker has been employed for more than a year by the same firm, any termination of the labour contract has to be ratified by the union. According to the union statistics 3,330 such contracts were terminated in 1978.16/ The ratification can alternatively proceed through the local labour office; but it was found that, in the case of textile workers, the labour office only deals with a small proportion. In 1978 this came to approximately 10 per cent 17/ of a total of around 3,700 ratified terminations of labour contracts.

According to the union's own statistics, Americana had 14,701 textile workers in December 1978.18/ Thus the 3,700 recorded dismissals or resignations amount to an annual rate of turnover of 25.2 per cent or a monthly rate of 2.1 per cent. This is only the turnover of those employees who worked for the same employer for one year or more. The overall monthly turnover in the six sample firms was 3.3 per cent which means that over the year 40 per cent of the workforce changes employer.

What are the factors which cause this high turnover? We propose that it has its roots partly in the technological development and resultant skill requirements of the industry. Technological advance, as was shown before, has reduced the necessary training time of workers such that they have become more easily replaceable. This does not, of course, necessarily lead to high turnover. Even in the spinning and weaving industry low turnover would be advantageous for employers, but this does not seem to be of sufficient importance to them actually to pay for it, for instance by offering higher wages. The most useful way of bringing out the connection between technology and labour turnover might be to say that technology provides a necessary condition for high turnover to take place, but not a sufficient condition. What transforms such a potential effect into a real result is the labour legislation. Before moving on to this issue, it would be interesting to look at turnover rates at a more disaggregated level.

Table 4.24: Monthly Rates of Labour Turnover in the Spinning and Weaving Industry of Americana by Category of Labour and Firm 1978

Category of labour	Firm 1	Firm 2	Firm 3	Firm 4	Firm 5	Firm 6	Overall
Production managers	0.6	0	0	0	0	0	0.4
Supervisors and foremen	0.5	0.4	1.7	2.0	0.9	0	1.1
Maintenance workers	3.5	0.3	2.8	2.8	0	0	2.0
Machine operators and auxiliary workers	4.4	2.6	4.1	3.1	3.2	2.9	3.6
Overall	4.1	2.1	3.8	3.0	2.9	2.7	3.3

Source: The personnel departments of the sample firms provided for each category of labour the number of employees in December 1978 and the number of workers entering or leaving the firm during 1978. Because of inconsistencies in the figures given for machine operators and auxiliary workers, these two categories had to be grouped together. The turnover rate was calculated as the number of workers entering or leaving the firm (if they were different the smaller one was taken), divided by the number of employees, multiplied by 100.

Table 4.24 shows the turnover rates separately for the investigated firms, which are listed according to size (in terms of number of workers). Firm 2, the second largest and a multinational, has by far the lowest turnover as a direct result of paying relatively high wages and having established a labour market internal to the plant or internal to the company. Interestingly the other multinational (firm 1) has the highest turnover rates, even though it has a recruitment and training policy similar to firm 2; but its wages are low, which could be the main reason for its high turnover of 4.1 per cent per month which amounts to an annual turnover of almost 50 per cent! The turnover rates of the national firms vary less, ranging between 2.7 and 3.8 per cent per month.

In all firms, turnover is lowest in management, supervison, and maintenance, and highest amongst machine operators and auxiliary workers. In cases where separate turnover rates are available for specific occupations within the category of machine operators (not included in Table 4.24) one can find additional evidence that turnover is highest in those jobs which require the shortest training and have the lowest wages.

Our respondents put the blame for the high turnover mainly on the labour legislation. The law provides that employers deposit in the name of each employee a monthly amount equal to 8 per cent of their monthly wage in a government controlled bank. The money accumulated in this account is the so called Fundo de Garantia do Tempo de Serviço (FGTS), which will be called 'guarantee fund' henceforth. The fund is supposed to serve primarily as a resource which the employee can draw upon in periods of unemployment or when he retires.19/ In practice it has turned into a vehicle of increasing the fluctuations of labour in two ways.

The guarantee fund law came into force in 1967 as part of a package of new labour legislation introduced by the then new military government. The previous legislation had imposed high indemnity payments on employers, especially for employees with long years of service. Under the new law, the direct cost of dismissing an employee became very low. If a worker is dismissed without just cause he has the right to obtain the money from his guarantee fund, which has been deposited regularly in his name. The only extra cost for the employer is a payment of 10 per cent of the guarantee fund, which the employer must pay directly to the worker. So from the point of view of severance payments, there is very little disincentive for enterprises to change employees. In fact, in some industries the ease of replacing workers was reportedly used to lower wages by firing workers just before the new yearly wage settlement and then hiring the same or other workers at lower wages. According to the trade union officials this was a practice also applied by some enterprises in Americana.

The guarantee fund can also be a cause of turnover through the worker's own initiative. As mentioned above, the employee can dispose of his guarantee fund if he is discharged without just cause. All interviewed managers and trade union officials reported cases of workers seeking their own dismissal in order to obtain their fund. Either the employee simply tells his employer of his intention and asks to be dismissed without just cause, or in firms which are unwilling to do this, he provokes his own dismissal. This is done by not turning up in time, working less hard or less carefully, but by doing it in such a way that the employer cannot prove 'just cause' for dismissal.

Alternatively the employee can resign from his job and receive the fund, if he declares he needs the money in order to set up his own business. It is not rare for firms to be set up by one or several employers just for this purpose, only to be closed down again once they have received the fund money.

It is difficult to quantify the turnover which is due to these practices. The information collected from enterprises and the union does in most cases distinguish between workers handing in their notice (pedidos de demissão) and dismissals (dispensas), but since the dismissal is sometimes deliberately provoked by the worker for the reasons stated, this information cannot show what part of the turnover is due to employers' and what part due to workers' initiative. In some cases the turnover is believed to be only fictitious, as the worker is only dismissed on paper, whereas in reality he stays with the same firm. He is formally dismissed to enable him to draw his fund and after a certain time he is formally admitted again by the same firm. According to the union secretary, the real turnover is possibly up to a quarter lower than indicated by the data.20/

According to the trade union secretary, the main cause for the withdrawal of the guarantee fund is low wages. While wages in Americana are higher than in, for instance, Minas Gerais or the North-East, they are still low and the guarantee fund is often the only resource workers can draw upon in times of great need, be it for medicaments, house repairs or installments on a refrigerator or televison set. Some of the interviewed managers were keen on pointing out that the fund is not only used to help out in emergencies, but also to finance luxuries. Obviously in order to get a clear idea of the reasons for the withdrawal of the fund money, one would have to interview the workers themselves.21/

A Case Study from the North-East
Research carried out on the same branch in the North-East confirms most findings from the Centre-South but also reveals some important differences.

First, there is virtually no subcontracting to be found in the North-Eastern spinning and weaving industry; in fact there are hardly any small firms of the kind found in the state of São Paulo. This cannot be explained by a lack of textile tradition in the North-East. As mentioned above, the region is one of the country's traditional areas of textile production. A supporting industry which provides textile technology, however, has never developed in the region. All technology and knowhow comes from the Centre-South or abroad. Machinery suppliers are concentrated primarily in the state of São Paulo. In a previous study (Schmitz 1982) we have suggested that this fact enhances considerably the growth prospects for small enterprises in that state. Such enterprises often rely on secondhand machinery and the proximity of machinery manufacturers gives them a greater chance of obtaining spare parts quickly. Where spare parts are no longer available, small firms can fall back on a number of secondhand dealers or small engineering firms which can repair or copy a part. In other words, the lack of a well-developed integrated structure in the supply of technology probably to some extent explains why in the North-East small firms are of little importance in providing employment in the branch considered.

Even though government incentive policy for the North-East has generally favoured the textile industry, this policy has if anything aggravated the position of small firms. Incentives are not available for purchasing secondhand equipment; firms which do receive incentives are obliged to destroy their old machinery (compensatory scrapping). This has probably prevented the development of a local or regional secondhand machinery market. Apart from this technological aspect, the government's industrialisation programme is such that small firms can never qualify because the amount requested for their projects would be too small and because they do not have the required juridical form of business organisation.

The utilisation of labour in the medium and large sized firms was studied in Fortaleza, capital of the North-Eastern state of Ceará. The sample covered five firms of different technological outfit and size. Three firms were large and had more than 500 workers. Two were medium sized with between 100 and 500 workers. As in the previous study, the information comes from interviews with the firms' managers and their personnel departments. In addition we had access to the data which all firms have to provide to the Ministry of Labour in April of each year. From this data we can derive an aggregate view of the composition of the labour force in the five firms examined (see Table 4.25).

These firms employed a total of 2,779 people (excluding administrative workers). Of those, 88.9 per cent were machine operators or auxiliary workers. A major characteristic of this group of workers is their low wage level. They earn between 1.1 and 1.8 minimum wages. This is certainly low in relation to comparable workers in the state of São Paulo where earnings are about twice as high.

There can be little doubt that this regional difference reflects primarily the much greater labour surplus in the North-East. The region has continuously constituted the greatest labour reserve in South America. This is the background against which the employment practices of North-Eastern firms must be seen. We will begin with the recruitment and training practices before investigating the wage question in greater detail. Wherever possible, the general picture emerging from Table 4.25 will be disaggregated in order to evaluate how technologically modern and old firms differ in their demand for labour.

Table 4.25: Gender, Age, Education, Length of Service and Average Wage of Workers in the Spinning and Weaving Industry of Fortaleza by Occupational Category

Occupational category	Total	Gender		Age						Education					Length of service						Average wage* (in multiples of regional monthly minimum wage) ranging	
		Men	Women	Less than 20	20-29	30-39	40-49	50-59	60 and more	Illiterate or non-completed elementary school	Completed elementary or non-completed middle school	Completed middle school or non-completed high school	Completed high school or non-completed university	Completed university or equivalent	Less than 6 months	6 months - 1 year	1 - 2 years	2 - 4 years	4 - 6 years	6 years or more	from	to
Managerial and technical staff	15	15	-	-	3	8	-	3	1	-	-	1	8	6	2	3	3	2	2	3	15.9	37.4
Supervisors, Foremen and instructors	131	129	2	1	50	38	19	19	4	2	50	32	45	2	8	23	26	36	14	24	2.7	10.9
Machine operators	1376	909	467	145	648	308	160	89	26	287	803	281	5	-	103	212	345	335	177	204	1.2	1.8
Auxiliary workers	1096	786	310	116	569	240	144	25	2	116	731	246	3	-	291	197	190	238	91	89	1.1	1.7
Maintenance workers	161	161	-	4	70	40	18	24	5	9	63	74	14	1	10	36	40	30	25	20	1.9	4.8
Total	2779	2000	779	266	1340	634	341	160	38	414	1647	634	75	9	414	471	604	641	309	340	1.3	2.8

*Averages were calculated separately for each firm

Source: Firms' employment records prepared for the Ministry of Labour.

Recruitment and Training. Given that Fortaleza is a city with considerable tradition in the spinning and weaving industry, it seems remarkable that 57.8 per cent of the workforce is under the age of 30 (Table 4.25). In the case of the firms with the oldest machinery, the under-30s only make up 38.6 per cent whereas the technologically most advanced firm has 72.3 per cent in this age group. The other three firms with combinations of old and new machinery lie in between. This association between young workforce and modern technology is, however, not quite so straightforward because presumably the age of firms has to be taken into account. In our sample, the mill with the most outdated equipment is at the same time the oldest (66 years), whereas the most modern is the youngest (7 years in operation).

In any case, our interest is not so much in the workers' age as such, but in a related question, namely their skills. (The older the worker, the greater the likelihood that he has accumulated certain skills.) The technologically most advanced firm prefers shop-floor workers (machine operators and auxiliary workers) without previous textile experience. Another firm with a mixed machinery park had the same preference.

The significance of this recruitment policy depends, of course, on the availability of skilled workers in the local labour market. From the views expressed by the respondents no clear answer emerged as to whether the labour surplus included skilled workers. This difficulty is partly due to a tendency amongst employers to complain about a general shortage of skilled workers even though in reality such shortages only arise in relation to a few specific occupations. Whatever the reliability of the respondents' answers, the two firms with the discussed recruitment practice paid higher wages for machine operators (1.7 to 1.9 minimum wages) than the other firms (1.1 to 1.3 minimum wages); so presumably the option of luring experienced workers from other firms was open to them, but was not in fact pursued.

How does the size of firm affect the recruitment policy? In the case of Americana we suggested that there were important economies of scale in setting up an internal recruitment and training programme, and that only technologically advanced firms which are of a large size do therefore reveal a preference for unskilled workers. The Fortaleza data to some extent support this suggestion. The two firms which pursued the above policy were large in size (the third large firm, the one with the most outdated machinery, did not). The two medium sized firms tried to employ experienced workers whenever they could at the wage level offered. In relation to our hypothesis this is not necessarily supporting evidence since these two firms had a technologically mixed outfit. However, it is interesting to add that one of the medium sized firms was preparing to move to an entirely new plant with increased capacity. No recruitment and training strategy had been worked out for additional workers required, and the firm's ad hoc approach was to be maintained. This approach was also characteristic of the medium sized firms in Americana. It seems that the definition of a management strategy in labour questions is largely a function of the size of firm.

The process of finding new recruits is almost the same in all firms. It is their workers who spread the news if new people are sought; in addition vacancies are announced through signs at the factory gate. Radio or newspaper advertisements are rarely necessary.

As regards training, this is minimal for auxiliary workers. What they mainly need is a few days to get used to their new environment and the rules applied in the firm. Machinery operators need more training. In all firms and for all machine-minding jobs this was given on the job. There was only one exception; in the largest firm investigated, weavers received the first phase of the training on looms which had been set aside specifically for this purpose.

On the question of whether training requirements on modern machines were lower or higher than on older machines, the respondents confirmed that the skills tended to diminish with the advance of modern machinery. The significance of this reduction was, however, difficult to establish. In the largest firm we had the opportunity to discuss the question with a panel of four managers with long experience in textile production. They warned us not to make too much of the technology related de-skilling thesis; they argued that the reduction in training time was at least as much due to a change in training methods. Formerly new recruits tended to work for a considerable time alongside experienced workers, often in auxiliary positions, picking up the ins and outs of the job gradually. In contrast, nowadays training is much more organised and directly geared to the tasks to be performed.

The policy towards recruitment and training of foremen (contramestres) is the same as that observed in the previous case study. They are recruited from amongst the machine operators in all firms investigated; this experience in direct production work is exactly the preparation considered necessary for the role of foreman. Further up the hierarchy in the second layer of supervisors the situation is not so clear. A variety of practices was found which did not seem to depend on technological factors. Some supervisors (mestres) had been recruited directly from other mills, others from technical schools, and a third group from within; in the latter case they were generally sent to a special textile school for a course of approximately six months. Similarly in the case of managers and engineers no pattern emerged; except perhaps for the technologically most modern firm which belongs to one of the most powerful national textile groups. They aimed at recruiting supervisory, technical and managerial staff from other plants in the group; in practice however there were many exceptions to a labour market internal to the group. Probably this was so because the group had grown more through the acquisition of existing plants than through the building of new ones. (In contrast, a multinational group referred to in the Americana study had a strong intra-firm, or better intra-group, labour market. The plants in the various parts of the country were built by the group itself, and staffed in the upper part of the hierarchy by people who had been tried out in other plants before and who were requested to adopt the group's general recruitment and training policy).

In the case of maintenance staff, all firms were reluctant to put many resources into training. They preferred to recruit experienced mechanics and electricians from other firms or from the vocational training institution SENAI. Since there is a shortage of such workers, employers had to adopt additional measures to fill their vacancies. Generally they selected from amongst other workers those who showed an inclination or aptitude to work as auxiliary to a mechanic or electrician.

Wages. To analyse the remuneration of work we can draw on two sources: on the data given to the government (Table 4.25) and on the information provided by managers in the interviews (Table 4.26). While the data from the two sources does not coincide in all details, variations amongst firms come out very clearly.

Amongst machine operators and auxiliary workers the wage range is smallest. Nevertheless it is of great importance because of the number of workers involved, apart from the fact that for a worker who is at the bottom end of the wage scale, the difference between earning 1 or 1.5 minimum wages is enormous. Further disaggregation of the data by firm shows that those with older technology pay lower wages. Taking machine operators for instance, the technologically most advanced firm pays 1.8 and the most backward pays 1.2 minimum wages. The technology and wage characteristics of the other three firms fall neatly in between.

A firm-by-firm comparison of the wages of foremen shows exactly the same trend. This is to be expected since all firms recruit the foremen from amongst their machine operators. Further up the hierarchy, the picture is not quite as clear; the particular circumstances of individuals in the higher category (such as their history in the firm, their relationship with the owner) mean that salaries do not conform in any obvious way, with one exception: their salaries are comparable with those paid in the Centre-South for equivalent positions (compare Tables 4.23 and 4.26). Probably this reflects the fact that supervisory, managerial and technical staff are often recruited in the Centre-South. In contrast, machine operators and auxiliary workers fare very differently. As mentioned before, in the North-East they earn considerably less than the fellow workers in the Centre-South. Thus the intra-firm wage differentials in the underdeveloped North-East are greater than in the industrial Centre South.

To sum up, our main finding is that the technologically advanced firms in Fortaleza's spinning and weaving industry pay shop-floor workers better wages. This is somewhat surprising if we remember that they recruit primarily young workers without previous textile experience. In other words, their recruitment policy should enable them to pay relatively low wages. The conclusion we must draw is that in a situation where the general wage level is low, the preference for unskilled workers reflects mainly a strategy of forming a disciplined workforce. Its importance for a low wage policy comes to bear only in regions where the wages are not already at a very depressed level.

Table 4.26: Monthly Wages in the Spinning and Weaving Industry of Fortaleza by Occupational Category (in multiples of minimum wage)

Category of labour	Wage range	Most common wage
Managers and engineers	10 - 30	20
Supervisors (mestre)	6 - 16	−
Foremen (contramestre)	2.5 - 8.4	3.5
Machine operators	1.2 - 1.8	1.5
Auxiliary workers	1.0 - 1.5	1.1

Source: Interviews.

Labour Turnover. Overall turnover rates were close to those found in Americana. Monthly turnover in the five Fortaleza firms ranged from 2.5 to 4.2 per cent with an average of 3.5 per cent in the industry. Also the explanation for this fluctuation of labour seems to be the same as that found in the Centre-South; at least, the interviews with management and personnel departments in Fortaleza did not reveal any different reasons.

According to the respondents, turnover is highest amongst machine operators and auxiliary workers. Unfortunately we do not have separate turnover rates for the various categories of labour to enable us to examine this view. We can, however, draw on a complete record of length of service of all workers for one year earlier. As borne out by Table 4.27, length of service records are remarkably similar between the various types of labour. Fluctuation among auxiliary workers is higher than for others though not by a large amount. Hence the view of our respondents on differing incidence of turnover is not

The Cotton Spinning and Weaving Industry

entirely supported by the data. Certainly there is not the clear division which we noted in Americana between the relative stability of maintenance, supervisory and managerial staff on the one hand, and a concentration of turnover amongst machine operators and auxiliary workers on the other (compare Table 4.24).

Table 4.27: Length of Service of Workers in the Spinning and Weaving Industry of Fortaleza by Occupational Category (in percentages)

Length of service

Occupational category	Less than 6 months	6 months – 1 year	1 – 2 years	2 – 4 years	4 – 6 years	6 years or more	Total
Managerial and technical staff	13.3	20.0	20.0	13.3	13.3	20.0	100
Supervisors, foremen and instructors	6.1	17.6	19.8	27.5	10.7	18.3	100
Machine operators	7.5	15.4	25.1	24.3	12.9	14.8	100
Auxiliary workers	26.6	18.0	17.3	21.7	8.3	8.1	100
Maintenance workers	6.2	22.4	24.8	18.6	15.5	12.4	100
Overall	14.9	16.9	21.7	23.1	11.1	12.2	100

Source: Firms' employment records, see Table 4.25.

What about the differences between the Fortaleza firms? Let us compare the firm with the most out-dated equipment with the firm that is technologically most advanced. Table 4.28 suggests that there is no substantial difference in their length of service records. One could have expected a greater stability in the technologically advanced firm since it pays the highest wages in the industry (locally), but the firm with the old machinery does not reveal a greater turnover of labour despite its low wages. Possibly the fact that the modern firm, while paying relatively well, is also more demanding in terms of labour intensity and discipline plays a role here. Indeed, its manager explained that the turnover is largely enforced by the firm for these reasons in order to 'weed out the unsuitable elements'. The fact that the instability is more concentrated in the first half year (18.3 per cent were employed for less than six months) would support this.

Table 4.28: Length of Service of Workers in Firms at Different Technological Levels by Occupational Category (in percentages)

Category of labour	Length of service in technologically advanced firm							Length of service in technologically backward firm						
	Less than 6 months	6 months - 1 year	1 - 2 years	2 - 4 years	4 - 6 years	6 years or more	Total	Less than 6 months	6 months - 1 year	1 - 2 years	2 - 4 years	4 - 6 years	6 years or more	Total
Managerial and technical staff	0	33.3	0	0	66.6	0	100	0	0	0	0	50.0	50.0	100
Supervisors, foremen and instructors	0	50.0	0	20.8	4.2	25.0	100	8.6	5.7	22.9	34.3	14.3	14.3	100
Machine operators	9.3	2.7	19.8	52.7	15.4	0	100	3.6	6.3	24.6	26.6	25.0	13.9	100
Auxiliary workers	34.2	13.9	15.2	29.7	7.0	0	100	13.7	19.1	25.7	17.4	17.0	7.1	100
Maintenance workers	8.1	27.0	13.5	24.3	21.6	5.4	100	20.7	6.9	27.6	13.8	13.8	17.2	100
Overall	18.3	12.6	16.1	38.9	12.1	2.0	100	9.1	11.8	25.0	22.4	20.4	11.3	100

Source: Firm's employment records.

81

Table 4.29: Gender, Age, Education, Length of Service and Average Wage of Workers in a Technologically Advanced Firm of the North-East by Occupational Category

Occupational category	Total	Gender		Age						Education					Length of service						Average wage (in multiples of regional minimum wage)
		Men	Women	Less than 20	20-29	30-39	40-49	50-59	60 and more	Illiterate or non-completed elementary school	Completed elementary or non-completed middle school	Completed middle school or non-completed high school	Completed high school or non-completed university	Completed university or equivalent	Less than 6 months	6 months – 1 year	1 - 2 years	2 - 4 years	4 - 6 years	6 years or more	
Managerial and technical staff	6	6	-	-	1	4	1	-	-	-	-	-	3	3	-	-	1	1	2	2	45.9
Supervisors, foremen and instructors	36	35	1	-	11	23	2	-	-	-	14	16	6	-	-	-	1	1	4	30	9.3
Machine operators	198	160	38	13	141	42	2	-	-	32	143	23	-	-	25	31	9	36	34	63	2.9
Auxiliary workers	354	304	50	54	242	49	9	-	-	65	238	49	2	-	317	17	5	12	1	2	1.7
Maintenance workers	95	95	-	-	66	22	3	4	-	8	49	30	8	-	11	31	9	7	16	21	4.3
Total	689	600	89	67	461	140	17	4	-	105	444	118	19	3	353	79	25	57	57	118	3.3

Source: Firm's employment records.

Let us sum up our findings on the North-Eastern spinning and weaving industry. They confirm that advanced technology does not mean greater skill requirements. On the contrary, given the relatively short training time needed on modern machines young unskilled workers are recruited because they conform more easily to the demands of discipline and efficiency of such firms. While this relationship between technology and skills makes it increasingly easy to replace workers, the technologically advanced firms do <u>not</u> show higher turnover rates; nor do they pay lower wages than the firms with machines of an older vintage.

This picture finds its clearest expression in a very modern mill which we visited in another city of the North-East, and with which we will complete this chapter. The mill is a show -piece in terms of layout and technological outfit. It is located in an area where other spinning and weaving firms had dismissed large numbers of workers either due to closures or rationalisation. Interestingly these were not the workers who found employment in the new firm. Its manager made it very clear that he preferred shop-floor workers without previous textile experience. This recruitment policy is reflected in Table 4.29 which gives the composition of the workforce. The firm had just completed a phase of expansion, as can be seen from the high number of workers with less than six months service. (In this case this does <u>not</u> mean high turnover.) The majority is recruited as 'servente' (hence the high proportion of auxiliary workers) and then trained to become machine operators. The Table suggests furthermore that most of them are in the younger age brackets and therefore probably not those who had lost employment in the other textile firms. Despite this recruitment policy (or partly because of the rigorous selection), turnover was low (according to management well under 2 per cent per month) and wages were relatively high (on average, 1.7 minimum wages for auxiliary workers and 2.9 for machine operators).

NOTES

1. We refer to the cotton industry, but this does not always mean that cotton is the only raw material used. There is an increasing trend to blend cotton with other fibres, in particular with polyester, but this has no major bearing on the technology or labour used in the industry.
2. A description which is more detailed, but also for laymen, is given by Rothwell (1976a) in a summary of technological developments over the last three decades.
3. I wish to thank the Departamento Nacional of the Serviço Nacional de Aprendizagem Industrial (SENAI) for financing this study. The objectives and the work procedure were formulated by myself during an assignment to the UNDP/ILO Human Resources Planning Project in Brazil (see IPEA/PNUD

1979). Líscio Camargo of the Institute of Economic and Social Planning (IPEA) helped to make the institutional arrangements. The detailed technical work was carried out by members of the Centro de Tecnologia da Indústria Química e Têxtil (CETIQT): Luiz Gonzaga Lopes (Director), Lucio Geraldo Taboada Tenan, Geraldo Xavier de Andrade, Daltro Rangel Peganha, Augusto Bolivar Cerqueira, José Maria Simas de Miranda. Their collaboration is gratefully acknowledged.

4. For a general discussion and case studies on the problematic of technological choice see Bhalla (1975) and Stewart (1978).

5. Unfortunately there is no detailed breakdown of the managerial and technical staff of the 1950 and 1960 plant in the original ECLA study (1966). This complicated the comparison with the 1970 and 1980 plant in the subsequent CETIQT study (1980). The figures in the above tables do not entirely correspond to those arrived at in CETIQT (1980, Table 15B) due to slightly different categorisation, but this does not affect the emerging trend in this staff category.

6. The figures for 'simple locomotion' in the 1980 factory look exaggeratedly high. Unfortunately they could not be re-checked.

7. These include discussions with machinery suppliers held at an International Textile Machinery Exhibition in São Paulo and discussions with users of the technology. Valuable advice was also received from the Shirley Institute in Manchester.

8. Another question is what skills are required in order to induce incremental technical change in the form of modifications or adaptations of machines to local conditions. This question was not investigated, and indeed would constitute a research project in itself.

9. Interviews with foreign suppliers revealed that they were keen on starting up machinery production in Brazil itself (often in joint ventures), partly because of their favourable assessment of the Brazilian market, partly because new government levies introduced in 1975 made its imports prohibitively expensive. In this context it is interesting to add that Brazil's textile machinery industry owes its existence not so much to a conscious effort on the part of the government to build up this industry, but to pressures arising from the balance of payments. The above mentioned levies (particularly the 'depósito compulsório') had been introduced to stem the foreign trade deficit. In the wake of these measures the textile machinery industry expanded very rapidly; however only 45 per cent is under the control of national capital, according to information from the Industrial Development Council.

10. The increase is probably due to rising wages.

11. Wages fell from 1960 to 1970, so the fall in labour content (increase in capital intensity) is slightly exaggerated by the data.

12. For instance, Goodman and Cavalcanti (1974), while very critical of SUDENE practices in general, accept the validity of its survey results and make no reference to the corresponding Census data. On the other hand, Sandmeyer (1976) bases his study on the Industrial Census figures only.

13. At the time of writing, Liliana Acero was carrying out research on the labour process in the Brazilian spinning and weaving industry. The findings of her very detailed case studies could not be incorporated in this study, but provide very interesting material; parts of it support or further qualify some of our own conclusions, others cover issues not dealt with in this book. Most of her excellent work is contained in Acero (1983).

14. See chapter 8 for details on the selection of firms.

15. Most of Americana's textile firms are only involved in weaving and buy the yarn from outside.

16. Based on: Sindicato dos Trabalhadores na Indústria de Fiação e Tecelagem de Americana, 'Homologações de Rescisões Contratuais de Trabalho Efetuados durante o Ano de 1978' (unpublished statistics).

17. Estimated on the basis of information for eight months of 1978.

18. Sindicato dos Trabalhadores de Fiação e Tecelagem de Americana, Relação dos Estabelecimentos Têxteis em Dezembro de 1978, Baseada nas Guias de Recolhimento de Contribuição Assistencial (unpublished statistics prepared by the union).

19. The money in the fund cannot be used by the employer as working capital. It remains in the hands of a government bank which uses it to finance public housing programmes.

20. A study on labour in the metal working industry of Porto Alegre (Ely 1978) confirms both the importance of the guarantee fund in explaining the labour turnover and the difficulties in providing a quantitative picture of the reasons. Interestingly, a third of the managers interviewed for that study admitted that they were sometimes involved in fictitious dismissals.

21. Indeed, a drawback of our case study is that the information comes primarily from management. For an excellent study of textile workers, though with a different focus, see Pereira (1979); this is a study carried out in Rio de Janeiro, based on the workers' own perceptions of the world of work.

Chapter 5

THE CHEMICAL FIBRE INDUSTRY

Chemical or man-made fibres are included in this study since
they are made in continuous flow production. Our main
objective is to observe the labour utilisation which such
technology brings about. To this end we will first give a
brief account of the development of the industry in Brazil;
second, describe the production process in some detail and
third analyse the employment practices of firms operating in
Brazil.

CHEMICAL FIBRES IN BRAZIL

Depending on the raw material, chemical fibres can be
classified into two groups: cellulosic and synthetic fibres.
Brazil produces both; initially it produced mainly cellulosic
fibres such as rayon and acetate, but now synthetic fibres such
as nylon and polyester dominate. Even though Brazil is a major
producer of natural fibres - mainly cotton, man-made fibres
have increasingly gained ground, particularly since the
sixties. In 1963, their share in total production of fibres
was only 8.2 per cent; by 1970 it had risen to 11.5 and reached
28.7 per cent in 1980 (see Table 5.2). The share of chemical
fibres in total fibre consumption is a little higher; the
difference is due to exports of natural fibres and imports of
chemical fibres. Internationally Brazil fares as follows:
world wide, man-made fibres account for 44.2 per cent, in the
USA for 71.7 and in Brazil for 31.9 per cent of total fibre
consumption (see Table 5.1).

 Production in Brazil of man-made cellulosic fibres
began in 1931 and of synthetic fibres in 1955. In both cases,
it was the subsidiary of a French multinational which started

production first and which had for many years a virtual monopoly over the market until it was challenged by other foreign and national firms. Foreign capital, however, continues to dominate the industry.

Table 5.1: Consumption of Textile Fibres in the World, USA and Brazil in 1977 (in percentages)

| | Natural fibres | | Chemical fibres | |
	Cotton	Others	Cellulosic	Synthetic
World	50.7	5.0	11.7	32.5
USA	27.3	1.0	7.9	63.8
Brazil	54.6	13.6	5.8	26.1

Source: Associação Brasileira de Produtores de Fibras Artificiais e Sintéticas, A Indústria Brasileira de Fibras Químicas, São Paulo 1978

In 1977, the fifteen largest plants accounting for approximately 95 per cent of the industry's output, employed a total of 18,415. Of these, eight had between 500 and 1,000 workers, six had between 1,000 and 1,500 workers and one over 4,000 workers.1/ We visited and carried out interviews in four of these plants, which employed together almost 9,000 workers. Interviews with managers and factory visits took between one and two days in each plant. In addition, the personnel departments provided detailed written information on the firms' workforces.

Understanding the production itself was an important step in the research. This was done initially through the reading of introductory technical literature, and above all through the plant visits. What mattered was not the technical detail, but grasping the fundamentals of such continuous flow production and where and how labour intervened.

THE PRODUCTION PROCESS

As already stated, man-made fibres fall into two broad groups, according to the origin of the fibre-forming substance. The first group, of which rayon and acetate are examples, is produced by using natural fibre-forming materials such as cellulose. The second group, generally called synthetics and including such fibres as nylon and polyester, is produced from synthetic chemicals. Like natural fibres, chemical fibres are

Table 5.2: Production of Textile Fibres in Brazil, 1963-1980 (in 1,000 tons)

Year	Natural fibres			Chemical fibres			Total
	Cotton	Others	Subtotal	Artificial	Synthetic	Subtotal	
1963	467.7	85.7	553.4	38.9	10.4	49.3	602.7
1964	504.0	100.3	604.3	40.6	12.6	53.2	657.5
1965	405.0	164.4	569.4	38.3	14.5	52.8	622.2
1966	540.0	112.6	652.6	45.9	19.2	65.1	717.7
1967	445.0	108.4	553.4	45.2	18.1	63.2	616.7
1968	617.0	119.7	736.7	53.4	27.3	80.7	817.4
1969	721.0	117.4	838.4	48.4	31.5	79.9	918.3
1970	580.0	137.2	717.2	47.9	45.6	93.5	810.7
1971	595.0	129.6	724.6	53.2	55.1	108.3	832.9
1972	680.0	142.0	822.0	54.5	77.2	131.7	953.7
1973	651.0	154.0	805.0	59.3	116.2	175.5	980.5
1974	535.0	118.9	653.9	53.7	130.4	184.1	838.0
1975	532.0	128.7	660.7	49.2	145.4	194.6	855.3
1976	400.0	129.8	529.8	53.7	178.1	231.8	761.6
1977	590.0	125.5	715.5	50.5	190.8	241.3	956.8
1978	488.0	111.5	599.5	46.5	218.2	264.7	864.2
1979	541.0	130.2	671.2	49.9	211.4	261.3	932.5
1980	572.0	123.8	695.8	51.4	229.1	280.5	976.3

Source: Sindicato da Indústria de Fiação e Tecelagem no Estado de São Paulo, Carta Têxtil, Edição Especial, Maio 1981

composed of long thread-like molecules. A substance that is to be converted into fibre must first be converted to a liquid or semi-liquid state, either by dissolving it in a solvent, or by heating it until it melts. In this first stage of the process the long molecules are freed from close entanglement with each other, allowing them to move independently. The resulting liquid is extruded through small holes, or spinnerets, emerging as fine jets of liquid that are hardened to form filaments. This second stage is called spinning, not to be confused with the spinning process described in the previous industry study. In a third stage, the fibres are further processed including operations such as stretching, washing and drying. Finally the filaments are wound onto cones for dispatch to the purchaser. Alternatively they are cut into short lengths of staple fibre,2/ which is compressed into bales for transport to the customer.

These are the main stages of production common to chemical textile fibres. The details vary with each type of fibre. Of the four plants which we visited, one specialised in the production of the cellulose fibre rayon, the others in the synthetic fibres polyester and nylon. Let us look at these processes in greater detail.

Figure 5.1 shows the production process of the rayon factory. The raw material for rayon may be cotton linters, the short fibres adhering to the cotton seed, or wood pulp from soft timbers. The cellulose (a) contained in these materials is purified and formed into thin sheets that are steeped in caustic soda, forming powdery crumbs (b). During the ageing period that follows, the caustic soda reacts with the cellulose, forming alkali cellulose (c). This is mixed with carbon disulphide in a revolving drum (d) and then treated with a diluted solution of caustic soda, forming sodium cellulose xanthate, a thick orange-brown solution (e). This is allowed to mature for several days at carefully controlled temperatures (f). After repeated filtering the solution is forced through tiny holes bored in the metal cap forming the spinneret. Emerging from the spinneret hole, the jet of viscose enters a bath of acids and salts, in which it is reconverted to cellulose, which coagulates to form a solid filament (g). The filaments are then washed free of acids and sulphur (h) and fed into a cutter which produces fibres of the desired staple length (i). The staple fibre is bleached (j), passes through pipes into the drier (k) and is then sucked into machines (l) which press it into bales (m). (If continuous filaments are the end product, the rayon is taken through similar washing, purifying and drying processes before the final winding on to bobbins).

Of prime interest to us is the degree to which this process is continuous, in the sense that major damage would be caused if it were interrupted. This could engender a particular concern with the reliability of workers and hence a policy

The Chemical Fibre Industry

Figure 5.1   Flow Chart of Rayon Production

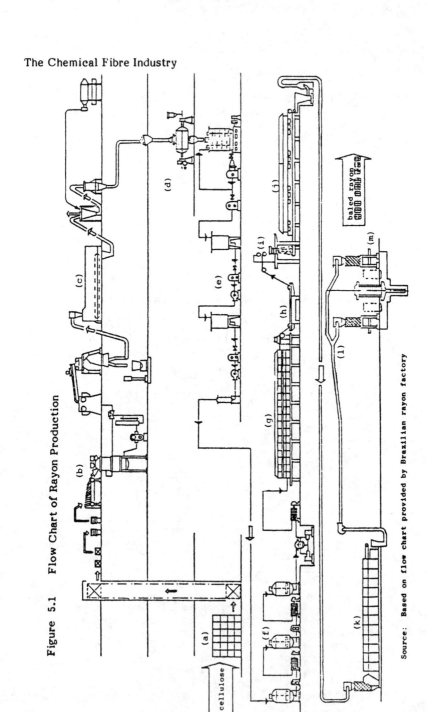

cellulose

(a) (b) (c) (d) (e) (f) (g) (h) (i) (j) (k) (l) (m)

baled rayon

Source: Based on flow chart provided by Brazilian rayon factory

towards labour which reflected this concern. Most of the rayon process is continuous in the strict sense, i.e. the preparation of the viscose spinning solution and the extrusion of the fibre-forming material must not be stopped or interrupted. Otherwise the materials are lost and machinery and installations are difficult to recover for further use. A clear example is solutions which solidify prematurely in pipes or reaction tanks. Once the filament has been extruded and hardened, more flexibility is possible; in further processing (purifying, washing, drying etc.) delays do not lead to such severe damage to materials or equipment, but of course an uninterrupted flow is still desirable.

Before analysing the labour utilisation in such production let us describe the process of making synthetic fibres. Man-made cellulose fibres are manufactured from naturally formed materials whose molecules are merely rearranged. In the case of true man-made fibres such as nylon or polyester, the molecules first have to be synthetically built up from derivatives of mainly coal or petroleum, and formed into polymers or chainlike structures of linked molecular units.

Polymerisation is the first stage in a synthetic fibre plant (see Figure 5.2). The raw materials are fed into reaction vessels and processed at a high temperature. The resulting liquid is discharged from the reactor in the form of a ribbon which solidifies and is cut up into chips. These are conveyed through pipes to the spinning building. Here they are dropped into a drier and then gravity fed into a melter hopper. The molten material is forced through holes in the spinning head. As the jets of molten nylon or polyester emerge they solidify by contact with a stream of cold air, forming solid filaments. These are drawn together and wound on to cylinders. From here the yarn is fed onto a draw twist machine, where it is hot-stretched to several times its original length before being wound onto bobbins. This filament yarn is then supplied to the customers, who often texture it (to make it fuller) before use. Alternatively the texturising may be carried out in the synthetic fibre plant itself.

Synthetic staple fibre is made in the same way, up to the spinning operation. A great number of filaments emerging from the spinning head are brought together to form a thick tow. This tow is drawn, crimped mechanically (to make it fuller) and the crimp is set or stabilised by heating. The tow is then cut into specified lengths of a few inches according to the textile process for which it is intended. Finally the staple fibre is baled and dispatched.

Again there is the question of how continuous this process is and how serious its interruption would be. The polymerisation process is very sensitive to disturbances. Once the raw materials are fed into the reaction vessels, the chemical process has to proceed according to a precise schedule. If it stops for say ten minutes, this will affect the quality of the end product. If the conditions for the chemical reactions are changed for longer, it can mean that the material has to be thrown away. The importance of continuity in this stage is highlighted by the fact that all plants have their own electricity generators for use in emergencies. Electricity failure is one potential danger. The other one is workers' negligence. This can cause serious damage, but unless there is a series of errors, individual failures are unlikely to bring the whole process to a standstill. The plants have built-in checks; for instance, all work on the reactors is monitored on a central panel, so that major divergencies lead to alarms. The day-to-day problem is regularity and precision; slight errors in the dosing of raw materials, feeding in of additives at the right time, regulation of temperatures and so on, can lead to inferior quality of large amounts of fibres. In an industry where <u>constant</u> quality is a condition for success in the market, such errors mean considerable financial losses.

Figure 5.2: Flow Chart of Polyester Production

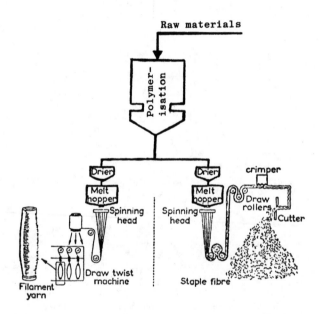

Source: after Moncrieff (1970).

The production process can be interrupted <u>after</u> the polymerisation is completed, if the polymer solution is converted into solidified polymer chips which can be stored. The most modern processes, however, channel the solution directly to the spinning stage. As in polymerisation, installations of the spinning process are connected to the plants' own electricity generators. Complete stoppage of all spinning operations caused by labour can hardly occur unless there is sabotage by a group of workers. In the rare case of one spinning machine being forced to stop, the material would be lost and the machine put out of action for some time; it has to be dismantled, the solidified material has to be removed, and the machine put together again. Relaunching the machine can take weeks. A more common risk arises at the point where the molten filaments solidify and are collected and guided over rollers. If the stream of solidifing liquid is broken, the filament immediately piles up underneath the spinning head instead of being continuously taken up and passed on. Workers with special equipment have to be on guard to re-establish the flow quickly. Otherwise large amounts of solidified waste material accumulate, in the order of 4,000 metres of wasted filament underneath one spinning head in one minute.

The subsequent processing is not quite so delicate. If filament yarn is the end product, there is a certain buffer because the filament is wound onto a package before being put on the draw twist machine. Such a buffer does not exist in the processing of staple yarn and operators have an important role in preventing waste production. The machinery and installations, however, are not at risk in the case of a breakdown.

Hopefully this characterisation of the processes3/ conveys some sense of the particular problems in continuous flow production. Breakdowns and interruptions are of course costly in any type of process, but in cotton spinning and weaving for instance, a standstill for one hour merely means one hour of lost output. Raw materials and machines are not at risk; the quality of the end product would not be affected in any significant way. As we have seen, this is quite different in the production of chemical fibres. We now wish to examine how this technological difference influences management's policies towards labour.

LABOUR UTILISATION

The managers of the chemical fibre plants visited showed a common concern in relation to labour reliability. Since the only way to find out about a worker's reliability is by employing him over a period of time, there was a common policy of trying to maintain the worker in the enterprise, in order to have a stable labour force. The managers interviewed were not equally successful in achieving stability, but clearly the worker's commitment and cooperation are of special importance in continuous flow production.

Recruitment and Training
How was it done? The strategies were not all identical. One firm put particular emphasis on getting the right people in the first place; recruitment policy was directly geared towards the goal of labour stability. The general recruitment principle for all posts was a) to work out a detailed job profile, including the mental and physical aptitudes required, and b) to look for the person who best adapted themself to the post. This might seem obvious or trivial, but is not. Of several candidates the person who adapts themself best to a job, might well not be the person who is brightest or learns the job most quickly.

Let us first take the case of machine operators and auxiliary workers. For these categories, the manager formulated his policy as follows: 'We look for the type of people who are likely to be happy in the enterprise...the new employees must have a future within the enterprise, therefore we don't seek people with too much formal education'. It should be added that illiterate workers were not admitted, since the reading of notices and instruments is part of the daily job.

The concern with stability was also reflected in other criteria. For machine operating the firm preferred married men between 25 and 35 years. For many auxiliary jobs, particularly the dull ones, slightly older workers were recruited, preferably those in their mid or late thirties. It was felt that younger workers would have too much pride, too much ambition and move quickly out of such jobs. Recruitment policy in the other two synthetic fibre plants was similar, but there was not so much concern with avoiding the over-ambitious. As we shall see later, they put greater emphasis on opening up channels for upward mobility in order to incorporate these workers.

The question of recruiting skilled versus unskilled workers does not arise in chemical fibre plants. Since there is only a small number of such plants (15) and since they are not concentrated in one small area, workers with the required experience are almost impossible to find. Training usually begins with a two- or three-day introduction covering topics such as lines of communication, hierarchy, obligations and benefits, security measures etc. After this, the training is on the job. Indeed, it could hardly be otherwise, since it would be too costly to have the production process duplicated in a separate training department.

Training is on the job, but not quite in a learning-by-doing fashion. Learning from mistakes would be too risky. Special instructors introduce the recruits to the machines and materials being processed and explain the tasks which have to be performed. The new operator is only allowed to handle machinery or products under direct supervision of the instructors. An operator of polyester spinning, for instance, stays for four weeks under the responsibility of the instructor, before being handed over to the production supervisor. At this point the operator is believed to be able to perform his tasks without help, or judge when he has to ask for assistance. After that he is given a maximum of five months to reach the productivity standards established by the firm. By way of an example, there follows the job profile for such an operator as drawn up by the firm.

Job profile for operator in polyester spinning
Educational requirements: The post requires the ability to read, write and perform the four basic operations of algebra.
Training: Up to six months (maximum period given to satisfy the standards of job performance set by the enterprise).
Room for initiative: Work is of a routine nature, in which operator receives instructions of norms to be followed from immediate supervisor; there is some room for decisions and initiative in solving simple problems.
Precision: The post requires precision in controls and operations.
Materials: There is a probability of wasting large quantities of materials due to carelessness of operator.
Machines and equipment: Operator negligence can lead to damage of machinery or render it inoperative.
Physical effort: Work implies light physical exertion, standing or walking, handling light materials and using tools during most of the shift.
Environment: work under conditions of considerable noise, high temperature, and pollution during the entire shift.
Risks of injury: Possibility of small cuts and bruises, not leading to absence from work.

The job profile of the operator in the polymerisation process is somewhat different. It emphasises more the need for precision in reading various instruments which measure and control temperature, pressure and duration of process, and also for being able to apply rules which determine when he can take action to solve problems and when he has to refer to his immediate supervisor. The training time is the same as that of the spinning operator. For operators of stretching, winding or texturising machines, training time is shorter. They have three months to reach the established productivity standards. Their work is more repetitive and leaves less room for serious mistakes.

Let us next review the recruitment and training policy for those higher up the hierarchy. The general policy in the firm was to recruit from within and to provide the training required for those who move into posts which are more complicated or carry more responsibility. There were, however, limits to this procedure due to the general educational and technical standards stipulated in higher positions.

Foremen were invariably recruited from amongst existing machine operators, and were given some extra training and instructions about security measures. Further promotion to supervisor was a problem because workers generally did not have the educational and technical standards required. The largest enterprise, however, was so keen on using its own workers for these positions that classes had been organised to make good this deficit. Classes were outside working hours, but held at times which meant that workers from all shifts could attend. Regular attendance at the course took the participants up to middle school level (nível ginasial). Those who were actually selected for promotion in the enterprise then received a further job specific training. Clearly, the large size of the enterprise helped to make this a workable scheme.

The other enterprises which were not quite so large turned to recruitment from outside. Thus they had a second entry point at the level of supervisory and technical staff. (In the largest enterprise, this entry point was pushed one level higher.) Their preferences were recently graduated textile or chemical technicians or engineers. The objective was to 'build up' their graduates so that they could finally move into higher technical and managerial positions. The general experience, however, was that it was difficult to reap all the benefits of this training and keep them. Hence all enterprises also recruited experienced engineers.

In general, recruitment from within was more pronounced than in the spinning and weaving industry. Building up a labour market internal to the firm was seen as one way of stabilising the workforce. In the largest firm, the promotion ladder seemed to be the main means of achieving this objective; the clearest indication of this was the above mentioned attempt to push up the ceiling for promotion of ordinary workers as high as possible by way of educational and training courses.

Obviously these measures are unlikely to be successful if not backed up by a corresponding wage policy. In order to analyse the wages paid by chemical fibre firms, we have to take into account their location. As seen in the previous study, regional wage differentials can be considerable. Three of the four plants were located in the state of São Paulo. Table 5.3 gives the range of their monthly wages by occupational category.

How do these wages compare with those in the spinning and weaving industry of the state of São Paulo (see Table 4.23)? The range of wages in each occupational category indicates that precise comparisons are difficult, but it is clear that wages in the chemical fibre plants are higher. The differences are, however, not dramatic; they are in the order of 25 per cent.

Table 5.3: Monthly Wages in the Chemical Fibre Industry in the State of São Paulo by Occupational Category (in multiples of minimum wage)

Category of Labour	Wage range
Managers and engineers	25.8 - 50.7
Supervisors	9.3 - 22.0
Foremen and instructors	5.3 - 11.6
Machine operators	3.0 - 5.1
Auxiliary workers	2.1 - 2.7
Maintenance	
Mechanic/electrician	4.1 - 7.6
Assistant	2.3 - 3.0

Source: Interviews with management and personnel departments.

Table 5.4: Monthly Wages in a Chemical Fibre Plant in the North-East by Occupational Category (in multiples of minimum wage)

Category of labour	Average wage
Managerial and technical staff	46.2
Supervisors, foremen and instructors	9.3
Machine operators	3.0
Auxiliary workers	1.9
Maintenance workers	5.7
Overall	4.8

Source: Firm's employment records.

Table 5.4 gives the wages for the plant located in the North-East. Its machine operators and auxiliary workers earn clearly less than their fellow workers in the Centre-South, whereas supervisory, managerial and technical staff do not lag behind. (The same was found in the spinning and weaving industry). North-Eastern machine operators and auxiliary workers are, however, better off in chemical fibre production than in spinning and weaving. A comparison with wages paid in the latter industry (see Table 4.26) reveals a substantial difference. There is, however, a problem in this comparison, because the synthetic fibre plant is located in a different metropolitan area known for a slightly higher wage level. Comparable wage data from that metropolitan area is available, though not disaggregated. Even so, it is worth noting that the average wage in the synthetic fibre plant was 4.8 minimum wages (Table 5.4), whereas the average wage in the spinning and weaving industry in the same area was 2.7 minimum wages.4/ Even though the evidence is patchy, we would suggest that in the underdeveloped region of the North-East, the wage differentials between the chemical fibre industry and the spinning and weaving industry are higher than in the industrialised Centre-South.

Labour Turnover
Let us now see how successful these policies were in stabilising the labour force. The average monthly rates of labour turnover in the four plants were, respectively: 1.0, 1.3, 1.7 and 3.0 per cent.

Table 5.5: Monthly Rates of Labour Turnover in a Chemical Fibre Factory by Occupational Category

Category of labour	Average labour turnover
Managerial and technical staff	0.0
Supervisors, foremen and instructors	0.2
Machine operators	2.0
Auxiliary workers	9.7
Maintenance workers	1.7
Overall	3.0

Source: Firm's personnel department.

In the firm with the highest turnover rate, a management strategy towards labour did not in fact emerge quite as clearly as in the other three. Its managers were concerned about the high turnover, but tended to put the blame on the workers for not having the right industrial mentality, or wanting to cash their guarantee fund (which requires dismissal). Measures to reduce turnover (such as company housing) had been discussed by management but there was not the pronounced and comprehensive effort to stabilise the workforce which was discernible in the other three firms. At the same time, it should be pointed out that labour turnover which mattered was not so different. This can be concluded from a disaggregation of the 3.0 per cent average turnover rate. As can be seen from Table 5.5, turnover is heavily concentrated amongst auxiliary workers and much lower for the other occupational categories.

Internal differences in the other three plants were much smaller. Unfortunately we do not have comparable disaggregated turnover rates, but since the overall rates are much lower, there is clearly little room for pronounced internal differences. In fact, one manager was very explicit in extending the concern with reducing turnover to the entire workforce. In his words: 'If you want to keep your house in order, you can't allow rubbish in your backyard'. Nevertheless, even in his plant, which had an average turnover of 1.7 per cent, some internal differences can be detected, if we compare the various stages in the production process (see Table 5.6). In the stages where stability and reliability matter most, namely polymerisation and spinning, turnover was only 0.9 and 1.3 per cent respectively. In the subsequent stages where the risk factor is lower, turnover rates were higher (except in twisting and winding). But as suggested before, differences were not very pronounced.

The lowest average monthly turnover rate of only 1.0 per cent was achieved in the largest plant. In previous years the rates had been 1.1 and 1.3 per cent. We tried to get further disaggregated figures, but it soon became clear that at such a low overall rate, internal differences were of necessity so small, that nothing systematic could be read into such figures.

Table 5.6: Monthly Rates of Labour Turnover in a Chemical Fibre Plant by Stage of Production Process

Production process	Labour turnover
Polymerisation	0.9
Spinning	1.3
Drawing	3.0
Twisting and winding	0.4
Dyeing	3.1
Texturising	1.6
Packing	3.3
Overall	1.7

Source: Firm's personnel department.

A particular strength of this firm lay in its credit cooperative. This enabled it to deal relatively smoothly with workers who ran into financial difficulties. A worker was allowed to apply for credit after three months of service. The credit limits varied; for an auxiliary worker it was the equivalent of 3.2 monthly minimum wages, for a machine operator 6.4 and for workers higher up the hierarchy it could reach over 12 minimum wages. Judging from the yearly reports of the cooperative, this credit system was heavily used. While it is impossible to quantify the contribution of this credit facility, it seemed to form an important element in the firm's policy of keeping the turnover down and binding the worker to the enterprise. The other elements were the already discussed elaborate internal career structure (including educational courses), good wages, and fringe benefits such as medical assistance and canteen services at low rates.

By way of summing up this industry study, we can conclude that the technological characteristics of continuous flow production lead management to greater concern with the stability of workers. Through careful selection, emphasis on internal training and promotion, better remuneration and fringe benefits, three of the four chemical fibre plants had achieved turnover rates well below those in cotton spinning and weaving, which are basically discontinuous processes. Our experience in this sector can best be summarised with the reactions of one of the plant managers interviewed. Asked why he was concerned with labour turnover, he immediately produced a chart which showed the waste production in his factory. He had been in charge of the plant for three years and he regarded the reduction of waste product as one of his main achievements. Over the same time period, labour turnover in his plant had also decreased.

NOTES

1. According to information from the Brazilian Association of Chemical Fibre Producers (Associação Brasileira de Produtores de Fibras Artificais e Sintéticas).

2. Staple fibres can be spun into yarns by techniques similar to those used in cotton spinning or indeed often chemical and cotton fibres are mixed or blended. For many applications, continuous filament yarns are less satisfactory than the looser and fuller staple yarn.

3. For a detailed account, see R.W. Moncrieff (1970). A good introduction for lay persons is given in the 15th edition of the Encyclopaedia Britannica (1970) under the entry 'Fibres, Man-Made'.

4. According to employment records ('Relação 2/3') provided to the Ministry of Labour and processed by SUDENE.

Chapter 6

THE CLOTHING INDUSTRY

Clothing manufacture provides an interesting contrast to the previously studied industries. In comparison with the chemical fibre industry the main difference is that its production is completely discontinuous and is labour intensive. With the spinning and weaving branch, garment manufacture shares the reputation of being a traditional industry; but technical change in the former has been very rapid and in the latter it has been rather slow. For the last century the clothing industry has been dominated by the sewing machine which is a relatively simple, cheap and long-lived tool. More recently attempts at automation got under way in the wake of the diffusion of micro-electronics, but their impact is still very limited.

THE PRODUCTION PROCESS1/

The manufacturing operation may be broken down into five main categories: 1. design; 2. laying and cutting; 3. sewing; 4. pressing; 5. inspection and finishing. Leaving aside the design stage and taking the British clothing industry as an indicator, the workforce is distributed over the various jobs as follows (NEDO 1971):

laying and cutting	7	per cent
machining operations	77	per cent
pressing	7	per cent
inspection and finishing	9	per cent

The above figures show that the machining operations would be by far the most important objective in the process of improving the garment manufacturing process. These activities can be grouped in two categories: general seaming and unit operations. General seaming constitutes the bulk of the manufacturing process and is only marginally affected by the type and style of garment being produced. The operator (virtually always a woman) is in most cases presented with two or more parts, printed or verbal instructions, and puts the pieces together to form the garment. Unit operations may be described as small repetitive operations that are common to many or all garments; for example, button-setting, button-holing, strap-fixing, attaching labels, pocket – setting. The machinery for these jobs comprises obvious extensions of the sewing machine which have been developed by machine manufacturers to a degree requiring little more of the operator than to insert the work piece.

New machines have therefore been developed, but there have been great problems in breaking the one machine/one operator ratio. This has to be seen against the development in spinning and weaving: 'in an installation in Formosa, a single female operative on roller skates can adequately look after 150 of their looms which are producing high quality poplin for the North American market' (Rothwell 1976b, p.103). Admittedly, this is an extreme example, but our detailed account of the changes in this industry (chapter 4) further underlines the point.

As a result of this relatively slow technological development, entry into the clothing industry has been and still is easy, as far as capital requirements are concerned. This, combined with the seasonality of the market and fashion changes, accounts for the fact that throughout the world a considerable part of the clothing industry consists of small firms. Small units, however, do not always mean independent producers. A further characteristic of the clothing industry is that small firms are often subcontracted by large factories or buying groups. In this system of 'cut, make and trim' small firms or women working at home are supplied with the material only to produce garments or parts of garments for the parent firm.

In firms with long production runs, productivity increases have been achieved mainly by applying principles of Taylorism and Fordism to the organisation of work. Time and motion study in the production of clothing has been developed to a very sophisticated level. This has led to a division of labour in the factory which leaves the individual machinist a very narrow range of repetitive operations. Roller conveyors or conveyor belts connect the individual operators. This segmentation of work tends to de-skill jobs. According to the manager of a successful German trouser factory, the training time required for a sewing machinist in his factory can be kept down to 12 weeks.[2] The preconditions for this are: a) no machinist should do more than two or three operations, b) no operation should last longer than two minutes or less than thirty seconds. Machinists in small firms tend to be more skilled, because they have to be more versatile than their colleagues in large fully 'rationalised' factories. This, however, need not be the case in small subcontracted units, to which only parts of the production process have been farmed out.

Even though the assembly or machining stage accounts for almost 80 per cent of labour costs, this is the stage where mechanising and automating has proved most difficult.

> The use of micro-electronics has, however, allowed for two types of semi-automatic sewing which although they do not completely replace the operator, do increase productivity while at the same time reducing skill levels and training time. The first incorporates a dedicated microprocessor in specialised pieces of equipment for small parts, i.e. collars, cuffs, belt-loops and pocket setting. These machines...allow a high volume producer to increase productivity by anywhere from 50-300 per cent... (Hoffman and Rush 1982, p.38)

However, long runs, infrequent style changes and more than one operating shift are necessary for these reliable, extremely efficient, but relatively inflexible machines. The second category of sewing innovations is distinguished by the use of programmable memory chips. This means that sewing machines can be programmed and controlled to perform a large variety of stitches in either decorative or functional sewing tasks. Such programmable machines are not only of interest to large-scale producers. They are, however, still in their first generation and the inherent technical problems are such that the productivity increases achieved are only incremental, certainly in comparison to the highly specialised machines mentioned above.

Technical innovation has been most fundamental in the operations leading up to the cutting of material. Grading, laying out, making and cutting have traditionally been highly skilled manual tasks carried out by men. Given the value of the cloth in the total cost of the finished product (generally reaching 50 or more per cent), the phase of laying out patterns on the cloth is crucial if wastage is to be kept to a minimum. Likewise, cutting the cloth precisely according to the lay is important, particularly since error at this stage can lead to defective garments at the assembly stage. The sequence of tasks from grading through to cutting has been the only operation for which automation with micro-electronics has significantly bridged the gap in what were previously discrete activities. However, the costs of these new systems are enormous (US$300,000 to US$1,000,000) limiting their diffusion to very large firms. Even there such highly technical schemes cannot have a fundamental effect on the overall economy of the industry, given the relatively small number of workers required in the cutting room. The same is true for finishing operations which have in fact been relatively neglected. New pressing equipment, incorporating micro-electronics, has been developed for jeans, slacks and suits, but these machines have not been used under production conditions long enough for an assessment of their operating performance to be made. What is currently evident is that all the micro-electronics related innovations can be used to reduce both the training time and the skill of the operator which were previously required to ensure quality (Hoffman and Rush 1982).

THE BRAZILIAN CLOTHING INDUSTRY

Little comprehensive information is available on the technological 'outfit' of the clothing industry in Brazil. Judging from our factory visits and interviews,3/ it is safe to say that traditional technology still prevails. Automatic equipment has not come to be used on a significant scale.4/ The manager of one firm with close to 1,000 workers indicated that wages would have to rise at least four-fold before he would try to automate parts of the production process. Another manager of a similarly large firm emphasised that apart from the high capital costs of automatic machines, maintenance would be an exorbitant problem because it was so costly, and speedy repair could not always be guaranteed in Brazil. Obviously the pace at which new technology is being developed could change their reasoning, but as indicated in the previous section, for the time being innovations are likely to be of relevance for the larger enterprises only.

Table 6.1: Enterprises and Workers in the Brazilian Clothing Industry, 1950-75

	1950	1960	1970	1975
Enterprises	1,076	2,687	5,050	6,421
Workers	26,557	45,174	112,626	177,889

Source: IBGE, Censo Industrial
Note: The figures in the Census relating to the clothing industry are not all grouped together. For details of the Census classification and how it was used, see Schmitz (1978).

The larger share of Brazilian production and employment is accounted for by medium and small-scale enterprises. Unfortunately this is difficult to document since the breakdown by size of enterprise in the Industrial Census is not

sufficiently disaggregated to identify the clothing industry.5/
Special tabulations from the Statistical Office could probably
remedy this difficulty, but there is a more fundamental problem
in that the small-scale garment sector is seriously
underestimated in the Census. Before examining this, let us
look at the available data (Table 6.1).

Table 6.1 shows a steady growth of the clothing industry,
but these figures underrate its real importance, as is made
clear by comparing the employment data in Table 6.1 with the
occupational statistics of the Demographic Census, according to
which the numbers of 'tailors and seamstresses' were as shown
in Table 6.2.

Table 6.2: Tailors and Seamstresses, 1950-70

Year	1950	1960	1970
Workers	257,804	388,814	405,328

Source: IBGE, Censo Demográfico
Note: A Demographic Census was not carried out in 1975 and
the results of the 1980 Census had not come out at the time of
writing.

There are several problems in using the figures in Table
6.2 as indicators for employment in the clothing industry. For
example, the industry does not only employ workers who work on
sewing machines; from this point of view the figures are too
low. On the other hand, some of the tailors and seamstresses
are engaged in the repair of clothes rather than in the
production of new clothes. Also, not all of them work full
time in this occupation, but according to the latest Census, 76
per cent work 40 hours per week or more. These and other
problems have been discussed elsewhere (Schmitz 1978) in a
detailed examination of the relevant data of the Industrial,
Services and Demographic Censuses. The conclusion reached was
that the total number of people engaged in clothing production
in 1970 was probably around three times the number given in the
Industrial Census. It should be emphasised that this
conclusion was based on some rather crude estimates, but in all
likelihood they constitute a lesser evil than taking the
Industrial Census figures at face value.6/

The question arises as to why the Industrial Census is so
inadequate. First, it does not cover outworkers, which is a
serious omission in the case of the clothing industry.7/
Second, it leaves out many small-scale enterprises, largely
because they are not registered. For instance, for the entire
state of Rio de Janeiro a mere 30 knitting and 25 clothing
firms of less than 5 workers were listed (in 1970), whereas in

Petrópolis alone (a town in that state) hundreds of such small enterprises existed (Schmitz 1982). Thus the Industrial Census gives at best an indication of the size of the internal workforce of the medium and large enterprises. Interpreting Table 6.1 in this light, we can conclude that this workforce increased substantially over the period 1950 to 1975. How total employment in the small-scale sector developed is hard to say. Casual observation would suggest that there are two conflicting tendencies. On the one hand, production of garments made to measure for private customers seems to be declining. On the other hand, there are signs of a considerable increase in small producers who make clothes in series, be it for other larger manufacturers, shops, boutiques, stallholders in markets or for itinerant salesmen.8/

Not all small firms are subcontracted by large ones. Many manage to find room in the market and grow, because the demand for clothing is channelled through a very diffuse distribution network which in turn calls for a flexible production network. Indeed flexibility is the main advantage of small firms in a branch where changing seasons and fashions are further obstacles to advance planning and organisation. A manager of Brazil's second largest clothing firm cited the need to cope with the country's extremely changeable market as his main challenge: 'I was hoping for the day when this volatile demand could be disciplined by the supply. I have given up this hope.' At the same time he pointed to a positive aspect of these market conditions, which his enterprise was beginning to appreciate: the market structure helped to keep foreign companies out of the industry. 'It is indispensable for the multinational to have a stable market; its responses are slow because of its structure; its extensive lines of delegation make it slow.' The conditions of the internal market are certainly a major reason why foreign capital is of relatively little importance.9/ Ninety-six per cent of capital invested in the industry is national (Visão 1977). As long as the industry produces primarily for the internal market, this is unlikely to change.

LABOUR UTILISATION

Given the large segment of employment in the clothing industry which exists behind the curtain of official statistics, research at the micro level is indispensable if one wants to understand the pattern of labour utilisation in the branch. For this study we investigated the industry of Fortaleza in the North-East.10/ Fortaleza probably has the most interesting clothing industry in the region, because it covers all sizes of enterprises, from the very large plant with over 1,000 workers to the small backyard manufacturer who relies primarily on family labour. Table 6.3 provides the best available statistics, but it is accurate only for enterprises with 100 or more workers. Particularly in the category of enterprises with less than 10 workers it shows only a small fraction of the real number of producers involved.

The information that follows is based on research in: two large enterprises with over 500 workers; two medium-sized enterprises of between 100 and 500 workers; four small enterprises of more than 10 but less than 100 workers; and 17 non-registered enterprises with less than 10 workers. Useful complementary information came from interviews with two suppliers of machinery and a supplier of raw materials. As explained before, within this study, employment in the small-scale economy is of interest to the extent that it represents an extension of the labour utilisation of the medium or large-sized firms.

Table 6.3: Enterprises and Workers in the Clothing Industry of Fortaleza 1977-78

Size of enterprise (workers)	Number of enterprises	Number of workers
500 and more	3	2,803
100-499	16	3,635
10-99	29	1,266
less than 10	20	104
Total	68	7,798

Sources: 1. Survey carried out in 1978 by the Associação da Indústria de Confecções do Estado do Ceará (Employers' Federation of the Clothing Industry) amongst its members.
2. Federação das Indústrias do Ceará, Instituto Euvaldo Lodi, Cadastro Industrial de 1977.
Whenever possible, data were taken from 1. which were then complemented by 2. for those enterprises which did not belong to the Employers' Federation of the Clothing Industry.

Labour Utilisation in Large and Medium-sized Enterprises

Let us begin with the employment within the medium and large-sized firms. Table 6.4 presents the aggregate data of the four firms investigated, by occupational category. Before we concern ourselves with the influence of technology on labour, let us pause and absorb what this table tells us about clothing employment. Four features stand out: the labour force is predominantly: 1. female; 2. single; 3. young; 4. earning just above the minimum wage. None of these features would be particularly surprising, but they deserve closer scrutiny, not least because the clothing industry is supposed to be one of the pillars of employment creation in the region. In fact, all four enterprises were set up or expanded with the help of government incentives.

Employment has certainly been created by these clothing firms, but it has to be recognised that this employment is generally temporary (for the individual) and poorly paid. The temporary nature of the employment arises from the fact that the women generally have to give up their job once they marry. All managers interviewed emphasised that this is not a strict rule, but the data for sewing machinists, by far the largest occupational group, suggest otherwise: virtually all machinists were women and almost 98 per cent were single. The temporary nature of the employment is further supported by the low percentage of workers with more than two years of service (although this could partly reflect the net expansion of these enterprises).

The poor remuneration undoubtedly reflects the large labour surplus which the industry can draw upon. This has already been commented upon in the case study on the spinning and weaving industry in the North-East. Another recurring feature is that this labour surplus is not entirely unskilled. Fortaleza has a considerable tradition in the making of garments particularly through domestic production. In fact this was mentioned as an advantage by managers in three of the four enterprises (although the fact that they all recruit primarily young women must mean that this advantage is not of overriding importance).

One firm considered this to be of no advantage at all. The recruitment policy of this firm is of particular interest since it was the one which used the most advanced methods of production, both in terms of technology and organisation of work. The lay-out of the factory was determined by an automatic conveyor which took the garment through its successive stages of production. This was part of a package of imported technology and know-how which included detailed instructions about the execution of each operation, a system of quality control and even a programme for job enrichment through music (for example: slow, calm music early in the morning; then faster, more rhythmic music in the second half of the morning). Most importantly for us, this system of production was associated with a specific recruitment policy, as evidenced by the following interview excerpt:

> Question: In implementing this system of production and control, did you have any problems with the local labour force which is not used to these methods?

Table 6.4: Gender, Marital Status, Age, Education, Length of Service and Average Wage of Workers in the Clothing Industry of Fortaleza by Occupational Category

Occupational Category	Total	Gender		Marital Status			Age						Education					Length of Service						Average Wage* (in multiples of regional monthly minimum wage)	
		Men	Women	Married	Single	Other	Less than 20	20-29	30-39	40-49	50-59	60 and more	Illiterate or non-completed elementary school	Completed elementary or non-completed middle school	Completed middle school or non-completed high school	Completed high school or non-completed university	Completed university or equivalent	Less than 6 months	6 months - 1 year	1 - 2 years	2 - 4 years	4 - 6 years	6 years and more	from	to
Managerial and technical staff	16	13	3	11	5	-	-	5	8	2	1	-	-	2	4	7	3	1	2	3	4	5	1	16.9	35.9
Supervisors, foremen and instructors	147	60	87	30	116	1	2	106	33	4	4	1	4	55	67	19	2	12	16	37	26	33	23	2.5	5.0
Machine operators	1519	11	1508	33	1485	1	264	1141	103	8	1	1	93	1128	297	1	-	347	385	583	111	55	38	1.1	1.4
Auxiliary workers	887	320	567	66	820	1	289	506	68	15	4	5	70	604	203	10	-	167	261	361	51	32	15	1.1	1.3
Maintenance workers	45	44	1	19	26	-	6	23	7	7	2	-	5	24	16	-	-	6	11	14	11	3	-	2.9	6.3
Total	2614	448	2166	159	2452	3	561	1781	219	37	9	7	172	1813	587	37	5	533	675	998	203	128	77	1.3	1.6

*Averages were calculated separately for each firm.
Source: Employment records of sample firms.

109

Answer: Exactly, the right kind of recruitment and training are fundamental in this system. Therefore, point one: we only recruit in the age group of 16 - 24 years, because this is proven to be the age range in which the girl has the greatest facility to adapt to our pattern.11/ Point two: we don't accept machinists who have experience from elsewhere; we seek only girls who have never worked on a sewing machine before to make sure they are without pre-set work habits.

Question: How long does it take you to train a machinist to reach average productivity?

Answer: That depends on the operation in question. Nobody makes an entire garment, everybody carries out only one operation...There are operations which a girl can learn in a week, since we consider her trained once she reaches 80 per cent of the objective. She will reach the other 20 per cent with time and practice. So we have operations where one week is sufficient and others where we would need 12 weeks. The great majority of operations can be mastered in up to eight weeks.

Question: How do you select who should be trained for what?

Answer: We have a little school [training department] here in our factory and also instructors on the production line. In the school we have set up a series of basic exercises with and without machines ... By the results of each of these tests we know which direction the girl should take. The instructors on the line are there to see to those who for one reason or another are not keeping up their productivity.

What emerged was a clearly defined recruitment and training policy with the prime objective of moulding each worker to the rules and standards of the enterprise. The attempt to achieve real subordination of labour was highlighted by the conveyor along which the machinists were placed and which seemed to impose an 'objective' pace and flow into the system. In the personnel policy it was highlighted by the insistence on unskilled recruits. To make sure, other elements of the recruitment and training policy were very similar in the other enterprises.

The absence of a conveyor in the other enterprises and the hustle and bustle which this involves cannot necessarily be taken as a sign of inefficiency, a point we should briefly elaborate upon. The enterprise which we called the 'most advanced' in technological and organisational terms was so in the sense that it came closest to European or US methods of production. This was because it was a firm which sought long production runs and tried (with varying success) to get a foothold in the export market with good quality trousers and shirts labelled with its own trademark.

The other three firms investigated had shorter production runs. In the case of the two medium-sized firms this was not surprising, but the case of the other large firm presented an interesting contrast to our above-mentioned firm. It had taken a conscious decision against the most advanced methods of (handling) technology and the organisational sophistication that goes with it. The reason lay in its assessment of the Brazilian clothing market, which was considered excessively volatile:

> If you have this relatively expensive transport system implanted in your factory and are then surprised by changes in the market, it takes you backward rather than forward ...The flexibility is more important than productivity gains achieved through a more 'rational' handling system and lay-out.

Indeed in this factory, as well as in the other two, the handling was all done manually. In the actual transformation process (the individual machining operations) however, the four firms showed no major differences. They all adhered to the principle that no worker sews an entire garment and each operation is carried out by a different person. As regards the machines, we have already explained that technological change was not of a kind which could have opened up huge gaps between the various producers. In sum, the difference lay more in the organisation of the collective worker in the 'advanced' firm.

This difference is, however, not reflected in a different composition of the labour force (except for a lower percentage of auxiliary workers in that firm). A disaggregation of Table 6.4 by firm (given in Table 6.5) shows above all the similarities amongst the four firms. The reason is that other factors override technology or organisational principles as an influence on labour utilisation. The high percentage of women (83 per cent overall and 99 per cent amongst machinists) is socially determined and reinforced by the cheapness of female labour. The high percentage of single and young women is not restricted to the 'advanced' firm seeking workers without previous experience, but found in all firms, since they avoid the costs and problems which can arise when women are pregnant or have children. Overall, only 10 per cent of workers are over 29 years of age; amongst machinists the proportion is even lower at 7 per cent. Surprisingly none of the respondents mentioned the poor health conditions of much of the population in the North-East which would presumably further shift the balance towards young workers, particularly for strenuous industrial work.12/ The importance of the health factor can be

Table 6.5: Gender, Marital Status, Age, Education, Length of Service and Average Wage of Machinists in the Clothing Industry of Fortaleza by Sample Firm

Firm	Total	Gender		Marital Status			Age						Education					Length of Service						Average Wage (In multiple of regional minimum wage)
		Men	Women	Married	Single	Other	Less than 20	20-29	30-39	40-49	50-59	60 and more	Illiterate or non-completed elementary school	Completed elementary or non-completed middle school	Completed middle school or non-completed high school	Completed high school or non-completed university	Completed university or equivalent	Less than 6 months	6 months - 1 year	1 - 2 years	2 - 4 years	4 - 6 years	6 years and more	
1	675	1	656	4	652	1	128	522	7	1	1	1	-	591	66	-	-	147	150	359	-	1	-	1.1
2	530	9	521	12	518	-	53	416	55	4	1	1	58	253	219	-	-	127	131	111	77	49	35	1.2
3	194	1	193	13	181	-	29	127	33	5	-	-	20	166	8	-	-	55	41	68	22	5	3	1.2
4	138	-	138	4	134	-	54	76	8	-	-	-	15	118	4	1	-	18	63	45	12	-	-	1.4
Total	1537	11	1508	33	1465	1	264	1141	103	9	1	1	93	1128	297	1	-	347	385	583	111	55	38	1.1 - 1.4

Source: Firms' employment records.

gathered from the recommendation of a consultancy firm: 'The provision of meals for the operators at an accessible price is a necessity, as well as the free provision of bread and coffee with milk early in the morning' (Capelin Associados do Brasil 1977, p.87).

As already stated, the overall picture is one of temporary employment, and for those who remain, the chances of upward mobility are not overwhelming, at least not for women. Whilst among machinists the percentage of men is as low as 0.7, in the category of supervisors, foremen and instructors it rises to 41 per cent (Table 6.4). All firms said that they prefer to recruit instructors and supervisory personnel from inside, but also confirmed that it was not rare for them to have to seek candidates with the required leadership qualities outside the firm. (This is not of course surprising, since the attributes sought in the recruitment of machinists are manual dexterity and willingness to follow instructions rather than the ability to take initiative or give orders). For managerial and technical staff there is a separate entry point; they generally come from higher technical schools and/or the families which own the enterprises. In contrast to the industries covered before, maintenance workers are very few, overall only 1.7 per cent of the workforce.

Labour turnover was high; the rates varied between 3.2 and 4.5 per cent per month.13/ All personnel managers seemed to feel uneasy about this high turnover, but one must wonder about the likelihood of any significant improvement. The (almost automatic) dismissal of women who get married or become pregnant is one major cause of turnover. Then there are the fluctuations in demand which impose a certain instability from outside. A third factor is the labour legislation and guarantee fund (FGTS) for which the rationale has already been explained in chapter 4; in all four firms, at least part of the labour turnover was attributed to this factor. Finally there are the 'normal' causes of turnover due to dissatisfaction with the conditions of work and pay on the part of the worker, or dissatisfaction on the part of the firm with the performance or behaviour of the workers.

Clearly turnover could be lowered by a change in employers' policies, but probably this will not happen so long as there is no technologically-imposed necessity to do so.14/ The fragmentation of jobs keeps the necessary training time low and facilitates the replacing of workers. The production process is discontinuous (even with conveyors), and reliability of workers is not a factor in the sense that it is in the previously analysed chemical fibre production. If the production process is interrupted, the damage is limited to the loss of output in the section concerned and during the period for which the interruption occurred. Damage due to the operator's negligence is limited to the specific piece of equipment or garment which she is handling.

The low wages bear testimony to the employers' policy towards labour. Given the production and market characteristics outlined above, higher wages would not be an 'efficient' solution. Indeed, the wage ranges given in Table 6.4 were confirmed in the interviews. The standard pattern is that machinists and auxiliary workers earn a basic minimum wage which they can top up with productivity bonuses by up to 50 per cent. This payment by results is calculated on the basis of standards which are determined by employees specialised in time and motion study. Fore(wo)men and supervisors start with two and can earn up to six minimum wages in the larger enterprises, which have two layers of supervisory personnel.

Labour Utilisation in Smaller Enterprises
The study of some smaller firms in the size category of 10 to 99 workers complemented our understanding of labour utilisation, particularly as regards organisation of work and skills.

Four such enterprises were visited and clearly one of their main problems was to make the transition towards an organisation of production which was found in the larger enterprises. In simple terms, the problem is getting away from the organisation of work around a complete garment (i.e. one woman carrying out the entire assembly) to one divided into stages with every worker specialising in certain operations. This was most visible in an enterprise of 70 workers, where the owner had brought in a young 'técnico', lured away from a large enterprise, and had put him in charge of reorganising the production process. Indeed he approached it with the conviction of a Frederick Winslow Taylor, but encountered huge problems. Re-training women used to different methods of work proved difficult. Moreover the firm's size put severe limits on the drive for 'rationalisation'. Dividing up the labour is not a great difficulty even in small firms, but doing it effectively is. As already mentioned, the larger enterprises use time and motion studies to work out training schedules and schemes for payment by results. In enterprises with shorter production runs this is not always economical.

That re-training is a problem was confirmed by one of the local machinery suppliers. He referred to a number of his clients who had reorganised production, but believed this could be done simply by introducing their former seamstresses into the new fragmented process. Reporting on one of these small factories he said:

If I'd been manager there, I wouldn't have accepted half the machinists; they pick up a bit of material, look at it, turn it round, put it in the machine, position it, sew a bit, stop the machine, get another bit in position, sew it...That's no good. What's important is machining time.

It's the machine which is supposed to do the job, not the seamstress. Sometimes you can see a very neat seamstress, she looks busy, but the machine is at a standstill. So you have to get to the point where she can position the materials in the machine and sew it all in one go. If you translate that into hours, months, a year, it's one hell of an increase in production.

The point to be re-emphasised here is that even where a firm tries to reorganise, it is difficult to achieve the productivity increase without thorough re-training, even though (or better, because) work has been simplified and routinised. This machinery supplier, for instance, who used to be a production manager, preferred to train people from scratch. The skill of being able to produce an entire garment can thus become an obstacle in 'advanced' systems of clothing production.

The above experience ties in perfectly with that of another producer who had 16 workers and supplied exclusive models for boutiques. He explained that:

a firm like ours can't produce a garment in stages like other firms do. Our sewing women have to know everything from start to finish...They all come with experience, because we can't train them here. They come from small enterprises where they often worked without registration, or they were self-employed. There's no room here for machinists from large enterprises. They can only do a single operation.

Seamstresses able to produce entire garments are apparently available in the market. This is of course of considerable importance for producers of the type referred to above. The training time required for their workers would be six to eight months (for somebody who starts from zero) to reach average productivity, whereas two to three months training is sufficient in those enterprises which have broken the process into separate operations.15/ The availability of these workers is also important in terms of the wages small producers have to pay. Even though their seamstresses are more skilled (in terms of necessary training time) they pay just above the minimum wage (1.1 to 1.3 minimum wages). It may be remembered that this is also what sewing women in the larger enterprises receive.

Outwork
The labour force of the enterprises so far considered extends beyond their factory walls into the 'informal economy', where small family enterprises or individual homeworkers carry out piece – work. Often this 'domestic industry' goes unregistered

with the statistical office and taxman, but not always. In this section we analyse under what circumstances this form of labour utilisation occurs and whether/how changing technology influences this practice.

Informal enterprises constitute an important part of Fortaleza's clothing industry. Sometimes they are only a one-person enterprise, but more often other family members join in, and not infrequently these are further complemented by some wage workers from outside the family. Nineteen such enterprises were visited; they all had less than ten workers in total and operated from domestic premises. Trying to quantify the size of this segment of the local industry is an almost impossible undertaking. One respondent suggested: 'count the number of houses in and around town and divide it by three!' This would overestimate the number of such enterprises, but in some areas of Greater Fortaleza it is probably not too far from the truth, if we include individual homeworkers.

To be sure, not all domestic producers are subcontracted by larger enterprises. Many are independent, buying their own raw material and selling their produce as best they can; others work in semi-subcontracting arrangements for wholesalers or retailers. The numbers and types of distribution channels are bewildering. One major distribution centre is the central market, where stallholders sell to both consumers and retailers. In many cases the home manufacturers go there to sell their produce and with the money received buy material for the next round. Sometimes it is a neighbour or friend who regularly collects the garments and re-sells them in the central market. The local tourist market (ENCETUR) and boutiques are other outlets. Some work directly for the consumer. Others send the clothes by mail or bus to acquaintances in other areas of Brazil where they are re-sold. Many people leaving Fortaleza for other destinations take with them a parcel or suitcase full of clothes for re-sale. In other words, the small-scale, informal, domestic production feeds into an equally informal distribution network through which some of this production reaches all corners of Brazil.

The formal enterprises make use of these producers, but rarely for the manufacture of complete garments, generally only for one specific operation, namely embroidery. The state of Ceará, of which Fortaleza is the capital, has a reputation for embroidered textiles throughout Brazil. Traditionally this industry relied primarily on external workers. Indeed, both our medium-sized enterprises and two of the smaller ones had been able to accumulate and grow partly on the basis of this form of labour utilisation. A study of artisan production in the state of Ceará, carried out in the early sixties, gives some idea of how the production was organised. The study (Rios 1962) refers to those firms which have hundreds of women working for them, some in the capital but most in the interior of the state:

There are many different ways of conducting business. In some towns the enterprise has an agent, in others the work is distributed directly. In some cases the agent is a local firm which works for the parent enterprise in Fortaleza. In other towns an individual, who may or may not be an embroiderer, picks up the material in Fortaleza and takes it to the groups [of embroidery women] of varying size. In the interior, groups sometimes get together and nominate a representative to deal with the enterprise. This person may get a commission from the enterprise or may take something out of the wages of the local embroiderers...(p.91)

Most of these goods leave the state without invoice...Some organised firms pay taxes, but the majority work outside the system...(p.92)

Embroidery work is poorly paid and because the business is badly organised and firms do not pay taxes 'the one to suffer most is the embroidery woman' [said the representative of a firm. Another representatative, referring to the avoidance of social security payments said] 'if one of these embroidery women were to be considered a registered employee, we'd be lost. If we were to close down, there'd be a huge crisis in the interior, because embroidery work serves a tremendous social function' [source of income]. (p.93)

The advantages to the employer of this system were three: he was spared investment in buildings and machinery, he could easily adjust to changes in demand, and he had access to the cheapest of all workers, women who had often no alternatives of gainful employment.

Gradually, however, this work is being transferred to within the factory. For instance, one of the medium-sized enterprises which used to have over 800 external embroiderers had reduced this number to 180 and instead increased its internal production. The other medium-sized enterprise continued to have over 300 outworkers, but had also installed an internal embroidery department.16/ Most respondents agreed that in the long run the external work would only play a minor part, if any at all. There was, however, visible disagreement as to the pace and form this transition would take.

Our way into the discussion was by asking: 'Is it not cheaper to farm out this part of the production process than to bring it inside?' Answer: 'At the moment it is about equal. The greatest problem is the control we need. The costs of administering this system and the loss of quality are considerable. Another problem is that our enterprise requires quicker responses when it comes to delivery of the goods.'

Quite clearly the most <u>immediate</u> problem with the putting out system was quality control, together with reliable and fast delivery.

A more decisive factor, however, was and is going to be technical change. Generally outworkers carried out embroidery work on their domestic sewing machines, equipment which most women had anyway for making and repairing clothes for the family; if they had to buy a machine, they could probably get one cheaply second-hand or pay the equivalent of 1.5 monthly minimum wages for a new one. The embroidery work carried out inside the factories was all done on specialised industrial machines, which allowed a three-fold increase in labour productivity. On the other hand this machine was also much more expensive. Depending on the brand and model, it cost the equivalent of between 14 and 24 monthly minimum wages, an investment which very few outworkers were able to afford.

The temporary solution found by both firms was to operate both systems. They had acquired 64 and 41 industrial machines respectively in order to guarantee speedy and constant quality production when it was most required. But why did they hesitate to go all the way? One reason lay, of course, in the considerable investment which these machines involve. What made the completion of this process particularly difficult was the uncertainty about utilising this new capacity. First there was a yearly seasonal cycle in embroidered textiles which reached its peak during the months of September to November and had its low from January to March. Then there was the more general problem that embroidery, especially on women's garments, was in some years more fashionable than others.17/ So the decision only partially to bring the embroidery operation inside the factory was not technology- but market-determined. Clearly, maintaining a network of external workers provided both firms with a very convenient way of coping with the ups and downs in demand.

There was a third solution which both firms were exploring with great enthusiasm. Through cooperation with a machinery supplier and a bank they wanted to enable outworkers to buy their own industrial machines. The machine was to be purchased from this supplier by way of a loan from the bank, while the clothing firm played the role of guarantor (where required) and helped with training. The initiative actually came from the machinery supplier, when he felt that the clothing firms were hesitant to increase their internal capacity further. The only partner in the scheme who showed some reluctance was the bank, which was, however, finally persuaded to open a special credit line for this purpose. The scheme got under way with one of the firms, and the women who joined were registered, not however as employees but as self-employed.

It was too soon to assess how this scheme changed the pay structure for outworkers, but some indication came from two women who had acquired the new machines. Judging from their

information on rates of pay and time per piece, they could earn
1.8 monthly minimum wages (calculated on the basis of an 8-hour
day). This compared well with the average 1.3 minimum wages
earned by internal workers, but they had to pay the monthly
instalments on the machines acquired on hire purchase. Their
greatest headache was the risk of not being able to use the
machine. 'It must not stop, because the investment is so
high', said one of them. Obviously with more women acquiring
the industrial machine the piece rates might fall and the risk
of under-utilisation rise. Those with domestic sewing machines
will probably be marginalised, except for the case of some
complicated types of embroidery which apparently cannot be done
on an industrial machine.

Looming on the horizon is an even more advanced technology
which might completely revolutionise embroidery: the multi-head
automatic embroidery machine. It can be visualised as four,
six, or more conventional machine-heads in a row, whose
operations are determined by a tape. In other words, this is
programmed embroidery. 'Simple' versions only use one yarn
colour, sophisticated versions include automatic change of
yarns. Several such machines can be operated by one person,
whose training time is only a fraction of that required in
conventional embroidery.

We saw such machines (imported from Japan) at an
International Textile Machinery Exhibition in São Paulo and
also the managers of the Fortaleza firms were familiar with
their technical features; but they were not considering the
purchase of such machines in the near future. The main reason
lay in their cost (from the equivalent of 360 monthly minimum
wages upwards) and their greater suitability for long
production runs. It is, however, conceivable that
micro-electronics-based innovations will over time make such
machines both cheaper and more flexible for frequent embroidery
changes. Whether automatic machines will eventually be used on
a significant scale in low wage areas such as North-East
Brazil, and whether they might even have an impact on the use
of outworkers, is too soon to predict but the possibility must
be considered seriously, particularly for those lines where
constant quality is important.

Finally we should broaden the question of outwork in the
clothing industry and consider it beyond the specific case of
embroidery.18/ The widespread use of outworkers and
subcontracted enterprises for seaming operations has already
been mentioned. In this Brazil is no exception, as can be seen
from Table 6.6.

Even though this table should be treated with great
care,19/ it underlines the importance of external labour use in
the clothing industry. São Paulo is particularly well known
for its extensive subcontracting network and is generally
referred to as the centre where this practice is most firmly
established.20/ Spindel (1981) shows that increasing numbers

of sizeable workshops with 80 or more workers are being set up in the interior of the state with the sole purpose of producing garments or merely carrying out sewing operations for parent firms in the capital. In the North-East, however, subcontracting is not so common, at least not in larger firms set up with government incentives.21/

Table 6.6: Farming Out of Sewing Operations in Brazilian Clothing Firms by Product and Region (in percentages)

Product	North-East	Paraná Rio Grande do Sul	Rio de Janeiro Espírito Santo	Santa Catarina	São Paulo
Trousers	3	20	18	–	17
Shirts	3	19	16	–	28
Underpants + Undershirts	–	–	–	–	9
Lingerie	8	20	8	–	15
Jeans	4	40	45	–	40
Dresses	15	28	20	–	36

Source: Capelin Associados do Brasil 1977, Vol.II, p.130-A.

A point which is not borne out by Table 6.6 and which should be made explicit is that subcontracting is not only used by large capital. It is our impression that in relative terms it is even more important for small-scale capital engaged in the clothing industry. This capital often has a stake in both production and distribution. A good example of this was found in a centre of knitted clothing, Petrópolis. The rapidly growing industry in that town included a large number of clandestine domestic producers. They worked primarily for firms which sold the knitwear directly to the consumer or to retailers and at the same time had their own internal production department with 20, 30 or more workers.22/ Also in Juiz de Fora, another knitwear centre, it is primarily small capitalists who make use of individual homeworkers or small domestic workshops.23/ Similarly in Fortaleza we have already referred to the large number of domestic producers in that town; many of them make garments to order for local traders (stallholders in the market, shops) who also have their own production facilities. A study on outworkers in Rio de Janeiro provides further evidence. The enterprises of Rio's fashion industry rarely have more than 30 internal employees, but they have a high proportion of external workers. Abreu (1980) estimated that for each internal seamstress eight external sewing women were employed.

It is quite clear from these recent micro-studies that the

main reason for this form of labour utilisation lies in the volatile market. To some extent the demand pattern and its impact on the organisation of production is a result of the skewed income distribution in Brazil, which means that more of the effective demand goes into high priced, exclusive boutique clothes. The clearest, almost extreme, example is Rio's high fashion industry, where:

> the influence of fashion, so important in women's outerwear in general, seems to reach its paroxysm, forcing the launching of three collections a year and often the changing of models within the season. This exaggerated product diversification is determined by the system of distribution, since the main clients are boutiques which buy three or more examples of each model and demand a constant supply of novelties from the producers; this in turn creates a structure of production which - in order to cope with the instability of demand and to meet the sought-for quality, diversification and sophistication of details - must allow a flexibility totally incompatible with a large industrial organisation. Therefore, the clothing firms are relatively small, producing two to five thousand articles per month, with an internal workforce of 20 to 30 people...The extreme versatility...is achieved through a structure which centralises in the enterprise the stages of creation, preparation (design and cutting) and sales, but where the largest part of the production is carried out by external sewing women. (Abreu 1980, pp.132-135).

In the other examples referred to, the enterprises were not quite so much at the forefront of high fashion, but were still confronted with similar problems further down-market. Hence the use of external labour. Clearly, there are also other advantages in this form of labour utilisation (apart from the flexibility it provides): the saving on fixed investments in buildings and machinery, and access to cheaper, often non-registered, labour. For most enterprises, however, these are secondary.

Finally, we should re-emphasise that this form of labour utilisation is only possible because of the technological characteristics of the industry. The technology is divisible and cheap, which makes the farming-out of production relatively easy. Several innovations are on their way, as we have seen at the beginning of this industry study, which might change these features. But most of this new technology is still in its first generation, and its diffusion is more or less limited to large-scale producers operating in predictable markets. It is probably safe to predict that those clothing manufacturers who operate in volatile markets are the last to adopt the new technologies. Since it is they who make most use of external workers, outwork and subcontracting are likely to remain important features of the employment pattern in the clothing industry.

NOTES

1.　This section is based on NEDO (1971), Hoffman and Rush (1982), and our knowledge of the industry gained in factory visits and interviews.
2.　Training time required to reach average productivity. Based on discussion with the author.
3.　Including machinery suppliers interviewed at an International Textile Machinery Exhibition in São Paulo.
4.　A study by Capelin Associados do Brasil (1977) suggests that 3.7 per cent of Brazilian enterprises possess automatic sewing equipment, but there is no indication of the share of sewing operations which is carried out with this equipment.
5.　There are two problems: a) clothing manufacture is lumped together with shoe production, and b) part of the clothing industry, namely knitwear, is included in the textile industry.
6.　As in a recent study of the clothing industry which was commissioned by the government and carried out by a private consultancy firm (Capelin Associados do Brasil 1977).
7.　As shown by Abreu (1980) for Rio de Janeiro, by Spindel (1981) for São Paulo and in the following case study for Fortaleza.
8.　This is based on conversations with persons who have a good knowledge of Brazil's main centres of garment manufacture. Further support can be found in Abreu (1980), Schmitz (1982) and Spindel (1981).
9.　Significantly Brazil's largest clothing producer, which is a multinational firm, specialises in jeans and matching shirts which suffer relatively few modifications.
10.　We shall also draw briefly on the results of a previous study carried out in the state of Rio de Janeiro (Schmitz 1982) and three other studies on the clothing industry in the Centre–South (Abreu 1980; Caulliraux 1981; Spindel 1981).
11.　It is hard to resist adding here a quote from a report on training practices in the British clothing industry: 'There was a marked preference among employers for taking on 15 year-olds straight from school because as one said: "You can discipline children of 15 into your own methods and behaviour patterns".　Younger girls were said to be more amenable to discipline and to have lower absenteeism than the older ones' (Stewart 1963, p.13).
12.　The intensity of labour, stress and occupational disease in fragmented work are emphasised in a study on the labour process in some large and medium-sized clothing

enterprises in Rio de Janeiro by Caulliraux (1981).

13. We cannot read too much into the data on 'length of service' in Tables 6.4 and 6.5, because the enterprises had been expanding, which probably explains to some extent the low numbers amongst those with two or more years of service.

14. Again, a brief reference to the British industry may be of interest. 'Labour turnover is widely recognised in the clothing industry as a major problem. Turnover for the industry as a whole was well over 40 per cent throughout the '60s and in 1969 rose to 50.4 per cent although it fell again in 1970 and 1971. These figures are well in excess of those for manufacturing industry as a whole. Moreover the engineering and light electrical goods sector, an important competitor for female labour, maintained its turnover at well under 40 per cent throughout this period.' (NEDO 1972, p.5)

15. The higher skill requirements in small firms, especially if they operate in the high fashion market, are also emphasised by Abreu (1980, p.146): 'the quality of the garment and its complete assembly [by one person] requires skills much greater than those of a sewing woman in a large factory who only carries out a few tasks in the assembly process. Generally they are women with many years of experience and none of the firms investigated accepted very young girls'. A useful characterisation of the different labour processes in large · and small firms can also be found in Caulliraux (1981, chapter 3).

16. Both firms were among the leading producers of embroidered textiles. Discussions with their managers, complemented with information from the machinery suppliers, helped us to obtain a hopefully accurate picture of the changes which were occurring.

17. Embroidered textiles were major product lines in both firms, but not the only ones.

18. The town of Ibitinga in the state of São Paulo is another centre of embroidery where, even more than in Fortaleza, domestic production prevails. 'The register in the town hall includes 47 small firms and only 200 self-employed embroidery women; but the mayor confesses the existence of at least 6,000 machines installed in people's back-yards. Some postulate that the number of embroidery units comes to 9,000...' (O Estado de São Paulo, 15 June 1977, p.21; see also same paper of 17 June and 2 July 1977).

19. The main shortcoming of the table is that it does not give an indication of the weight · of external production/employment in those enterprises which use it. Also the sampling procedure is not always clear. For the state of Santa Catarina the sample seems too small to allow the generalisation that no outwork/subcontracting occurs, even though it is probably correct to say that it is very limited.

20. Based on conversations with machinery suppliers and garment producers in various parts of the country.

21.   The North-East data in Table 6.6 comes largely from such firms.

22.   For a detailed examination see Schmitz (1982).

23.   Based on reports from Líscio Camargo of the Instituto de Planejamento Econômico e Social, Brasília.

Chapter 7

THE HAMMOCK INDUSTRY

Let us now turn to an industry where technological advance has been even slower than in the clothing industry. In the manufacture of hammocks, technology has virtually stagnated. Up to the present day, most stages in the production process are carried out manually. Elsewhere we have described the functioning of this industry in detail (Schmitz 1979b, 1982). The objective here is merely to draw out its main technological features and analyse how this is connected with the pattern of labour utilisation.

HAMMOCKS IN BRAZIL

The custom of sleeping in hammocks originated with the indigenous Indian population of Brazil; the first hammocks were made by indigenous Indian women. 'After manioc flour, the hammock was the next important element in the adaptation of the Portuguese conqueror', said Cascudo (1957) in a study that describes the way in which, for four centuries, millions of Brazilians were born, lived, loved, died and were even buried in hammocks. Up to the present day a hammock is preferred to a bed by the majority of the population in most states of the North and North-East of the country.

From being initially a purely domestic product, the hammock came to have exchange value and to be produced by specialised artisans and their families. From the thirties onwards hammock production began on an industrial scale, that is with wage labour, without the existing technology altering very much, however. In fact, still today the production process is almost craftsmanlike, compared with that in other textile branches. As we shall argue later, this is the main reason why large capital does not enter this branch in spite of the size of its market. The population of the states where it is most used (Amazonas and neighbouring territories, Pará, Maranhão, Ceará, Rio Grande de Norte and Paraíba) accounts for over 21 million people. There is also a market for luxury hammocks which are sold all over Brazil and abroad, but for the industry as a whole the standard hammock is the main product.

According to official statistics (Table 7.1), the industry is of only minor importance, but they do not adequately represent its size. The explanation lies in the way the industry is organised. Hammock production takes place both in enterprises based on wage labour and in domestic workshops based on family labour. The employment practices of the former include non-registration of part of the internal workforce, the subcontracting of non-registered domestic workshops, and extensive use of individual outworkers. Many domestic workshops produce independently (are not subcontracted), but are more often than not clandestine, using outworkers in addition to their internal workforce. It is for these reasons that official establishment surveys cover only a fraction of the real number of workers involved.1/

Table 7.1: Enterprises and Workers in the Hammock Industry of Brazil in 1975

	No. of enterprises	No. of workers
Enterprises with 5 or more workers	171	2,732
Enterprises with less than 5 workers	148	365
Total	319	3,097

Source: IBGE, Censo Industrial.

Most, if not all, of the industry is located in the North-East. The largest centre of hammock production is the capital of the state of Ceará, where most of the information for this study was collected. The best available statistics are given in Table 7.2. In the course of the research it was estimated that the real number of workers engaged in this industry was at least six times the figure that can be derived from official sources (Schmitz 1979b, Appendix). Estimates made in a study on another centre of hammock production suggest that the extent of non-registered labour is even higher (Rocha 1979a). As we shall see in the course of this study, these conditions of clandestine employment are not unrelated to the technological conditions prevailing in this branch.

The respondents for this research included: the owners of eight enterprises (all registered), none of whom had more than 100 workers but who all had more than 10 internal workers; the owners of eight domestic workshops with up to 10 people working in them, seven of the workshops being clandestine;2/ ten persons engaged in carrying out or distributing outwork; four suppliers of yarn or machinery. Also three hammock enterprises in the state of Paraíba were visited to discuss with their owners some of the findings emerging from the Fortaleza interviews. Useful supporting information comes from a comprehensive study on the hammock industry in the state of Paraíba, carried out by Rocha (1979a,b).

Table 7.2: Enterprises and Workers in the Hammock Industry of Fortaleza in 1976

Type of enterprise	No. of enterprises	No. of workers
Enterprises with 10 or more workers	19	788
Enterprises with less than 10 workers	19	78
Total	38	866

Source: Ministry of Labour, '2/3 Survey'. The hammock branch belongs to the textile industry (branch 106 of '2/3 Survey') and its data is not published separately. Only through a detailed register of textile enterprises, provided by the Human Resources Department of SUDENE was it possible to compute the above data for 1976.

THE PRODUCTION PROCESS

The fieldwork in the hammock industry was carried out at the same time as that in the spinning and weaving industry. Coming out of a modern spinning and weaving mill and entering a typical hammock enterprise gives one the impression of going back in time, since it is so much like a pre-industrial revolution workshop. The main stages of production are carried out manually in most enterprises; in some small workshops the only source of power available is human muscle.

The raw material used is thick cotton yarn and the quantity necessary varies according to the size of hammock desired, that is, whether it is for a child, or whether it is a single or double hammock. The cotton yarn reaches the enterprise wound on cones; it undergoes three different processes: dyeing, weaving and finishing.3/

Dyeing: the yarn must first of all be wound into large hanks, so that during the dyeing process the dye is distributed

127

evenly.   This is a simple but tiring operation; the yarn is wound onto a wooden frame (2m by 5m) which has, along the vertical sides, a series of pegs around which the yarn is wound.   This protracted operation is usually done by women or children, walking back and forth from one end of the frame to the other, holding a wooden baton through which the yarn passes and which serves as a guide.

When sufficient yarn has been wound, the hanks are gathered together to form one large hank.   This is then put into a large metal cauldron containing the dye and is left until the desired shade is obtained.   Then the yarn is put on a line in the open air to dry.   This job is very messy - the dye goes everywhere - and is usually done by men.   The subsequent disentangling of the yarn is a time-consuming process.

Weaving: before beginning the actual weaving, it is necessary to prepare the warp (threads which run the length of the cloth) and the weft (those which run across the cloth), which when woven together form the 'cloth' of the hammock.   The warp threads are wound onto the beam of the loom.   Only some of the large producers use a mechanical process for this beaming. The weft thread is wound onto spools (pirns), which are placed inside the shuttle, and propelled from side to side, weaving in and out of the warp threads and so forming the cloth.   In the bigger enterprises, the winding onto pirns is mechanised, whereas in the small ones it is done manually.   This preparation for weaving is done by men and women.

In most firms, the looms are wooden and operated manually. A loom has two foot pedals on which the weaver stands; using his body weight, he is able to change over the two sets of warp threads.   His leg movements have to be coordinated with his arm movements.   The shuttle is sent back and forth by pulling two ropes which are on the loom, at head level.   Pulling the left hand rope sends the shuttle to the right and vice versa.   This work requires skill, especially when several different colours are being used.   In all the firms visited, the looms were operated by men.

Finishing: this stage is sent out to women who do the work manually in their own homes.   The woven cloth received from their employer has about 20 cm of loose threads at either end; these are plaited together in groups of about 12, to form a string; each string has a loop on the end.   To strengthen these strings and loops, they are incorporated in two narrow bands which run the width of the hammock.   These bands are woven by women with manually operated equipment.

A cord is threaded through the loops, itself in loops which are about 60 cm long; these are gathered together at the end farthest from the cloth and bound to make one single large loop.   This large loop (one at either end) is used for hanging the hammock and can be hooked onto a special metal fixture in the wall, or some other projection.   The cord used is bought

128

ready-made by the small enterprises, whereas the bigger ones have their own machines to produce it.

The final stage in the finishing of the hammock is the decorative fringe which runs along the two long sides. This may be very simple, a series of interlinking knots, or may be an intricate and beautiful lace-work fringe which takes several days to produce. The high quality of the fringe is one of the things which distinguishes a luxury hammock from a standard version.

So it can be said that to this day hammocks are made largely manually,4/ even though there are changes under way which will be evaluated below. It was surprising to find a branch of activity within the textile sector which had remained almost untouched by the rapid technological changes which have affected the world's cotton textile industry. How is it that the branch is technologically so backward? As far as is known, hammocks have never been produced by the countries which are the main technological innovators for the textile industry (Britain, Germany, Switzerland, USA, Japan). This is not to say that Brazil is incapable of developing its own machines, but, within the country, hammock production is concentrated in the region where labour is cheapest, giving little incentive to invest in the mechanisation of hammock production. This seems to be the most plausible explanation of the present · day technological conditions; these are backward but at the same time appropriate to the needs of the region which is characterised by great underutilisation of labour.

Let us now assess the likelihood of technical change affecting the industry, beginning again with the dyeing process. The most common way of dyeing is described above. It is a cheap method used by the majority of the large and small enterprises. It does not, however, give fast colours. There are, in the main centres of the branch, enterprises which do industrial dyeing with fast colours for their own use and/or for other hammock producers. This process is much dearer, and requires investment in sophisticated equipment, which goes beyond the resources of most, especially the small, enterprises. Even so, if demand changes in favour of fast colours, this in itself would not necessarily alter the structure of the industry because, instead of buying brute yarn, it could be bought ready-dyed, or sent to be dyed by a specialised firm.

The major technological challenge to be faced in the medium and long term is in weaving. Some large producers (particularly in the state of Paraíba) already use mechanical looms. Their hourly production is higher, and also one weaver can look after two machines at once. They are usually bought second hand, costing approximately US$1,400 including accessories and installation, as compared with US$280 for a new manual loom.

It is surprising that all the producers who had experience of mechanisation said that hammock firms with manually operated looms could continue competing in the market, for the following reasons. First, the necessary investment goes beyond just the cost of the new looms, since mechanical looms do not work well with yarn prepared by hand. As a result, anyone who mechanises the weaving must also mechanise the preparation of the yarn for the weft and the warp. The high investment in equipment would therefore slow down mechanisation. Second, weaving is only one item in the total cost and the reduction in total production costs achieved through mechanical weaving is so small that it can hardly render manual weaving obsolete.5/

If this is correct, it should also hold for more sophisticated machines. Automatic shuttle looms would anyway present problems because of the thick yarn used in hammock-making. Shuttleless looms would solve this technical problem, but are very expensive, around US$28,000 including accessories and installation. The high investment makes it unlikely that they will be used on a significant scale.6/ Some larger enterprises have a type of hammock made from ready-made cloth bought from weaving companies in São Paulo and Santa Catarina in the South of Brazil. According to the producers this practice is, and will remain, limited to a small number of more sophisticated hammocks.

The stage of production which is least likely to change is the finishing. Two old machines were seen, adapted to make simple fringes, but the end results were of poor quality, and the machines were not a solution in terms of mechanisation of the work. All those interviewed believed that finishing would continue to be a manual process, except for one producer. He thought mechanisation was possible, since there are operations conducted by textile machinery which are much more complicated than hammock finishing. According to him, the problem would be to find a mechanical engineer with an interest in hammock production and with the financial resources necessary. These technological innovations are unlikely to come about, since the textile machinery industry, and mechanical engineering in general, are concentrated in the Centre-South, which does not show much interest in hammock production.

For the moment it must be concluded that present-day technology in this industry will not see radical changes in the near future and that there are no substantial economies of scale in the industry, at least not in the production process.

LABOUR UTILISATION

Our next task is to examine the pattern of labour utilisation which is associated with these backward technological conditions. To this end we start from the following classification:

	Internal labour force	External labour force	
Large enterprise	Wage labour	Home workers	Labour of sub-contracted workshops
Small workshop	Family labour	Wage labour	Home workers	—

As already mentioned, hammocks are produced in two types of enterprises: first those based on wage labour, which we call large enterprises; second, those based on family labour, called domestic workshops or small enterprises. In reality, the division between the two types of enterprise is not a rigid one, because the domestic workshops also employ some wage workers. However, their owners are generally forced to engage themselves directly in the production process and their capacity to manage and supervise is thus severely limited.

Both large and small enterprises have in addition to their internal labour an external workforce, mainly women who carry out the finishing process at home. Moreover some domestic workshops are tied to the large firms in a kind of subcontracting system and are therefore included in the diagram as external labour force.

Of the entire labour force engaged in hammock making, only the internal workers of the larger enterprises are registered, and not all of them. It was noted that the men are generally on the official pay roll, whereas women often are not. Employment linked to the domestic workshops (be they independent or subcontracted) is clandestine, given that the enterprises themselves are not registered (with few exceptions). For these reasons it is difficult to quantify the size of the various categories of labour. The best we can do is give some crude orders of magnitude, based on estimates of respondents. The domestic workshops (taking independent and subcontracted producers together) probably employ nearly as many people as the large firms.7/ The size of the homeworker contingent is greater than the internal workforce of the large and small enterprises, but it is difficult to be more precise, because many homeworkers cannot work full-time. In what follows, the internal workforce will be examined first, before turning to the external workers.

Internal Labour Force

Hammocks are widely considered an artisan product, but as we
have seen above, the production process, while still largely
manual, is divided up into a number of separate stages, carried
out by different workers, except in the very small enterprises.
The key occupation is that of the weaver. To learn the
technique and reach average productivity (on a manual loom)
takes between two and three months. Other tasks are generally
easier to learn. Thus skill requirements (in terms of training
time) are not necessarily high in a craftsmanlike process,
particularly if this process has been divided up.

Hence the recruitment and training of workers is a
relatively easy matter. The labour surplus in the region
explains why none of the manufacturers suffered from any
shortage of labour. On the contrary, they mentioned that there
were always people seeking work. They prefer workers with
previous experience in the branch and can often afford to
reject those who have none, especially when some enterprises
shed labour due to problems in access to raw material (which is
not uncommon in the branch; see Schmitz 1982). When training
is required, it is always done on the job. There are no
vocational training courses.

Labour turnover is high. In the case of registered workers
it is linked to labour legislation, a factor also found to be
important in the other branches investigated. The pattern is
repeated: the guarantee fund (FGTS)8/ makes it easy to dismiss
the worker when the firm wants to; at the same time it invites
workers to provoke their own dismissal in order to receive
their guarantee fund. In the case of hammock production it is
difficult to quantify turnover, even though data is available
on the length of service of employees.

As can be seen from Table 7.3, one third of the workers has
a length of service record of less than six months, and
approximately one half less than one year, which indicates high
turnover. But, according to various respondents, it is quite
common for a worker to hand in his notice and leave in order to
take out his fund money, only to join again a short while
afterwards. So a worker may have been working for many years
in a firm, but according to its official records has only been
working there for a short time. This makes it very difficult
to have a more exact idea about labour turnover of registered
workers and about the differences between firms.

Amongst non-registered workers, the instability also seems
high. 'It's normal [the turnover] in hammock production.
Today you've got ten weavers; in 60 days' time you've only got
one or two of them left. Others have already replaced them.
People who aren't registered, they're always on the move', said
the owner of a firm which had 18 employees.

Table 7.3: Length of Service of Registered Workers in the Hammock Industry

Length of service	Weavers (percentages)	Other workers
Less than 6 months	30	38
6-11 months	17	18
12-23 months	26	19
2-3 years	19	18
4-5 years	7	7
6 years and more	1	-
Total	100	100

Source: Firms' employment records prepared for the Ministry of Labour. Data refer to five of the registered enterprises included in the sample and, within these enterprises, only refer to those workers who are registered. All firms had been in operation for more than six years.

The same is happening with the workers of the small firms. 'How long have your two weavers been with you?' 'They're new, not even two months. They come and go, work here and there. They never work for a whole year, at the most three to five months.' This quote represents well the observations of the other workshop owners who have more than one worker from outside the family. Why this high turnover? It is believed that low wages are at the root of it, as in the case of the registered workers who take out their guarantee fund in order to make up their income. The non-registered workers are prepared to change workplace or take up other employment wherever they have the chance to earn a little more, even if it is only for a short time. 'They leave one job for even the smallest rise in the next one', said one of the small workshop owners. What the respondents did not say was that in many cases the workers are obliged to move because of the instability of production, caused by fluctuating demand or lack of raw materials.

Wages are low in the hammock industry. However, they are not lower than in comparable occupations in large spinning, weaving or clothing firms, and indeed that would be difficult, given the low levels in these industries. No production worker in the hammock industry earns more than two minimum wages. It is the weavers who earn most. They are all on piecework and earn on average 1.4 minimum wages (on the basis of 48 hours a week). There is no difference between the money wage in the large and the small firms; the difference is that most weavers in the former are registered and have certain legal rights, while in the clandestine workshops they have no protection whatsoever.

The rest of the workers earn less, about one minimum wage. Those who are registered are declared as earning one minimum wage but in fact, they are on piece-rates, too. In order to calculate the piece-rate, the boss divides the minimum wage by the amount of work he considers reasonable. 'I count how many hammocks they have to make to earn that wage. Anyone who produces more, earns more'. But there are those who do not even earn a minimum wage, especially women. One job, which is not paid piece-rates, is that of day workers who carry loads both inside and outside the workplace. This is done by men and they are paid one minimum wage.

Except for weavers, it is difficult to compare wages in the larger enterprises and the workshops, since in the latter these other jobs are generally done by members of the family. For grown-up children and relations, the remuneration is not all in the form of a direct wage, but also through board and lodging. These family ties make any comparison of wages difficult. The owner, his wife and children do not receive a wage; as we have already seen, their work is not fully taken into account in a calculation of the labour costs. On the one hand it can be considered non-remunerated or under-remunerated labour, even in relation to the low wages of the larger firms. On the other hand, if the profit from the workshop is bigger than what they could earn together as wage-earners, then one could say they earn well. But in this case one should also ask whether the owner has an adequate return on the capital invested in his workshop.9/

External Labour Force: Homeworkers

All the large enterprises use homeworkers for the finishing of the hammocks; this system is also used on a smaller scale by workshops. In total, this external labour is larger than the workforce inside the enterprises. It is almost impossible to quantify the external labour force, because the manufacturers themselves do not know. This is because they often use intermediaries who pass the work on, and because many of the people involved only work part-time. The owners were always asked 'If everyone involved in finishing had to work here inside, do you know how many people you would need?' A typical reply was 'No idea at all. But I do know we wouldn't survive economically, nor would they all fit in here.'

There are two ways of organising external work: one is for the firm to distribute the made-up cloths directly to the finishers; the other is through intermediaries. A firm which works without an intermediary saves on their remuneration, but on the other hand has to administer this work, which is 'pretty complicated' as one producer said of his colleague who used the direct system: 'He wants to see everything there in the office. There come 20 or 30 women and their children into his office with finished hammocks. He thinks it's good business, but it's really difficult to keep track of.'

The bigger firms generally work through intermediaries. Depending on the quantity and type of work, the made-up cloths and/or yarn are delivered to the intermediary's house, or she/he has to collect it at the factory.

Here is part of an interview on the production of fringes:

Question: Can you please tell me how a fringe is made, how the work is distributed?

Answer: We don't make the fringe here, we have people who collect the yarn and distribute the work. When the completed fringes are returned, we pay the intermediary piece rates. We don't know how much she pays her people.

Question: Do you give out the yarn, and then take it off the price?

Answer: No, we give out the yarn and then pay per fringe. What we give out has been weighed, and then we check the weight of the completed fringes.

Question: How many people do you have working for you, to your knowledge?

Answer: I really don't know, because here [internally] we only keep a register of the intermediaries...I have no idea how many women she has working for her.

Question: But how many people come here to pick up the work?

Answer: We've got about 80, 100 or more. But each one of them has some five people working for her. So I reckon we've got at least 700 people just working with the fringes. They don't work full-time, only when they can.

Question: But for your production, how many people would you need working full-time?

Answer: I reckon about 400 people. All over the Fortaleza area. Not just in the districts near here.

Question: Do you think it's possible to earn a minimum wage doing this?

Answer: Just by making fringes it would be difficult, because it's a time-consuming thing, crochet takes a long time. There's one family whose only source of income comes from making the fringes - two elderly women, and they don't make that much, on average about Cr$600-700 [the two women together, in one month; one monthly minimum wage = Cr$1,111].

Question: One person working at this for eight hours a day can earn how much?

Answer: Maybe Cr$600. One of my fringe-makers manages Cr$1,500 or Cr$1,600, but her whole family helps.

Question: Are there registered people who do this?

Answer: Very few. There's a lot in the hammock world that doesn't get registered. As I say, we've got a big pay-sheet here, but in the official accounts we pay out little.

The Hammock Industry

This extract is from an interview with a luxury hammock producer; he produces 70 hammocks a day, with only 15 people working in the factory. It is possible that he exaggerated when he spoke of 700 people working for him from home, but even if half that number is nearer the truth, then the size of the hidden workforce is still impressive.

Another bigger producer who uses crocheted fringes has a network of female labour which reaches into the interior of the state of Ceará: 'There are women who come by train every fortnight, bringing in what's ready. The leader [intermediary] pays the women right there in the station, they organise everything there. Anyway, the best fringes are made in the interior.'

This same producer has many fewer intermediaries, even though his production is greater:

> We've got eight women who work as leaders. We give them the hammock cloths and the necessary yarn for the finishing. They give them out to the dozens of women under them. All our dealings are with these leaders, our accounts are with them. There's a daily collection of hammocks. Each of these leaders is responsible for only one or two types of work, and the hammock is never passed on from one leader to another. It leaves here, comes back here, and then goes out to another one. You have to do it like this, otherwise you'd never be able to check them.

Two of these leaders were interviewed. The first gave out work to more than 100 women, and on entering the poor district where she lived and worked, one could see women taking hammocks away for finishing. Also, women and children arrived during the interview, delivering or collecting hammocks. From the information that the leader gave, it can be concluded that a woman working full-time can earn between 0.6 and 0.7 minimum wages. Many women, however, can only put in a few hours a day, though some have children to help. The leader herself said that she earned between 3 and 4 minimum wages with the help of her old man and two grandchildren. This woman was the 'star' of the enterprise and headed the biggest group of women.

The other leader gave out part of the work, and the other part was done by herself in her backyard shed with the help of a daughter and three young girls she employed. They earned 0.7 and the leader herself earned 2 minimum wages. She spoke very badly of other producers for whom she had worked and who 'pay really badly'. Both leaders emphasised in the interview that in their long experience of that type of work (roughly 20 years) their present boss was the first to pay health insurance for them.

One of the largest hammock producers entrusted the entire finishing process to two intermediaries. Five of the women working for them were interviewed and, using the information

136

given by them on payment per piece and time taken, it was possible to calculate that they earned (assuming an 8-hour day) between 0.3 and 0.6 minimum wages. One of them was so chronically ill that she was able to work only at home. It is worth mentioning that, according to one of the intermediaries, 20 per cent of the homeworkers' wages was already accounted for each month in advances. He also drew attention to the fact that there is a high turnover in this workforce. This was confirmed by another respondent who gave out hammocks in his district for finishing:

Question: Is it always the same people working for you, or do they change?'

Answer: There's a lot of change-over. They don't stay long. If someone else is paying better, they go there. Even if it's very little more.'

Considering the poor remuneration, this is not surprising.

The workshops also use this workforce; of the eight visited, only two completed the entire hammock. The rest farmed out most of the finishing work. Very simple fringes are not ordered, but bought from women with a stock of ready-made fringes, who regularly visit the workshops. As the production of the workshops is low, they do not generally use intermediaries to distribute the finishing, but arrange things directly with the women who do the work.

External Labour Force - Subcontracting of Workshops

The section of the labour force which remains to be analysed is that of the workshops which work directly for the big firms. In one sense, these workshops can be considered with the independent ones, but in fact they are an extension of the production network of the bigger firms.

From our sample of eight workshops, three used to work exclusively in this system, and two others only when they had no other means of getting yarn. From the sample of eight large firms, only one had a series of external workshops, certainly the firm to use this subcontracting system most in Fortaleza. Another firm had used it in the past, and the case of a third is uncertain; the owner said he did not use it, while others said that he did. According to various statements there are also firms who do not themselves produce at all, but simply distribute the raw material to workshops and then collect the finished hammocks. This type of yarn distributor did not fall into the sample.

From the point of view of the workshop owner, there is only one reason for him to enter the subcontracting system: he does not have access to the required working capital and/or raw material in order to become an independent producer. For the contractor one major motive is to avoid taxes or social security payments, because the workshops are clandestine. Also he makes the most of the cheap labour of the workshop; cheap

137

because he is again, in part, using non-remunerated family labour.

According to our information, the firm which most uses subcontracted labour in Fortaleza has 260 people working for it, excluding those who do the finishing at home. Of the 260, there are 100 working within the enterprise and 160 working outside in clandestine workshops. 'Look, if I pay a minimum wage, plus health insurance and social security, who am I going to be able to compete with?' said the owner, speaking of the external labour. One of his external producers was interviewed; he had seven looms, three of his own and four belonging to the contractor. The hammock cloths were made in the workshop and the finishing was distributed in the district. Of the total number of workers, only one was registered - the workshop owner; he was a registered employee of the contractor, but 'he never gave me a penny in wages, not a thing, everything comes out of here,' that is, the production of his workshop and its non-registered workers. 'But don't the inspectors know there's a workshop here? - Of course they know. - And so? - They ask who the workshop produces for, and so we tell them we work for Mr. X. Seeing as they know Mr. X, they go out there and sort things out with him.' It was clear that bribery is common practice. This was confirmed by another subcontracted producer interviewed: 'Since I work for Mr. X, I send them [the inspectors] to him.'

The case of the latter workshop owner illustrates another advantage which subcontracting offers the contractor. Since demand is irregular, external labour need only be used when there is a peak in demand. The interviewee had already been working for Mr. X for three years, but had spent several months without work. 'Taking the last 12 months, for example, how often was there no yarn? - I reckon that for 6 out of the 12 months he didn't send any.' This small producer was not an employee of Mr. X. in the same way as the other respondent, and worked with his wife and four children. They also had two employees, though only when there was work, since, 'if we have to stop because there isn't any yarn, we can't afford to pay a wage'. During the months when they did not get any yarn from Mr. X, the women of the family went round other enterprises to pick up any finishing work they could get.

It is difficult for the small producer to accumulate sufficient capital to get out of this subcontracting system, because of the instability in production and because his profit margin is low, only half of that of an independent producer. Nevertheless, it is thought that the number of independent workshops is greater than those subcontracted. However, when the former have problems in access to raw material or in selling their hammocks, they go to a large producer and exchange hammocks for raw material, in order to continue working. There the hammock is weighed and the small producer receives an equal amount of yarn in return. His labour is paid either in yarn, or in money. Obviously the price he gets for his work is very low because he is in the weaker position; he needs the money and cannot wait. Anyway, this too is a type of subcontracting, except that it only happens when the small producer is in need, which does not mean that it is not good business for the large producer; he gets the labour of the small one at a very low price.

The practice of exchanging hammocks for yarn is very common, according to practically all the respondents, because often the small producer, on his way to becoming independent, is left without the necessary yarn to be able to keep working in a stable, continuous way. The large firm gives him the yarn, sometimes only in exchange for completed hammocks, and sometimes it 'lends' the yarn to the small producer on condition that he return a ready-made hammock. Like this, the small producer who tries to work independently slips back into a type of subcontracted work.

Because of the irregularity of work, it is difficult to assess the small producers' earnings, but orders of magnitude can be given based on their information on output and profit margins per hammock. A subcontractor with three looms earns approximately 2.7 minimum wages including his own remuneration and that of his wife. An independent producer with the same number of looms earns about twice as much. This compares well with the 1.4 minimum wages of an employed weaver, but the instability of workshop owners' earnings would have to be taken into account.

The Future of the Putting Out System

It has been suggested above that the hammock branch is unlikely to undergo fundamental technical change in the near future. If this is correct the pattern of labour utilisation just described is likely to continue. In a labour intensive branch, where labour productivity is not increasing significantly, low wages are essential. In the North-Eastern context (where the general wage level is only slightly above the minimum wage, even though this wage hardly covers the costs of reproduction of labour power), lower wages can only be achieved by by-passing the law for example, registering somebody as earning a minimum wage, but paying less; not registering the worker at all in order to avoid social security payment; using external labour without registering it. It is also for this reason that big capital keeps out of hammock production.10/ The above employment practices are difficult to organise in a large company; they need a certain hierarchy, organisation and planning in order to function, which are difficult to construct within clandestine work relations. A smaller organisation is more efficient in this.

While closer government inspection might reduce the clandestine employment within the enterprises, it is unlikely to affect outwork. In contrast to the clothing industry, outwork in hammock production is not primarily a way of coping with fluctuating demand; it is essential to keep labour costs low. As explained above, the equipment used in the finishing of hammocks is simple, almost negligible. A substantial shift away from outwork, which we have seen in the embroidery work of the clothing industry, could only be expected if industrial machines were developed to carry out the labour intensive finishing work on hammocks. For the time being this remains a dream of the (large) manufacturers.

For the same reason, domestic workshops are likely to survive. Even though some larger producers have been able to mechanise the production process partially, technological conditions do not differ substantially. Where productivity differences do occur, they are not sufficiently large to drive the small enterprises based on family labour out of business. In a way the larger producers contribute to their continued existence by co-opting their labour, even though in an indirect way. The point has been well made by Rocha (1979a) in his study on the hammock industry in the state of Paraíba:

> ...perhaps the main factor explaining the survival of family production is that, from the point of view of the larger producers, it is good business to let it proliferate, because they are not only the main suppliers of the raw material, but also the main buyers of the products. In reality, by what was observed, the small producers are much more selling their labour (under bad conditions)...than producing independently. (p.104)

He concludes: 'In this way the non-registered producers subsist as an extension of the larger producers'(p.105).

NOTES

1. The occupational data in the Demographic Census of 1970 lists 6,078 hammock makers, but even this figure is an underestimate. Weavers, for instance, the most prominent occupation in the hammock industry, were probably classified with the weavers of the weaving industry.
2. In the case of the registered enterprises, a random selection was made from the register of enterprises used for Table 7.2. The inclusion of non-registered enterprises was governed by the possibilities of access gained through various informal contacts.
3. The following description of the production process is based on direct observation.
4. Even in the state of Paraíba, where mechanisation has gone a little further than in Ceará, most producers use only manual equipment (Rocha 1979b).

140

5. The share of weaving costs in total costs would decrease from about 8.5 to 3 per cent in a standard hammock.

6. One producer who had ordered such looms believed that in his case they were technically and economically viable, since he already used the better quality twisted yarn necessary for the smooth working of the loom, but only worthwhile in the luxury hammock, which was in any case his principal line of production. He declared that the shuttleless loom was not a good investment for standard hammock production, but even for luxury hammocks one wonders how he could amortise the high investment, unless he managed to increase (and sell) his output massively.

7. This is an estimate for Fortaleza. In São Bento, state of Paraíba, Rocha (1979a) counted 75 registered enterprises as against an estimated 490 clandestine producers. The former employed a total of 2,975 workers, of whom 528 were internal and 2,447 external workers. The non-registered enterprises employed a total of 3,155 workers of whom 1,772 were family workers and 1,383 non-family workers (both internal and external). While these figures have to be treated with great care, because they include both full and part-time workers, they support the picture given above. Above all they underline the irrelevance of the Census data; compare Table 7.1.

8. The FGTS (Fundo de Garantia do Tempo de Serviço) is built up by employer's monthly payments equal to 8 per cent of the remuneration paid to the employee in the previous month.

9. For a further examination of the profitability in small and large enterprises, see Schmitz (1982).

10. No big North-Eastern Brazilian (let alone international) companies are involved in hammock production. The producers which we called 'big' or 'large' are so in relation to the domestic workshops. In terms of the general industrial structure of the country, the 'large' hammock enterprises are owned by relatively small capitalists.

Chapter 8

THE SPINNING AND WEAVING INDUSTRY CONTINUED

Let us now return to an industry where technology is progressing fast: spinning and weaving. Chapter 4 showed in detail how technology changed over the last 30 years and what the implications are for labour, in terms of recruitment, training, wages and turnover. One aspect which was not covered was that of external labour. Having dealt with this form of labour utilisation for both the clothing and hammock industry where technology developed differently, it is thought to be important to examine how the practice of using external labour develops in an industry where technical change has been much more rapid.

To this end we consider once again the case of the textile industry in the Centre-South (see chapter 4), more precisely the weaving industry of Americana. As can be seen from Table 8.1, subcontracting is particularly important in that town. The high percentage of subcontracted firms in Americana does not necessarily set it apart as an atypical textile centre, at least not in the state of São Paulo1/, since a large number of the town's firms are subcontracted by firms from the capital city. Thus, Americana's industry should be conceived of as an extension of the capital's industry rather than being contrasted with it as a separate centre.

It is possible to find such comprehensive data as that in Table 8.1 (see also Tables 4.21 and 4.22) since the subcontractors, though small, operate in the open, virtually all being registered.2/ This also made the fieldwork somewhat easier than in the clothing and hammock industry. The respondents3/ included: three large and three medium sized enterprises (whose internal labour was examined in chapter 4); 14 subcontracted firms; two retired textile industrialists; and two machinery suppliers, one of them dealing in new, the other in second-hand machinery. A complete account of the subcontracting system based on these sources has been given elsewhere (Schmitz 1982). The emphasis here is on the effect of technical change.

142

Table 8.1: Distribution of Independent and Subcontracted Enterprises in the Textile Industry of the State of São Paulo According to Location 1976

Location	Independent	Subcontracted	Part independent/ part subcontracted	Total
Americana	129	467	5	601
São Paulo (capital)	829	42	10	881
Other towns	324	213	3	540
Total	1,282	722	18	2,022

Source: Sindicato da Indústria de Fiação e Tecelagem em Geral no Estado de São Paulo, Relação das Empresas Têxteis do Estado de São Paulo, 1976.

Note: An enterprise is called 'independent' as opposed to 'subcontracted' if it buys its own raw materials and sells its product on the market.

SHORT HISTORY OF SUBCONTRACTING

The textile industry of Americana dates back to the early years of this century when a cotton spinning and weaving mill was established. It took, however, a further two decades for a second mill to be set up - in this case a mill which produced silk cloth. At the beginning of the thirties, weavers of these factories began to invest their savings in second-hand looms which they upgraded and installed in their own home. They obtained yarn from their employers to be woven into cloth by wives and daughters working at home while initially they continued to work as internal employees. Gradually they left their employment and began working exclusively as subcontractors, either for their former employers or for yarn dealers from the capital city of São Paulo. These were intermediaries (commercial capitalists) who bought yarn, distributed it among small producers to have it woven into cloth and then collected and sold it in São Paulo.

It was during the forties that Americana's weavers took their great leap forward. The second world war had brought a rapid rise in Brazilian textile exports, in the wake of which new markets opened up, bringing Americana's weavers more work. In addition, one of Brazil's largest and most powerful yarn producers, Matarazzo, contributed to the multiplication of small subcontracted weaving sheds by delivering considerable quantities of cellulosic yarn (rayon) to Americana.

The end of the second world war and the subsequent regaining of world markets by the leading industrial nations brought an end to the period of rapid and easy growth, and crisis to Brazil's textile industry. How serious this crisis was in Americana is not clear from our sources of information. What seems clear is that over the following three decades the town's textile industry expanded; independent and subcontracted producers increased in numbers and some also in size. A few managed the transition from subcontractor to independent producer. Apparently the process of growth was interrupted by various crises caused by the introduction of new taxes, shortages of raw material and problems of overproduction. These hit the subcontractors particularly hard. In what follows we deal mainly with the current and probable future changes, pointing out the problems which are encountered from both the parent firms' and subcontractors' point of view.

THE PARENT FIRMS' INTEREST

Many of the firms which are now of medium or large size owe their growth to the use of external subcontracted workshops. In the case of four of the six sample firms of medium and large size, the putting out system was a major means of accumulation. (The other two firms were of more recent origin and subsidiaries of multinationals.) For many years all four firms had more looms working for them outside than inside their factories. In particular during their initial years of operation, their capital went to a large extent into the purchase of yarn which they distributed amongst small producers and then collected again in the form of cloth. This enabled them to expand production without investment in machinery or buildings.

Indeed, the parent firms emphasised that initially one of the main reasons for using subcontractors was so as not to immobilise their capital; or, in other words, to use their financial resources as circulating capital and not as fixed capital. Today the internal production of these firms is higher than the subcontracted part, for reasons to be explained later. However, the profits required to buy their own machinery were largely earned through the subcontracting system.

The second reason for using this system lies in the flexibility it offers the parent firms. Working with an external workforce enables them to adjust smoothly to irregularities in demand. In the words of the director of one of the firms, 'subcontracting is for us a resource to draw upon when demand is high, it enables us to increase our production quickly when we need to'. Of course, the same applies · the other way round; in periods of sluggish demand, it is easy for them to reduce production, or as another manager put it, 'the subcontractors provide a safety valve' to the parent firms. Four of the five medium and large firms which had, or used to have, subcontractors affirmed that this facility was one of the main reasons for continuing this form of labour utilisation. For example, the biggest firm to pursue this practice had reduced its number of external looms from over 1,000 in 1976 to 500 in 1978/79, mainly due to marketing problems.

Subcontracting can also help in coping more easily with 'awkward' orders. In fact, one multinational firm, geared to large-scale production, kept subcontractors mainly in order to cope with small orders. In relation to total production the subcontracting was of little importance to this firm, but it was important for its ability to respond flexibly to customer demand. (The other multinational firm included in the sample was not involved in subcontracting at all.)

A third reason for subcontracting is related to differences in labour costs between parent firms and subcontractors. All respondents affirmed that wages paid by the subcontractors were lower than those paid for comparable jobs in parent firms and in our comparisons they were found to be at least one third lower. However, opinions in parent firms were divided on whether subcontracted production cost them less than internal production. The main issue here is that the cloth woven by the subcontractors tends to be of lower quality. A few subcontractors have moved up-market and specialised in high

145

quality items, but they are the exception. Since the parent firms pay by the metre, the subcontractors' main concern is generally to maximise output rather than achieve high and constant quality, which suffers further because, paying low wages, the subcontractors cannot keep their best workers. The manager of one parent firm stated that his internal production costs were lower than those for subcontracted production because of this problem of quality. The other firms also emphasised this problem and therefore farmed out only that part of their production in which quality mattered least. In these lines they found that subcontracting did give them a slightly lower cost per unit of output.

THE SUBCONTRACTORS

The people who become subcontractors usually come from the internal labour force of textile firms. Of the 14 subcontractors interviewed, 13 had previously been employees and had worked either as weavers or foremen. This pattern was confirmed by all other respondents. Asked why they had left their wage employment, the subcontractors were unanimous: in order to improve their economic situation. Families relying on a weaver's wage can hardly escape poverty unless there are other sources of income. While foremen or supervisors earn a higher wage, employees' career prospects are not found sufficiently promising. Also they prefer to be their own masters. Thus, many try their luck and set up their own business.

What is needed to carry this through? The parent firm delivers the yarn which the subcontractors transform into cloth. The yarn for the warp is generally provided ready wound on a beam; the yarn for the weft is delivered on cones, which the subcontractors wind onto pirns to fit the shuttles of their looms. The machinery required consists of a winding machine and a minimum of four looms, as this is the number which one person can operate. The maintenance of the machines is up to the subcontractors. None of the respondents received technical assistance from the parent firms.

Generally, second-hand machinery is used, bought in most cases from independent firms or other subcontractors who have modernised or gone out of business; in some cases it is bought from a dealer in second-hand machinery. The initial investment in machinery is as follows: four mechanical looms, at around US$450 each, amounts to US$1,800 including all accessories. A mechanical winder costs approximately US$100.4/ Thus, the initial capital required for machinery is US$1,900 which is equivalent to around eight months' wages for a weaver employed by an independent firm.

Buying his own machinery is therefore feasible and not entirely out of reach for a weaver. In fact, some begin with a greater number of looms and most buy additional looms once they have gained initial experience as subcontractors. What is generally beyond their means is to become independent producers; that is, buy the raw material, transform it into cloth and sell it. First, the working capital needed to buy raw material is well above the investment in machinery. Second, the quantity of yarn required would be too small to be of interest to yarn suppliers. Hence the workers begin as subcontractors who are essentially disguised wage workers, but hope that it will be possible to accumulate and one day produce independently.

As there is a constant flow of new entrants into the branch, competition amongst subcontractors is intense. The interviews showed clearly that they find themselves unable to negotiate the piece – rates, having little choice but to accept the parent firms' terms. Differences in what parent firms offer are very slight. In the words of one small producer, 'it is easy for them to find subcontractors, there are always those willing to offer their services and accept their conditions'.

Payment is lowest for those who are secondary subcontractors, that is, for those who do not receive the work directly from the parent firm, but from an intermediary, the primary subcontractors. Such intermediaries generally, though not always, have their own production facilities and do part of the job received from the parent firm themselves, while giving out to other producers that part of the weaving they cannot do themselves. This two-tier system occurs mainly when the parent firm is not from Americana, but the capital city São Paulo. In total, approximately half the subcontracted production seems to be for parent firms from São Paulo and half for local parent firms.

Usually the months from December to February are slack and subcontractors have to reduce the number of hours worked or the number of looms in operation. For those with workers from outside the family this period is particularly difficult. The yearly wage increases for textile workers in the state of São Paulo come into force in November and producers reported that they generally do not manage to pass on the increased costs to the parent firms until March when business tends to pick up again.

What does most harm to the subcontractors are crises in which the parent firms give out little or no work for extended periods. Thus, the parent firm's ability to adjust easily to changes in demand constitutes the subcontractor's greatest problem. 'If they tell you tomorrow that they haven't got any work for you, there's nothing you can do...they have no obligation towards you except to pay the agreed rate for the quantity of cloth you make.'

The interviews produced many accounts of subcontractors who had to give up in such crises and to return to wage employment, or others who only just managed to survive. For example, '1975 and 1976 were good years and I had two employees, but 1977/78 was terrible and I had to fire them, cloth didn't sell, there was little work, and for one month I stopped completely. I was about to take on a job as an employee, but then some work came up and I got going again.' According to a former subcontractor who is now a supervisor in another firm: 'There were always bad periods: once it was eight months in a single year. I had to reduce working hours, and finally I sold the machines, I couldn't go on. I sold the machines to another guy who wanted to try, but he didn't get very far either.' Other subcontractors were keen on pointing out that not all parent firms are hit equally and simultaneously by sluggish demand and that through clever manoeuvring and with some luck they, as subcontractors, were able to avoid major crises. But also these respondents emphasised the instability faced generally by subcontractors. Although this is a major characteristic of subcontractor operations, it cannot be documented through detailed turnover rates of enterprises. However, corroborating evidence did emerge from the research. Thus, of the sample of subcontractors selected from a 1976 register of enterprises, only 50 per cent were still in business in 1979. This could partly reflect the quality of the register in that some of those producers might have gone out of business before 1976, but it reinforces the general impression of instability among such enterprises.

EMPLOYMENT AND INCOME

How does this combination of circumstances affect employment and income in the subcontracted sector? The tough competition and the consequent low piece—rates make it necessary for the small owner to participate directly in the process of production, unless he has an additional source of income. Indeed, in the initial period, the owner is generally the main worker, and is in many cases aided by other members of his family. Thus wives not only do the housework, but often help with the winding of the yarn and with other odd jobs or even replace the husband at the looms when he has to leave the workshop.

The working day in the subcontracted enterprises is long; in all cases investigated it went beyond the eight hour working day, which is the norm in medium and large-scale enterprises. All subcontractors said they worked at least 10 hours a day, some up to 12 or 13. Shift-work is impracticable for most subcontracted workshops since they are based to a large extent on family labour. Only one of the small subcontractors worked on a shift system; he had eight looms which were operated in the first shift by his wife and son, and in the second shift by two employees, the owner himself doing the additional work

148

necessary to keep both shifts going. The largest of the subcontractors also worked in two shifts with his total of 36 employees.

As for payment, the remuneration of family workers depends on whether they belong to the owner's household or not. If not, they earn what an employed non-family worker would receive. In the case of weavers, this amounts to between 1.9 and 2.5 minimum wages based on a ten hour working day. In comparison, the weaver employed by an independent firm earns between 3.2 and 3.8 minimum wages based on an eight hour working day, so that a weaver can earn up to twice as much if he works for an independent enterprise. This has immediate implications for the type of workers the subcontractor can attract. Some of these workers would not be accepted by independent firms because of advanced age or some handicap, others are not prepared to subject themselves to the tight rules and discipline imposed by most independent firms. More important, however, are the very young workers on whom the subcontractors rely heavily. They train them, work with them and then generally lose them once they have learnt their job. The young workers naturally move on to the independent producers who pay better and offer more stability.

If the wage earners in the subcontracted firms are so poorly paid, what about the subcontractors themselves? Given the intense competition and the power of the parent firms, can they earn more than the workers in independent firms? According to their information on incomings and outgoings, it was calculated that a subcontractor with eight looms and two (paid) assistants earns around 50 per cent more than a weaver employed in a larger firm. If, however, one were to consider all the benefits which the employee receives but which the subcontractor forgoes (such as paid holidays, thirteenth wage, guarantee fund) and consider his longer working hours, he is only slightly better off than the employed weaver. The situation would be somewhat better if the wife and children could do the auxiliary work. The income of a producer with only four looms (owner with one other worker) would lag behind the employed weaver's wage, unless the subcontractor is helped by a family member. The majority of subcontractors have between eight and 24 looms. Twenty-four machines, for instance, implies a total labour force of nine workers.

Obviously each step of expansion provides the possibility of higher income, but also increases risks. The major risk is that of periods of insufficient work for the machinery installed, which alternate with periods of working to full capacity. The subcontractor's income follows the ups and downs in the textile industry very closely. As one of them put it: 'There are good months when I earn a lot more than I could possibly earn as an employee and there are bad months when I would be better off if I was employed'.

THE FUTURE OF SUBCONTRACTING

None of the respondents saw the future of small subcontractors in rosy terms. Nevertheless, they said that workers continue to try to set up their own business, and indeed two of the producers interviewed were newcomers. Of those who had been in operation for longer, most wanted to continue as, on balance, they found they were doing better than they could have done as employees, but emphasised that this was as a result of hard work. What kept them going was also the ever-present hope of a couple of good years and making it in the end.

The disillusioned were carrying on, even though they fared no better than employees, for a variety of reasons: they preferred to be their own boss and wanted to organise their own timetable (even if it meant working, in total, longer hours); some also feared that because of their advanced age securing a good job as an employee (e.g. foreman) could be problematic; a machinery supplier also mentioned that considerations of pride and status kept subcontractors from returning to wage employment. Of those respondents who had given up, none was prepared to try it again, mainly because of fear of the instability of work and income: 'Working as a subcontractor gives more headache than money'.

As for the medium and long term tendencies of the subcontracting system, the majority of the respondents - parent firms, subcontractors and machinery suppliers - believed that it was in decline. All parent firms had cut back on their subcontracted production. Part of this was a short term phenomenon, because at the time of the fieldwork most of them were undergoing a relatively slack period. But all these firms also showed a clear long run trend to move away from subcontracting and towards producing inside their own factories.

One of the reasons relates to a point made earlier; parent firms repeatedly claimed that subcontractors could not meet the quality standards of their own internal production.5/ The explanation for the low quality can easily be deduced from what was said before: low piece rates force the subcontractor to (a) pay low wages and (b) outdo the parent firm whenever possible, both of which result in lower product quality. In turn, parent firms tend to farm out only those lines in which quality matters least and these are more often than not the lines in which competition is toughest and profits are lowest and in which they are least inclined to increase their payment of subcontractors. There are exceptions to this tendency, but the general situation is as described.

There is, however, a much more compelling reason for the decline in subcontracting, which has begun to make itself felt and which will develop its full force in the years to come, namely the technological developments in weaving. The majority of subcontractors use mechanical looms and one weaver can operate four or five of these at a time. The looms are bound to be replaced gradually by automatic looms, as the latter bring about at least a doubling in labour productivity; one weaver can operate ten automatic looms and their speed is greater.

This affects the subcontracting system first and foremost because the initial investment in machinery rises considerably. A new automatic loom costs between US$7,300 and US$9,100. Furthermore, if the producer decides to modernise he cannot change gradually from mechanical to automatic looms as he expands. Since one weaver can operate ten automatic looms at a time, he has to buy a minimum of ten machines. This means an investment of around US$90,000. If the producer can find ten looms second-hand and in good condition, he might be able to get them for US$36,400. In addition he needs at least two automatic winders which each cost US$2,700 new or around US$1,100 second-hand. So, taking second-hand machinery prices, the initial investment would be about US$38,600. This has to be compared with US$3,800 which is necessary to start up with, for example, eight mechanical looms and two mechanical winders. Hence the entry barrier into the branch is increased enormously.

To conclude, in most types of weaving, the mechanical looms cannot compete with automatic looms. The investment necessary for the more modern looms is generally beyond the means of subcontractors, considering that most of them are former employees who buy the machinery in instalments and with savings made from their wages. Given that the initial investment in automatic machinery corresponds to around 160 months' wages of a skilled weaver, the number of subcontractors is likely to decrease.

According to our respondents, some products will continue to be woven on the mechanical loom, in particular acetate and very fine or second-rate rayon and nylon. These yarns are not strong enough to be woven on automatic looms; they could be woven on these machines, but the frequent stoppages do not make it worthwhile. Machinery suppliers emphasised that future development would remedy this, but confirmed that for the time being the mechanical loom would continue to be used for these yarns. In these lines, the subcontractors are therefore less threatened by technological change.6/

Another factor working against the small subcontractors is the increasing difficulty in finding inexpensive premises. The visitor to Americana can hardly miss the presence of the weaving industry; the rhythmic noise of the looms accompanies one throughout most of the districts of the town, be they residential or industrial. The local government, in line with a programme of the state government, is now trying to reduce the noise pollution and move the weaving sheds out of the town centre and the residential areas and place them in special industrial districts. Buying a plot and building a new weaving shed in these districts is an investment which is beyond the means of small subcontractors.

The conjunction of these restrictions and the technological development is bound to bring about a decline in the subcontracting system. Such a decline is not likely to occur as a sudden exodus of subcontractors, but more likely through those who give up because of a temporary crisis or retirement not being replaced as they were in the past.

In this sense, we believe that a decrease in the number of subcontractors is almost certain to occur. It seems even clearer that subcontracted production as a percentage of total production is going to decrease; all the parent firms investigated had been increasing their internal production and cut back or at best kept constant their external production. Whether the total output produced by subcontractors will be reduced in absolute terms is difficult to say. First, there are those fibres for which the old machinery is still advantageous and where subcontracting can continue in small-scale operations. Second, it is conceivable that some subcontractors who specialise in the production of small quantities of high quality products can survive. Third, and most important, a few subcontractors interviewed had bought such machines second-hand and according to the machinery suppliers these were not isolated cases. Hence a smaller number of subcontractors might well produce the same or even greater output, but in relation to the internal production of independent firms there can be little question that it is declining.

If our analysis is correct, then an era of Americana's textile industry is gradually coming to an end. Until recently two of its main features were: first, the transition from wage employment to subcontractor which was attempted by many workers, even though only a few could finally manage to set up as independent producers. Second, those independent enterprises which managed to grow into large firms did so largely through the use of subcontractors. These features of Americana's industry are slowly but clearly declining in importance. The recent arrival of multinationals has not in itself provoked major changes in this growth pattern. It merely reinforced the tendencies described, since these firms are technologically very advanced and use subcontractors very little, if at all.

The multinational firms are also at the forefront of establishing a new pattern of labour utilisation in the textile industry, in particular with regard to recruitment and training. They were found to prefer production workers without previous experience in the industry. As already emphasised before, this was particularly puzzling as there was not just a surplus of labour, but the surplus included people who had previously worked in textiles. What seems to account for this policy is not so much foreign ownership in itself as the new technology. Since skill requirements have diminished with technological modernisation, large-scale firms find that higher training costs incurred by recruiting young unskilled workers are outweighed by gains in discipline and control over labour in the workplace. Thus, in terms of changes in the overall employment pattern in the industry, there is on the one hand the relative decline in external or indirect labour use (subcontracting) and on the other a relative increase in internal or direct labour use, accompanied by a process of de-skilling. In other terminology this represents a shift from formal to real surbordination of labour (Marx 1933).

NOTES

1. Comparable information is not available for other states, but our impression is that subcontracting in the state of São Paulo is more common than in other states of Brazil.
2. The reasons for this are that control and inspection are relatively tough, that parent firms only farm out work to subcontractors who are registered, and workers themselves demand registration. All this is perhaps connected with the stage of industrial development reached in the state of São Paulo which, in Brazilian terms, is very advanced.
3. The weaving firms were selected from a register of firms (used for Table 8.1) which was stratified by size of firm. From these strata a selection was made on a random basis, except for two large international firms which were chosen to explore whether foreign ownership made a difference to the issues investigated. Sample attrition would have been very high in the case of small firms, if only those producers had been interviewed who were originally selected and still in business. Given a high turnover of small firms it became necessary to adjust the sample in the course of the fieldwork. In cases where firms had changed owners, the new owner was interviewed. If the selected producer was no longer in business (for example, had gone bankrupt, moved on to a different industry, become an employee of another firm) an attempt was made to interview him whenever he could be traced.
4. These are average prices for second-hand machinery in 1979.
5. One should, of course, expect a tendency among parent firms to stress this quality problem as a way of 'justifying' the low piece rates. But the fact that they have cut back on subcontracting over the years would tend to confirm that their 'complaints' are not entirely without foundation.
6. Natural silk is also still woven on mechanical looms but the raw material is so expensive, and high quality weaving so important, that silk manufacturers prefer to weave inside their factories rather than subcontract others.

Part Three

TOWARDS AN UNDERSTANDING OF INDUSTRIAL LABOUR
PROCESSES IN DEVELOPING COUNTRIES

Chapter 9

CLASSIFYING TECHNOLOGIES

What have we learnt from these case studies?   Clearly there are
problems in drawing generalisations from such micro studies,
but it is believed that they can help to advance the discussion
on a number of the issues identified in the review of the
literature undertaken in Part 1:   To what extent and in which
way does technology affect the practice of using external
labour?   As regards internal labour, what is the impact of
modern technology on skill requirements?   Does it raise them
generally or only for some categories of workers?   Is the skill
trajectory different in the periphery from in the centre?   Does
modern technology lead to a privileged, highly paid, stable
work force?   Always?   Under what specific technical conditions?
To what extent does employers' concern with control over the
labour process enter the picture?   If control is important, how
does it influence employment relations in non-automated and
automated production?   What is the future of automation and
employment in developing countries?   These are the questions
which have to be taken up again and re-examined in the light of
the case study findings.   But this part of the report is not
limited to this.   The search for answers to the above questions
will trigger off some thoughts which go beyond the immediate
conclusions of the case studies.   Perhaps the best way to
organise the discussion is to explore the possibilities of
grouping technologies according to the pattern of labour
utilisation they are likely to produce.
     Implicit in our research approach is an argument for
branch-specific studies, because technological conditions
differ widely between industries.   The case studies illustrate
this clearly, not least because they were deliberately chosen
to draw attention to the wide range of technologies in use.
Such studies are an almost unavoidable first step.   However, in
order to rationalise further empirical research and allow
theorisation, one needs to group or classify industries.
Therefore it may be useful to discuss a number

classifications of technologies. One's grouping or classification depends, of course, on the objective of the analysis. In our case the interest was not in technology as such, but in the labour process as the combination of the material instruments of production with the social organisation of labour. At the beginning of Part 2 we suggested a classification which reflects the four stages in the historical development of industrial labour processes:

1. Workers are brought into one organisation either in the form of the putting out system or by bringing them together under one roof, without altering the existing technology.
2. The tasks are divided and special tools are developed for each operation.
3. This is followed by the development of machinery and the subordination of the workers to the machine (labour as an appendage of the machine).
4. Finally, there is the continuous automated production process, in which the worker's main task is to monitor the machines.

The first three stages represent the account given by Marx (1867), who traced the development of the labour process from simple cooperation, through manufacture to machinofacture. A fourth stage, we believe, has to be added, because of the degree of automation achieved and the potential implications for the utilisation of labour. The proclamation of such a fourth stage has been rejected, implicitly by Braverman (1974), and explicitly by the Brighton Labour Process Group (1977, p.20):

Developments in the labour process such as high-speed continuous flow mass production, automation, semi-autonomous groups do not...signal the emergence of a 'new era' in which all the brutalities of machine-based production would be left behind.

The problem with advocating such a fourth stage is that some authors believe it heralds the end of alienation (for example, Blauner 1964) and the beginning of the post-industrial society (for example, Davies 1971 a, b). We do not subscribe to these views; on the contrary, far from bringing to an end the real subordination of labour, new technologies tend to increase capital's command over the labour process. At the same time it is true that workers are no longer appendages of machines and have different functions. They are not necessarily more skilled, but employers are more concerned with reliability and have on the whole a different policy towards labour; at least this is our thesis and we shall later devote a separate section to it.

While the above classification is derived from the history of industrial production, it does not imply that all industries should go through these successive stages. For example, synthetic fibre production was 'born' in stage four. The clothing industry is still at stage two and cotton spinning and weaving, which did develop from stage one to three, has been only partially successful in reaching stage four. Overall there is a tendency towards automation, but reality still is, and probably always will be, characterised by uneven technological development. This is particularly true for developing countries. The continued existence of the hammock industry – still at stage one – bears testimony to this unevenness. It is an important but, as we shall later argue, by no means unique example of an industry with rudimentary technology, which facilitates a type of labour utilisation which is often no longer thought to exist, or to be irrelevant. Thus, for developing countries, a classification must cover this type of production.

What is being suggested here is that the above classification, while historic in origin, may be a useful way of grouping industries existing today. The Brazilian case studies underline this point, but cannot be taken as· an adequate 'test' of its usefulness. Certainly they should not pre-empt an examination of different ways of categorising the labour process. Such other typologies are discussed below, and the advantages and shortcomings of our own classification are brought out in the process.

Other researchers have used classifications which are in essence similar. Touraine (1962) distinguishes between three phases. Phase A is characterised by craftsmanship requiring only universal or flexible machines, not limited to the production of a single product. Phase B is characterised by mechanisation, or the feeding of machines by unskilled workers. In Phase C production is automated and direct productive work by human beings is eliminated. Blauner (1964) suggests four 'technological types': craft-technology, machine-tending technology, assembly-line technology and continuous process production.

The problem of finding an adequate typology of industrial technologies is discussed in greatest detail by Joan Woodward in Industrial Organisation: Theory and Practice (1965). Extensive empirical work in Britain, consisting of a cross-section survey and case studies of selected firms led her research team to an initial classification into three groups: a) unit and small batch production, b) large batch and mass production and c) process production. These were further subdivided as follows (Woodward 1965, p.39):

Unit and small batch production	1.	Production of units to customers' requirements
	2.	Production of prototypes
	3.	Fabrication of large equipment in stages
	4.	Production of small batches to customers' orders

....

Large batch and mass production	5.	Production of large batches
	6.	Production of large batches on assembly lines
	7.	Mass production

....

| Process production | 8. | Intermittent production of chemicals |
| | 9. | Continuous flow production |

These categories form a scale of 'technical complexity', a term used to mean the extent to which the production process is controllable and its results predictable. This criterion also entails a consideration of the degree of repetition which is important from a labour process point of view; where production is of the 'one-off' kind, labour requirements are likely to be different from standardised production. In our case studies this was highlighted by the small clothing firms, whose skill requirements for operators were higher than those in large-scale firms. Thus it is interesting to note that Woodward emphasises that firms in the same industry do not necessarily fall into the same category. She refers to the example of two tailoring firms which had different production systems; one made bespoke suits, the other mass-produced men's clothing. However, her scale of production systems does not merely re-classify firms on the basis of size.

This is an important point, because it suggests a weakness in our classification, which does not make allowance for the degree of repetition. If unit and small batch production occurred merely in small firms, one could 'solve' the problem, by excluding such firms from the analysis. However, medium and large-scale firms are not confined to long production runs. The capital goods sector, where production to customers' requirements is frequent, provides a good example. Firms involved in such production tend to rely more heavily on skilled workers, since each order creates different problems and requires individual attention. There are, however, signs that even technical workers in production of prototypes are increasingly subjected to de-skilling methods, including those engaged in research and development (Cooley 1980, 1981).

As far as this study is concerned, probably the most important aspect of Woodward's classification is the reminder of the importance of unit and small batch production. However, the detailed distinctions within the three broad groups are not all relevant for organising discussions on the labour process. Of course, it should be added that her concern was different from the present one; she studied the impact of technology on management organisation.

James Bright (1958, 1966) proposed a scale of technologies in the pursuit of a study closer to our own. He investigated the relationship between increasing automation and skill requirements; to this end he developed a scale of 17 'levels of mechanisation ' (see Figure 9.1).

Figure 9.1: Levels of Mechanisation as Charted by Bright

Initiating control source	Type of machine response			Power source	Level number	Level of mechanization
From a variable in the environment	Responds with action	Modifies own action over a wide range of variation		Mechanical (nonmanual)	17	Anticipates action required and adjusts to provide it
					16	Corrects performance while operating
					15	Corrects performance after operating
		Selects from a limited range of possible prefixed actions			14	Identifies and selects appropriate set of actions
					13	Segregates or rejects according to measurement
					12	Changes speed, position, direction according to measurement signal
	Responds with signal				11	Records performance
					10	Signals preselected values of measurement (includes error detection)
					9	Measures characteristic of work
From a control mechanism that directs a predetermined pattern of action	Fixed within the machine				8	Actuated by introduction of work piece or material
					7	Power-tool system, remote controlled
					6	Power tool, program control (sequence of fixed functions)
					5	Power tool, fixed cycle (single function)
From man	Variable				4	Power tool, hand control
					3	Powered hand tool
				Manual	2	Hand tool
					1	Hand

Source: Bright (1966) p.II-210

The concept of levels of mechanisation is based on the assumption that there are different degrees of mechanical accomplishment in machinery. One can sense this by asking: in what way does a machine supplement/substitute for the worker's muscles, mental processes and control over his work. On levels 1 to 4 of Bright's scale, the control is entirely up to the worker. Then as increasing degrees of fixed control yield the desired machine action, the worker carries out less and less guidance (levels 5 to 8). As the ability to measure is added to the machine, the information needed to act one way or the other is obtained mechanically for the operator (levels 9 to 11). At higher levels (12 to 14), more and more of the decision making and appropriate follow-up action is performed mechanically. Finally the machine is given the power of self-correction, until the need for its adjustment has been entirely removed from the worker (levels 15 to 17).

Even though Bright's study is generally recognised as one of the most thorough investigations of the relationship between technical change and skill requirements, the usefulness of his classification has been challenged. R. M. Bell (1972) finds that the exclusion of any characteristics concerned with technical differences of the handling functions in production is its most serious inadequacy. For example, into level 2 could fall equally well both the work on an assembly line of an automobile plant and the one-off assembly of specialised machinery. What differentiates the two production technologies is the associated mechanism for transfer and handling of parts: in the one case highly sophisticated, in the other probably non-existent. The labour requirements of the two would be markedly different.

We agree with Bell that labour requirements differ not only with levels of mechanisation, but also according to the function mechanised. Certainly a classification as detailed as that of Bright should reflect such differences. Bell himself conceives of the technological process as:

> an integrated complex of three functions or systems ...
> 1. The system which carries out the transformation process itself, which changes the state of the material being processed.
> 2. The system which transfers materials through the transformation process.
> 3. The system which controls the operation of the transformation and transfer systems. (Bell 1972, p.61)

Clearly these are useful distinctions, though one wonders why design and maintenance are excluded if the emphasis is on the function to be mechanised. Moreover, Bell does not build his distinctions into a new classification of technologies, probably because he recognises that the greater the number of dimensions used, the more detailed and complicated the classification becomes and the less operationally useful it is for assessing general patterns and trends.

A classification which is useful in this sense will never entirely satisfy the grouping of all empirical observations. The problem is less severe if one is only concerned with specific stages in the production process of any one industry. But as soon as one is concerned with the collective worker, with the entire production process, problems of categorisation become inevitable, since one often finds a combination of different labour processes. Nevertheless most firms/industries have their characteristic form of production which determines what type of work is carried out by most of the employees. Where this is not the case, it seems most sensible to point out the intra-firm or intra-industry differences, rather than refine the classification ad infinitum or proceed without one.

This discussion of alternative ways of classifying technologies has drawn entirely on studies carried out in advanced industrial countries. This largely reflects the absence of systematic work on the labour process in the periphery. Yet it is in these circumstances that a classification is particularly urgent. After all, research in this field tries to assess relative changes. Since most technology used in peripheral economies is imported, the jump from one form of production to another tends to be greater than in central economies; sometimes it is from zero to a very advanced technology. As we shall argue later, the size of the step taken explains why the relationship between technical change and labour utilisation is often different from that in the centre. Hopefully future studies can build these ideas into a scale of labour processes which reflects the different circumstances in the periphery.

Chapter 10

PUTTING OUT - PAST OR PRESENT?

The practice of farming out parts of the production process is much neglected in empirical research, even though in some branches the number of people earning their livelihood as disguised wage workers is considerable. Hopefully the case studies can serve as a reminder that this form of labour utilisation continues to be important (chapters 6, 7 and 8). Outwork cannot be discarded as a mere heritage of the past, surviving as an anachronism, and about to be replaced by more advanced employment practices.1/

How common it is, is impossible to tell. Comprehensive reliable information does not exist.2/ One can, however, state that external labour is not used in all industries, but only in some. The questions to be addressed here are: a) in what kind of labour processes can one expect to find outwork or subcontracting and b) in what way/to what extent is technical change affecting this kind of labour utilisation.

We start from our fourfold classification of labour processes. It is mainly at stages one and two that external labour is likely to play a role. The most obvious reason is purely technical. In production of synthetic fibres or cement, for example, farming out is a technical impossibility due to the continuous nature of the production process. Thus stage four eliminates possibilities of subcontracting, unless for ancillary operations.

Even where the production process is discontinuous, economies of scale often militate against this practice. Typically this occurs in stage three. The cotton spinning industry is a good example; so is the weaving industry today, even though it used to be a classical example of an industry where economies of scale were absent; but as we have shown in chapter 8 this is rapidly changing and with it the extent of subcontracting is declining. The economies of scale argument needs, however, to be treated cautiously, as can

164

be illuminated by reference to the car industry. Scale economies are of the utmost importance in the industry, yet subcontracting is a common feature. The reason lies in the fact that the car is a complex product, comprising thousands of components. The scale economies matter primarily at the assembly stage (apart from R & D), but not necessarily for the production of components. In some companies most components are produced 'in house', others rely on an extensive network of feeder firms. Brazil's largest car manufacturer, for instance, employed 25,000 workers directly; and indirectly as many or more workers in feeder units which constitute a hierarchy of primary, secondary and tertiary subcontractors:

There exist more than 4 thousand small, medium and large factories producing parts for the assembly line of the central unit (sometimes exclusively). These 4 thousand 'affiliates' or sub-factories of the larger system constitute an extension of the central unit, through which all elements are coordinated and combined in function of a big multinational company. Other characteristics of this mammoth system [are]:

a) All technological stages can be found among these different factory units ...
b) The employer's responsibility for employee benefits ... is transferred to these units that have nothing to do juridically with the central unit.
c) Since the central company determines the prices and volume of demand for the components entering its assembly line, the costs are also transferred. The small and medium proprietors of the 'affiliated' units, in their turn, guarantee their profit margin by transferring the whole burden to their workers through two basic mechanisms: 1. low salaries; 2. increasing the shifts and workhours. (Arruda et al. 1975, p.4)

While the labour process in the car industry, particularly in its assembly stage, is typically at stage three, the manufacture of components covers many different stages, emphasising the fact that subcontracting is not limited to any particular stage, especially when the subcontracted units are large. However, once the analysis is focused upon individual outworkers or small subcontracted workshops, one deals mainly with labour processes at stage one or two. At least the few recent micro studies would suggest so: carpets (Ayata 1979); lace making (Mies 1981); clothing (Abreu 1980; Alonso 1979; Hope et al. 1976; Reichmuth 1978; Schmitz 1982; Schmukler 1977; Sit et al. 1979; Spindel 1981); hammocks (Rocha 1979; Schmitz 1979b); shoes (Godard 1981); metal and engineering products (Bose 1978; Harriss 1982).

The reason lies in the technical divisibility of the

production process and its labour intensity. The latter makes the search for lower wage costs imperative, since mechanisation tends to be difficult. Access can be gained to cheaper labour through the putting out system.3/ As observed in the case studies on weaving and embroidery, mechanisation usually leads to a shift from external to internal labour a) because the wage difference becomes less important and the costs of high wages are outweighed by gains in speed and quality control, b) because at higher levels of mechanisation outworkers or small subcontractors can no longer afford the required investment in machinery.

The advent of micro-electronics might well upset this pattern. In contrast to previous technical innovations, micro-electronics promise to reduce capital costs and increase flexibility (Kaplinsky 1980). Thus in principle they open up the possibility of more decentralised production. In fact, this theme is explored by Huws (1984) in a recent study, The New Homeworkers, in Britain. Her main conclusions are as follows:

1. The combination of computer and telecommunications technologies has made it technically possible for large numbers of workers whose jobs involve information processing to work remotely, at terminals which could be in their homes.

2. Until now, however, it has not been economically feasible to introduce this form of working widely, except for professional computer staff with scarce skills, due to the cost of communication.

3. The advent of cable networks is likely to change this situation and make it cost effective to employ ordinary workers at long distance.

4. Those homeworkers who use the new technology (mainly computer professionals) are for the most part women in their thirties with children under five. They work at home because they also care for children.

5. Average pay levels are significantly lower than going rates for similar work on-site and some homeworkers also lack a number of benefits available to comparable on-site workers.

6. Periods without work were common, as were periods when the work load was too great to be managed during normal working hours, causing disruption to households.

7. Despite these problems, homeworking was felt by many to have considerable advantages, particularly flexibility and the opportunity it provided to combine work with childcare.

Cronberg and Sangregorio (1981) followed up the same question in Japan, but found little or no indication of new technologies fulfilling this potential:

> We were particularly surprised that there was no mention of the possibility of using the new data and communication technologies to decentralise work...Theoretically, people could easily be employed in the same company and even in the same department without necessarily being located in the same building.
> We can imagine several ways of decentralising the workplace. The most extreme, to quote an American magazine, would be to place a computer terminal in every living room. A better solution would probably be a local office where people who aren't necessarily employed by the same company but who live in the same area would be able to work with the aid of computer terminals and other technical equipment...When we took up the question in our interviews, everybody (all men) dismissed the thought as being against the Japanese character. The life-style of the Japanese man would be seriously threatened if he couldn't place a safe distance between himself and home every day. (Cronberg and Sangregorio 1981, p.76)

If this is so, the question still arises as to why the new technology is not used in Japan to employ women in their own homes. We have, however, some general doubts about the above 'cultural explanation'. It might be correct for existing internal employees of the large-scale corporations, but there is also the other side of Japanese industry: a multitude of small-scale firms, many of them working on a family basis, is linked through subcontracting arrangements with the larger companies (Shinohara 1968; Watanabe 1971). The new technologies might well reinforce this production and employment pattern. In fact Watanabe (1983) explores this question in a case study on Japanese electronics-based NC (numerically controlled) machine tools. While the diffusion of such equipment amongst small subcontractors is still small (31 per cent in enterprises of between 10 and 29 workers and only 8 per cent in enterprises of less than 10 workers), it is rising rapidly: 'As their direct motives for introducing NC machine tools, all the interviewed entrepreneurs mentioned the need for handling small lots of different work, rising labour cost and shortage of skilled workers, and increasingly severe quality requirements' (p.63). Those who introduced these machines in the last few years reported that it had become increasingly difficult to obtain attractive work without them, either because of the nature of available work or because of the low processing charge paid by the parent firms who assumed the use of NC machines.

One of Watanabe's main findings is that the very existence of the subcontracting network stimulated the development of small, relatively low cost NC machines. But even more sophisticated multi-purpose machines seem to find their way into the domestic enterprises: 'For entrepreneurs of the smallest size group, the machining centre is specially attractive, because a single machine can serve the purposes of different machines (boring, drilling, milling, etc.) and thus save the space as well as capital investment cost. Since its work cycle is between 30 minutes and 2 to 3 hours, household enterprises can continue to operate without interruption while the entrepreneurs and family watch TV, have dinner, etc.' (p.25). On a more cautious note, he warns that it is too soon to tell whether the new technologies are increasing or lowering the extent of subcontracting: 'The net effect of such machines on the extent of interfirm division of labour cannot be determined easily. We need to wait and see the general business trends for a number of years to come' (p.61). A case study by Murray (1983) on the Italian engineering industry suggests that the putting out is far from diminishing. On the contrary he observed a 'more systematic use of decentralisation, with the introduction of information technology into planning and the appearance of numerically controlled machine tools in increasingly specialised artisan shops' (p.82).

Clearly, any general conclusions on this subject would be premature. Even in the advanced countries the new technologies are only beginning to show their impact on employment patterns. Probably the main problem of more decentralised work is that many of the micro-electronics related innovations are still in their first generation and much of the decrease in capital costs and increase in flexibility is still to come. In developing countries, these problems are further compounded by the distance of users from technology suppliers who tend to be foreign. Proximity and close interaction between suppliers and users is essential for the new technology to function well, particularly in relation to maintenance.

How existing technologies affect the practice of external labour use has been set out above. Technology does, however, only explain half the story. Fluctuations in demand and marketing channels go a long way towards explaining the other half. The clothing industry shows this very clearly (chapter 6). From a technological point of view, all clothes could be produced in a putting out system, but typically it is found in those for which demand is most volatile and distribution channels are diffuse. For the same reason large capital keeps out of such lines of production, leaving the field to small capital which is generally more efficient in coping with the required flexibility and in farming out the production process, not least because often the cooption of external labour takes place in the twilight between legality and illegality.

NOTES

1.   The same point is made by Murray (1983) in a study on decentralisation of production in the engineering industry of Bologna, Italy: 'Putting-out...cannot be equated with an archaic and disappearing system of production' (p.84).

2.   This is even true for Britain.   'There are no national figures in Britain of the number of homeworkers, nor of the firms which use this type of labour; nor are there any accurate data concerning the kinds of work undertaken...the records kept are totally inadequate despite the fact that the 1959 Wages Council Act requires local authorities to keep up-to-date lists of homeworkers, and the 1961 Factories Act makes employers responsible for providing half-yearly returns to local authorities on the number of homeworkers they employ' (Allen 1981, pp. 41-42).

3.   The technical divisibility allows another advantage of subcontracting to unfold, namely a greater scope for specialisation.   Harriss (1982), for instance, noted that in metal work and engineering in South India, parent firms benefited from the efficiency of narrowly specialised subcontractors and also from associated capital savings.

Chapter 11

SKILLS AND CONTROL

This and the following chapters deal mainly with the <u>internal</u> workforce, in particular with the relationship <u>between</u> technology, skills, turnover and wages. In the discussion on technology and skills in developing countries one has to distinguish between two questions (even though they are interrelated): first, what skills are necessary in order to induce technical change and second, what are the consequences of technical change (once introduced) for skill requirements? The first is almost a separate field of investigation carried out under the heading of indigenous technological capability (see, for example, Cooper 1980a or Fransman and King 1984). Our concern is with the second question; it is taken up in this chapter in order to draw out some general points which emerge from the literature review (Part 1) and our case material (Part 2) and which are of special relevance to developing countries.

DE-SKILLING?

The Brazilian case studies show three trends:

1. The necessary training time for most shopfloor workers decreases. (This comes out most clearly where spinning and weaving mills at different technological levels are compared; here the de-skilling is undoubtedly an outcome of technical change. In the clothing industry it is more a result of changes in the organisation of the work process.)
2. There is a progressive concentration of know-how and skill in a small group of managerial and technical workers.

3.   However, the number of de-skilled workers (see trend 1) falls at a faster rate than that of managerial and technical workers; hence in relative terms, the skilled component of the workforce increases with technological modernisation, while a (shrinking) majority of workers suffers a process of de-skilling.

What we find therefore is a confirmation of the de-skilling thesis, but with the all important qualification noted in 3. above. We believe that in developing countries a further qualification is necessary which did not so much emerge from our case studies, but becomes obvious through mere reflection: when new industries are established which do not substitute for previous ones, there is no previous skill, so the de-skilling thesis becomes problematic.
Since so much of new technology or industry in developing countries means entirely new lines of production, let us reiterate the question: to what extent does it make sense to talk about de-skilling in the developing countries?   Sometimes it does.   The case of the Brazilian textile industry serves as an example because it has such a long history and has undergone substantial technological modernisation in its course. However, it would not make sense in the Brazilian textile machinery industry, for example, because most of it is of relatively recent origin; until a decade ago most textile machinery was imported.   Thus, in countries or industrial sectors where import (or export) substitution is a recent phenomenon, the de-skilling thesis is not always applicable. We emphasise this almost obvious point, because amongst students who take a critical stand towards issues of technology and skills in developing countries one sometimes finds an uncritical acceptance of Braverman's textbook.   This is not to say that observing industrial labour processes in the periphery through Braverman's lenses is an entirely futile exercise; on the contrary, some perspectives of his analysis, in particular the emphasis on control, are relevant.   (This is elaborated below.)   The point to be stressed here is that Braverman's trajectory on skills cannot be simply transferred to the situation in developing countries.
Strong adherents to the de-skilling thesis may object in one or two ways.1/   First they could query the national or regional context in which we have analysed the question and instead put forward a global perspective.   Indeed, de-skilling is an historical process which occurs at the global level, particularly when production itself is internationalised.   The sixties and seventies showed many examples of decomposition of complex production processes into elementary units such that unskilled workers (in any low wage site on the globe) could easily be trained to perform otherwise complex operations (Fröbel et al. 1977; Bienefeld et al. 1977).   Obviously such processes need to be studied in a global context and it would

be ludicrous to exclude developing countries from this international de-skilling scenario.

Other objections to our reflections on skills do not dwell so much on the international level, but focus more on the activities of the new industrial labour force. Generally such labour comes from various kinds of self- or family employment, often in subsistence production. The argument goes that the skills required to survive in this informal economy are considerably greater than those demanded of industrial wage workers. We have no doubt that this is correct, particularly if one were to compare the length of training required to survive by, for instance, producing crops, catching fish, or producing shoes, with the training time of wage labour in industry. However, we would suggest that the movement of labour from subsistence or informal production to wage employment, and the inevitable destruction of traditional skills which occurs in the process, is captured more adequately under the heading of proletarianisation. This is a well established area of research and it would confuse rather than help if these processes were dragged into the de-skilling debate. The latter, in our view, is, or should be, restricted to changes in the capitalist labour process.

Those who are anyway sceptical of de-skilling emphasise that this is only one side of the picture; their counter-thesis is that de-skilling in one branch is generally accompanied by increasing skill requirements elsewhere in the economy. The argument is certainly correct, even though it is difficult to assess at the macro level to what extent the generation of new skills in some sectors does offset the loss of skills in others. The new skills most frequently referred to are those which emerge in the launching of a new technology which may lead to de-skilling in the branches where the new technology is applied.

At the heart of this process of generation and diffusion of new technologies is the capital goods sector. More than any other sector of the economy it represents a pool of skills which is constantly faced with new challenges. This is where most of the compensatory skill creation takes place. When it comes to developing countries, this compensation thesis is more complicated, because generally the new technology is not produced locally. Even the so-called newly industrialising countries still rely to a large extent on the import of machinery. Some countries have made considerable progress in building up their own capital goods sector, which means that more of the new jobs and skills arising from industrial growth remain in the country. However, even where this has been successful, it does not always include the research and development of new technology. Since most capital goods producers in developing countries are subsidiaries of foreign firms, joint ventures or national firms operating under

172

licensing arrangements, the most skilled part of the labour process usually remains in the central economies.

In sum, the analysis of technical change and skill requirements, which has received much attention in the central economies, cannot easily be transferred to the peripheral economies. The processes of destruction of existing skills and creation of new skills are often different. The reasons lie in the younger industrial base and the technological dependence of developing countries.

CONTROL AND THE POLITICS OF PRODUCTION

Differences also emerge in the related issue of control. There is little question in the literature on developed countries about the connection between workers' skills and control over the labour process (see Part 1). In line with Edwards (1979) we can define control as management's ability to obtain the desired work behaviour from workers. He attempts to explain how the changing systems of control provide the key towards understanding the transformation of the workplace in the United States. In research on developing countries this perspective is rare to find.2/ There has been considerable concern with the impact of technological change on employment. Technology has been introduced into socio-economic analysis, but generally as a neutral factor; thus new technology tends to be seen only as an instrument of increasing labour productivity, which slows down the absorption of labour. It tends to be forgotten that it is at the same time an instrument in the employers' politics of production, an instrument of domination and control of the worker in the workplace.

In the case studies an attempt was made to bring this dimension into the analysis of employers' policies. The importance of this step was quickly revealed. It came out most clearly in the preference of the advanced textile and clothing firms for unskilled workers (chapters 4 and 6). Unless one understands employers' concern with discipline and precise execution of tasks according to instructions, it is hard to understand this policy. To remind us, the policy only becomes feasible because modern technology and methods of work organisation considerably lower training requirements. However, advanced machinery and work organisation are only a necessary, not a sufficient condition. For the above policy to work, careful selection and training procedures need to be followed, which in turn require specialised staff and facilities to carry this through. Such an apparatus is only economical for large enterprises. Thus we can conclude that, since skill requirements have decreased with technological modernisation, large-scale firms find that higher training costs incurred by recruiting young unskilled workers are

173

outweighed by gains in discipline and control over labour in the workplace.

A problem for employers is the fact that modern technology does not shift control in a clear-cut way. This becomes most apparent in continuous process production. On the one hand it is the kind of process where management has the greatest degree of knowledge and control over operations in that the physical limitations are known precisely and operator interference is minimal. On the other hand, reliance on the active cooperation of workers is more critical. The technical features which enable managers to predetermine the outcome so precisely, can be used as a lever against them, since non-cooperation results in much more severe damage of equipment and loss of materials than in discontinuous production. The chemical fibre study (chapter 5) highlighted these problems and in chapter 12 below we shall enlarge in more general terms on employers' policies towards labour which can be expected in production processes of this kind.

These considerations emerging from the case studies confirm the importance of control in understanding the pattern of labour utilisation. At the same time it must be recognised that in peripheral capitalist economies the issue of domination and control has three dimensions which make it different from the way it is in the central capitalist economies: 1. technology is imported, which means that it is not a result of the struggle between employers and workers in the periphery; 2. there is generally little trade union power and resistance on the shop-floor; 3. the labour surplus is considerably larger.

In order to explain the first factor, we have to engage in a short digression. Technology is not a neutral factor in the relationship between capital and labour. This has already been shown in relation to the consequences of technical change for labour. This conception of technology as a force in factory politics has to be extended by asking where technologies come from and what direction technical change takes. The danger is to view the origin of new machinery merely in attempts to solve technical problems in the pursuit of raising profitability. The politics of production must not be left out. As emphasised by Rosenberg (1976), historically the inducement for many innovations has come from capital's search for ways of (re-) establishing its control over the labour process:

> The apparent recalcitrance of nineteenth-century English labour, especially skilled labour, in accepting the discipline and the terms of factory employment provided an inducement to technical change ... the threat of worker noncompliance - in the last resort, strikes - served as a powerful agent in focusing the attention of decision-makers on obvious and major threats to their profit positions. (p.117) ... The preoccupation with substituting capital for

labour (especially skilled labour) was more than just a matter of wage rates. (p.120)

This is not a position specific to Marx; the most celebrated formulation comes from Andrew Ure (1835) who rejoiced that 'when capital enlists science in her service, the refractory hand of labour will always be taught docility' (p.368). In a more dispassionate approach, Rosenberg (1976) emphasises that numerous inventors have testified that they undertook the search process as the result of actual or expected problems in control over labour. A prominent example from the textile industry is the invention of the spinning mule: 'When a group of Manchester mill owners commissioned Richard Roberts to design a self-acting mule, their principal objective was to break the power of the very militant operative spinners' unions' (Catling 1970, p.147).3/ A more modern example is automatically controlled machine tools; Noble (1979) suggests that their design was heavily influenced by 'capital's attempt to minimise its dependence upon labour by increasing its control over production' (p.30).

Of course not all inventions or innovations can be explained in this way. Constraints in the supply of materials have been important in inducing the search for new processes, perhaps best evidenced by the oil crisis of the seventies. Technical imbalances constitute a further group of factors leading to the development of new machinery. The history of the textile industry with its changing imbalances between spinning and weaving provides some examples. Over the last few decades, experiments in the military sector have contributed greatly to technical change in industry. Ultimately virtually all search for new methods of production can be explained by economic pressure to raise profitability. But since economic incentives are so diffuse and general they cannot explain what form the new technology takes. This is why Rosenberg (1976) asks what forces determine the direction which industry actually takes in its exploration for new techniques: 'Since it cannot explore in all directions, what are the factors which induce it to strike out in a particular direction'? (p.111) The answer is that one important factor lies in capital's politics of production, in the issue of control. Hence technology is not an 'independent variable'. The form which technology takes (and the point at which it is introduced) often reflects previous conflicts between workers and management.4/ This is an essential feature of the labour process in the central economies.

In the periphery (our digression ends here) the connection between the history of factory politics and technology rarely, if ever, exists since technology (or at least the design) is imported. It is thought important to point out this difference. Probably it means that technology rarely comes into play as a means of breaking existing labour resistance, as a means of re-establishing management control in the workplace. The effect is more likely to be one of forestalling workers' resistance. This possibly also explains to some extent why trade unions in developing countries have some influence in general political terms but very little influence over factory work itself.5/

On the whole, however, labour unions in developing countries are not as important a political force as they are in developed countries. There can be little doubt that the main reason is repression, particularly in countries with a military government. This is where the second element behind the difference in the control issue lies; namely the question arises as to what importance the control aspect of technology has in a society where workers' resistance is repressed by the state apparatus.6/ A Brazilian student, in response to a lecture on the labour process, put the issue in a nutshell: 'You don't need Taylorism where you have Terrorism!'

Taylor himself probably would have disagreed, and rightly so because political control over the workers is not a sufficient condition for raising their productivity (which is ultimately the objective); general political control does not automatically result in control over working methods. At the same time one must realise that the two are related, when workers organise to defy management directives over pace and manner of executing work. The general political conditions determine to a considerable extent how far this resistance can go, or whether there is any organised resistance in the first place.

The third element altering the control issue is not unrelated to the second: the size of the labour surplus. Control, as discussed here, is about workers' compliance with management directives. There can be little doubt that the workers' alternative job opportunities influence management's ability to elicit the desired collaboration. The disciplining effect of the industrial reserve army needs no explanation. Equally there can be little doubt that this effect is greater in the periphery than in the centre. The world economic recession has brought high unemployment to the central economies, but also further increased the employment problem in most developing countries. Furthermore, the absence of a state social security network in the latter countries means that the pressure to comply is higher, probably substantially higher.

By way of summing up, we can say that the control aspect of technology has a different order of importance in developing countries for three reasons: the technology is imported; labour unions are weaker; and the labour surplus is larger. Nevertheless, the task of extracting labour from workers who have no direct stake in profits remains to be carried out. Conflicts arise over discipline, how the work shall be executed, and what work pace shall be established. The case studies show that management's employment policies can sometimes only be understood through its concern with control over the labour process.7/ The following chapter further underlines how its policies towards labour are influenced by the need to 'elicit cooperation and enforce compliance'.8/

NOTES

1.   I am grateful to students at both the Institute of Development Studies at the University of Sussex and at the Institute of Industrial Economics at the Federal University of Rio de Janeiro for engaging me in lengthy debates on de-skilling questions and thus forcing me to think these issues through more thoroughly than I otherwise would have.

2.   A notable exception is John Humphrey's excellent work Capitalist Control and Workers' Resistance in the Brazilian Auto Industry (1982). This study is not, however, very explicit on the relative importance of technological conditions.

3.   In the end this objective was not fully achieved with the otherwise successful innovation (see Catling 1970, chapter 9).

4.   Bruland (1979, 1982) provides an excellent general account of the argument, backed up with brief case studies of technical innovation in British industrialisation.

5.   At least in Brazil, the political power of unions (when they were not completely repressed) was greater than their power in the factory.

6.   Fleury (1978) suggests that advanced methods of work organisation are relatively underdeveloped in Brazil, without, however, linking this explicitly to union repression. In contrast, Vargas (1979) proposes that state repression is one factor which makes the introduction of Taylorism and Fordism less urgent in Brazil.

7.   In some of the case studies we made reference to the role of female labour, generally found in low wage occupations. The use of women workers is without doubt also influenced by considerations of docility and control. However, in order to limit the scope of the investigation, the gender variable was not made a focus of research. Our reference to it in the case studies is a by-product of research and, as such, casual rather than systematic. This is also why gender questions could not be dealt with in this general section on management policies towards labour. Amongst the studies which have taken on these questions more squarely are: Pacific Studies Centre (1978); Elson and Pearson (1981); Mars (ed) (1982); Joekes (1982); Arnold et al. (1982).

8.   Borrowing the words from Edwards (1979).

Chapter 12

LABOUR TURNOVER, WAGES AND RELIABILITY

The impact of modern technology on skills and control is intimately connected with its impact on labour turnover and wages. The first connection which comes to mind and which was revealed by the case studies is that a decrease in training time makes it easier to replace one worker by another. While this in itself does not produce high labour turnover, nor make it desirable, it means that high labour turnover where it occurs does not present major problems. In the case studies this was evidenced by the fact that employers in the textile industry did not make special efforts to reduce the high turnover rates. At least they were not prepared to pay for such a reduction through better wages or other means. Easy substitution of labour exercises a downward pressure on wages. In the textile industry, it certainly kept wages from rising in any significant way, even though substantial modernisation of equipment occurred and even though considerable gains in labour productivity were achieved.

These findings run contrary to what dual labour market theories suggest. They usually imply that modern, capital-intensive technologies lead to stable, well-paid employment. Rather, it seems necessary to disaggregate the notion of modern technology when it comes to employment implications. On the one hand we have the experiences referred to above: high turnover and low wages even under advanced technological conditions, most notably in the spinning and weaving industry (see chapter 4). On the other hand we have the experience from continuous process production, where employers' attitudes towards wages and turnover are markedly different (see chapter 5). Our case study on the chemical fibre industry revealed low turnover rates and relatively high wages and fringe benefits. The explanation cannot be found in high skill requirements; firms give operators a training time of three to six months to satisfy their standards of job performance. The reason lies in employers' concern with reliability. The continuous nature of the process means that breakdowns and interruptions are more costly than in processes lower

178

down the technological scale which are of a discontinuous nature. In the production of chemical fibres unexpected interruptions are particularly serious; if the processed substances solidify in reaction vessels, pipes or extrusion equipment, half the plant may have to be rebuilt. Through automatic control devices, firms attempt to safeguard themselves against such breakdowns, but they can never be ruled out completely. In the day-to-day running of the plants human errors or losses in regularity and precision are still a problem and the objective of minimising them pervades employers' policies towards labour. In this respect our case study confirms Blauner's (1964) analysis of the work of the chemical operator: 'Because of the high degree of responsibility that continuous-process technology demands, management is particularly interested in a permanent stable work force' (p.130). Quoting from Lester's 'The New Dimension of Industrial Employment', Blauner emphasises that:

> The employer and the prospective employee think of employment in terms of a whole work career - a long term relationship in which the employer takes on an increasing burden of fringe benefits covering the man and his family, and the employee acquires tenure, job rights, and rights to promotion opportunities. (p.130)

This assessment is very close to our own. However, having observed chemical operators at close hand, we find it difficult to agree with Blauner's suggestion that such work signals the end of alienation, that 'it provides new avenues for meaning and self-expression in work' (p.134) and that 'the special technological and economic characteristics of the continuous-process industries give workers a great deal of control over their immediate work processes' (p.135). While there is a difference from the machine paced work on the assembly line, the work of chemical operators is still narrowly defined by rules which determine their daily (or nightly) routine and which tell them in case of irregularities occurring when they can take action to solve (simple) problems and when to report to the supervisor. Applying these rules does not require an understanding of the chemical processes (as indicated by the short training periods). The one point which the operator does or must understand is that not following the instructions means trouble, often serious.

This is where the reponsibility factor comes in which leads to the kind of labour utilisation found in our case study: a high degree of labour stability achieved through:

- providing advancement opportunities; this included the opening up of mobility routes or job ladders and the offer of educational/vocational courses to make higher positions attainable (up to a certain level);

179

- paying relatively high wages and offering a range of fringe benefits such as medical assistance, good canteen services and credit facilities.1/

In the large plants of the other industries these elements were not all entirely absent, but management's desire to achieve lower turnover rates was not backed up by a sufficient preparedness to 'pay' for it. The reason seems to be in the different technical basis, since in those industries dependable work performance was not as critical as in continuous flow production. In addition there is an economic difference; labour intensity in the latter industry is low, hence an increase in labour costs 'hurts' less than in other industries. To give an indication, in synthetic fibres the share of wages in total costs is 12 per cent, compared with 21 per cent in spinning and weaving2/ (which is itself no longer a labour-intensive industry).

The rationale of the employment policy found in continuous-process production is perhaps best underlined by the experience of a plant which did <u>not</u> adopt it. The experience relates to cement production which is also carried out in a continuous process. Coriat (1981) found that in a Brazilian cement plant, a subsidiary of a French company equipped with the most advanced technology, breakdowns were frequent and efficiency was low. While the (French) management attributed this to problems encountered with the local labour force (attitudes to work, technical competence), Coriat suggests (convincingly) that the main reason lay in management policies towards labour. Internal promotion in the plant was not sufficiently guaranteed due to the absence of formal job ladders; wages, while not low for local conditions, were not sufficiently high to retain workers. The result was a high turnover of labour which prevented the smooth and efficient running of the plant.

Further evidence comes from a case study in the Brazilian steel industry by Borges (1983); her research on a modern integrated steel plant shows technological characteristics and employment practices very similar to those found in the chemical fibre industry. The production process is by and large continuous, consisting of a chain of physico-chemical reactions, in which <u>direct</u> human intervention is limited; in the main stages there is 'no direct relationship between the rhythm of work and the rhythm of production' (p.6). At the same time a dependable work performance is absolutely critical for the plant's efficiency. The degree of interdependence, the cost of interruption and the cost of producing waste or below-standard material, is extremely high. So is the responsibility of workers engaged in coordinating, monitoring, adjusting and maintaining the production process. Interestingly enough the plant studied (in 1980) had achieved an enviable degree of stability (average monthly turnover rates of 0.8 per cent for its 4067 workers; p.52). Instrumental in achieving the low turnover were the payment of relatively high wages3/ and emphasis on internal training and career opportunities. Management 'tries to exercise social control over the collective of workers and coopt them by way of a high wage policy, guaranteeing stability of employment, wage promotion, security training, etc., thus seeking their loyalty and forging an identity of interests between both parties (employers and employees) when it comes to production results' (p.53).

If the pattern of labour utilisation found in automated continuous process production is management's rational response to new technological conditions, do these industries portend future conditions of work and employment? The answer would seem to depend on two questions. First, how pervasive is the trend towards automation? Undoubtedly there is a long run tendency for industrial production to move up the technological ladder (towards stage four of our labour process classification). The advent of micro-electronics is speeding up this process, but their role in developing countries is still unclear (see chapter 14).

The second question is whether automated production, where it occurs, always increases the importance of the reliability factor. Bright (1966) raises some doubts:

> Responsibility can be thought of as increasing with more costly and more highly integrated machinery. However, it increases only to the extent that the worker truly has responsibility, and the ultimate effect of the higher levels of automation is to remove responsibility for performance from the hands of the worker. The detection of faulty operations, overloads, malfunction, shortages, changing material, power requirements, and so on gradually becomes vested in the machine. (p.212)

At the same time he acknowledges that:

> It would be a mistake, of course, to assume that the reduction of job content is the only effect of automation ...Because less attention is required on a given machine, the operator may be given more machines to tend. He becomes responsible for the manning of a physically larger portion of the production sequence or a larger number of identical activities. This may require a knowledge of additional machines, and hence additional technical skills on the part of the worker; it may also require more effort and attention. The net result may be a significant increase in responsibility because of the possibility and/or probability of more costly damage if the system under his control malfunctions. (p.213, emphasis added)

181

One could add that even though the expectation is that improvements in automatic processes would eventually eliminate the areas of uncertainty, each advanced stage of automation brings its own technical problems and potential for breakdown requiring human monitoring and intervention. Moreover, our own case study as well as the work of Blauner (1964), Coriat (1981), Borges (1983) and others, suggests that a focus on the efficiency or reliability of the individual worker is mistaken. The very technological conditions demand a concern with collective efficiency and collective reliability. In practice, a dependable performance of the collective worker can only develop over time and under stable work relations.

While it is difficult to assess authoritatively how important automated technology and the reliability factor will become, a pattern of labour utilisation is emerging which has wider implications for economic theory and policy. These turn on the argument that it pays to offer wages and employment conditions better than those demanded by the labour market. Advanced technologies create circumstances where the increased reliability and commitment obtained by offering conditions of labour above the supply price is worth more to the employer than the cost of doing so. If this is so, one would have, at the highest level of technology, an effect which divorces employment conditions (including the wage) from labour market circumstances. The higher wage, which one could call the reliability wage, has as its essential feature that it is endogenous to the firm and technology related and that it cannot be explained by exogenous factors such as imperfections in the labour market.4/ Thus, Alfred Marshall's (1920) words that 'highly paid labour is generally efficient and therefore not dear labour' (p.423) have special relevance at high technological levels due to the 'endogenous wage effect'.

This does not imply that all high wages can be explained in this way.5/ The proposition is merely that under certain technological conditions (which are likely to become more frequent), the high wage policy is the more rational approach for the enterprise. In as much as the reliability or efficiency wage becomes reality, it has far reaching economic and political consequences. In essence, this possibility breaks the link between flexible wages and employment creation and therefore severs the connection which establishes the market's supposed tendency towards full employment. In doing so, it destroys the very argument on which the defence of the market's social function rests. Politically, it means that attempting to achieve competitiveness with devaluation, reduction of wages and curbing of trade union power is misguided, though it does not mean that devaluation is never desirable nor that wages cannot be artificially high. It does, however, throw doubt on strategies which seek to restore competitiveness and full employment through 'union bashing' and other means of wage reduction.

It should be emphasised that at this stage these are hypotheses emerging from the research and not 'results'. Future research would have to seek evidence for these propositions at various levels. At the most general are all the instances where the effective elimination of trade unions has nevertheless seen the maintenance or even the widening of wage differentials whose explanation in terms of supply conditions is difficult or impossible. Past experience suggests the need to be aware of tautological explanations as when modern operations include 'new' jobs which are relatively highly paid and which are given new names making them new occupations or skills which, finally, are used to 'explain' the wage differential. In this process the objective content of these 'new' occupations or skills is often not examined at all.

This warning also indicates the need for complementary research at the micro level, probably along the lines of our case studies. One must hope that such research will be carried out, not least because a major wave of automation is on its way – at least in the central economies.6/ Advances in micro-electronics are at the heart of this process. The likely effects of the new technologies on labour are discussed in chapter 14 which looks into the future and asks what changes can be expected in employment, skills and wages. However, before moving into this somewhat speculative area, we keep on the firmer ground of our case studies and ask what are the policy implications emerging from them.

NOTES

1. In the literature this kind of employment pattern is often referred to as 'internal labour market' (see for example, Doeringer and Piore 1971). Our analysis implies a technological explanation for the existence of a labour market internal to the firm. It does not, however, imply that technology is necessarily the only explanatory factor.

2. The percentages are derived from the Industrial Census of 1975 and express the share of wages of workers linked to production in the 'valor da produção'. We wonder, however, about the reliability of this indicator, since one would expect the clothing industry to show a significantly higher percentage than the spinning and weaving industry, but this is not so.

3. Conversations with the researcher suggest that, in the region, comparable or higher wages were only paid in the petro-chemical industry, which is itself an example of continuous flow production.

4. I am grateful to Manfred Bienefeld for drawing my attention to the implications of the reliability or, as he prefers to call it, efficiency wage.

5. For instance, some Brazilian car firms pay relatively high wages which were, according to Humphrey (1982), 'neither a device for stabilising the labour force, nor a concession to

union power...high wages in the industry provided a basis for higher-than-average intensity of work, which also had an impact on health and safety in the plants' (p.90).

6.   See for example, the Special Report in <u>Business Week</u> of 3 August 1981, 'The speed up in automation'.

Chapter 13

SOME POLICY IMPLICATIONS

Drawing out implications for government policy from research on the labour process is a delicate thing to do. This piece of research, as any other that undertakes a realistic account of the relationship between machines and people in industry, cannot stop at the technical or economic level. One soon runs up against, or better into, the political field. We called it the politics of production, which arise from employers' need to obtain a certain behaviour pattern from their workers and from workers' reluctance or resistance to comply. This was an important, but limited, step to take; limited because the issue of control in the workplace was not followed through and connected sufficiently with the question of workers' unions and the role of the state in developing countries. In our empirical work much attention was given to the Brazilian experience; few can have doubts about the nature of the Brazilian regime, even though recent years have seen a decline in repression and a strengthening of the labour movement. Thus, the policy implications that follow cannot and do not assume a neutral, benevolent government. The suggestions might, however, be of some use to those working within the state apparatus trying to contribute to a more genuine concern with employment, training and working conditions in industry.

Some policy implications are general, others are specific. At the most general level, one must emphasise that advanced technology cannot be equated with privileged jobs. Intra-industry comparisons in the textile and clothing industry revealed that it is rarely an advantage to work in an advanced technology factory. If anything, work is more repetitive and strenuous. Pay is sometimes a little better, but not always. Labour turnover is considerable. Certainly, any expectation that technological modernisation would soon solve the problem of low-paid and unstable work conditions must be considered ill-conceived. A crucial factor is that in industries such as textiles and clothing, more modern technology tends to make it easier to substitute one worker for another. Hence the need for protection through legislation which improves job security and remuneration is no less urgent in technologically advanced firms.

There are, however, certain kinds of advanced technology, where replacing one worker by another presents problems; not because of high skill requirements, but due to the importance of dependable work performance. We have suggested above that this applies under technological conditions which are characterised by continuous production. Reliable performance requires job security for which employers are willing to pay through internal career opportunities and remuneration above the supply price of labour. The evidence from our case studies is only indicative, but policy makers should accustom themselves to the idea that under certain technological conditions, it is 'efficient' for employers to offer a package of employment conditions better than the law or the labour market demands. This package, including the wage, is explained endogenously and hence is not susceptible to government policies. In particular, general government polices which seek to influence employment or competitiveness by curbing wages would be futile for these industries. Future research will have to assess whether the 'efficiency' or 'reliability wage' effect can be expected to occur in all forms of automated production and whether the continuous nature of the process is a decisive criterion. Whatever the precise outcome of such research, it seems almost certain that the whole complex of modern technology and employment conditions needs disaggregating, before any useful conclusion about the desirability or consequence of government action can be made/predicted.

Policy implications of a more immediate practical value lie in the field of vocational training. Employers' complaints about the lack of trained workers are universal and too often governments are 'invited' or 'bullied' into supporting industrial training, all in the name of economic growth and paving the way for modern technology. We had the opportunity to examine a number of requests which were submitted to the Brazilian government, revealing employers' attempts to 'socialise' their training costs. In evaluating such requests, it is necessary to exercise great scrutiny; at least this is what our experience and the above case material suggests. At the risk of over-simplification we would formulate the following guidelines.

Do not subsidise or become involved in vocational training for machine operators and auxiliary workers. The reasons are simple. The training required for the jobs is short and the more modern the technology, the shorter the training necessary. If employers were interested in skills themselves, surely they would not avoid the recruitment of workers who had previously worked in other firms (as they do). The training they seek to provide is narrowly geared to the operation of a small range of machines and to the adoption of discipline. A subsidy for this training through tax reductions or provision of instructors1/ amounts to an investment in the company in question, not an investment in the country's human resources. The wording is perhaps extreme, but as a guideline it is believed to be correct. A more positive formulation could be: leave the training of operators to the companies; they are more efficient in catering for their needs and can be expected to carry the cost since training time is short.2/ If training costs are high due to excessive labour turnover, the solution must be sought elsewhere, not in government support for this kind of training.

For maintenance workers the recommendation would be different. The research revealed that in proportional terms their importance increases, but opinions were divided as to whether the length of necessary training time would increase. Whatever the answer, occupations such as mechanic, electrician, and electronics serviceman require a relatively comprehensive training, which in its basics is common to all industries. This is an area of training for which there is a great need and in which government must provide support. The Brazilian vocational training service for industry (SENAI) already has a training programme for these occupations, but in the course of the research it became apparent that it is not sufficient.

Shortages of skilled maintenance workers were frequently mentioned in the interviews and it seems that the problem was real, particularly in the North-East. This has two reasons: first, the availability of SENAI training in this region is much more limited than in the Centre-South. Second, being able to count on good maintenance staff is much more critical in the North-East. In the Centre-South, particularly in the state of São Paulo, firms have the advantage of physical proximity to machinery suppliers when they need spare parts or a specialised maintenance service; in addition there is a network of 'oficinas' which can repair or copy a part. In the North-East, the likelihood of finding the required maintenance or repair services outside the firm, but locally, is much more limited. Hence manufacturing firms require a more extensive internal maintenance department and would particularly benefit from increased training facilities offered by the government.

The suggestion of more and better government supported training of maintenance workers receives added weight from the concern with building up an indigenous technological capability in developing countries. The ability to maintain and repair technology is a first step towards the capacity to adjust this technology to local conditions and, at a later stage, possibly replace it with new designs. Obviously one is dealing here with long-run objectives, but these considerations should have a place in decisions on training policy. Perhaps it is also worth anticipating one of the messages of chapter 14. In future, the training needs for maintenance identified here will arise similarly, if not more urgently, in software skills (programming), particularly in systems analysis/engineering.

Finally, we should draw out some implications for employment orientated project evaluation. Employment policy, in order to be effective, has to be linked to the provision of government incentives. However, the government bodies examining industrial projects generally lack information on the amount and type of employment which can be expected from investment in determinate industries. This is, of course, not unrelated to the fact that often the concern with jobs is stronger in official documents than in reality. The problems are manifold. They are exemplified by the case of SUDENE, the Brazilian govenment's planning authority for the North-East, a region where the problem of un(der)-employment is most severe.

The first problem is that the organisation is not given sufficient financial and human resources to undertake a serious evaluation of industrial projects for which financial and fiscal incentives are requested. In fact, the organisation which started on a strong footing under Celso Furtado has been increasingly prevented from exercising any effective control over investment which would be geared to the needs of the region. SUDENE's textile group is a case in point. The textile department used to consist of a strong group of officials, both in terms of numbers and expertise. Over time this strength has been eroded to the extent that today the few remaining officials can do little more than administer the process of application for granting of incentives.

A second problem relates to the internal division of labour in the institution. In general, the Department of Industry deals with investment decisions. The question of employment is dealt with by the Human Resources Department which has no say in the project evaluation; it is limited to monitoring ex post the changes in the labour force and employment, mainly at the macro level. In a way the Human Resources Department fulfills an ideological function, because its existence and publications suggest a concern on the part of the institution with employment, but in reality it is excluded from the decisions on projects which in the end determine how many and what kind of jobs are created/destroyed.3/

All this does not mean that the concern for employment plays no role at all. The evaluation procedure works on a point system such that a high number of expected new jobs will improve the rating of the project and its chances of receiving government support. The problem is that the officials have to rely on the job figures which the enterprise provides in its application. Rarely do the officials have the means to examine this estimate. Even if they had the time to investigate this question, they face a formidable task. Let us assume the institution is given the resources to examine seriously the employment implications of the project. This would involve assessing both the probable number and type of jobs. Any such exercise requires a general understanding of the employment pattern that can be expected under different technological conditions. This is where case studies of the type presented above (Part 2) can be particularly useful.4/

However, such material will not always exist for all industrial branches in which projects are examined. In such cases there will be a need to derive at least some indications from those branches which have been studied and which are at a similar level of technological development. (The importance of a classification or typology of labour processes surfaces again.) Of course, such studies in themselves do not allow a quantification of the number and composition of the workers, but they should provide an idea of what can be expected in reality. These expectations can then be checked against information from three sources: a) machinery suppliers; b) other firms which already make use of the technology in question; and c) trade union or workers' representatives who are familiar with the technology.

This reads almost like guidelines for research, rather than for project evaluation; but most evaluation does involve a limited amount of research. The speed at which the required data can be collected and the accuracy of the data will depend to a considerable extent on the experience of the analyst. Most experience comes from doing the job, but precisely because the amount of research which can be carried out in the evaluation of projects is limited, more extensive studies are required from which the analyst can derive a theoretical and empirical framework for his or her project-specific work. It is hoped that this book can be of use in this respect.

NOTES

1. In Brazil, the 'Law 6.297' allows firms which engage in training programmes to apply for a reduction in income tax. If instructors are provided, the cost is usually carried by SENAI, the government body responsible for vocational training.

2. To avoid any misunderstanding, most training efforts in this category are shouldered by industry, but there are constant attempts to implicate the government.

3. This division of labour is not unique to SUDENE, it can also be found in other institutions, for instance the Institute of Economic and Social Planning (IPEA) which forms part of the Federal Planning Secretariat. The Institute's Industry Department used to be represented in the Council for Industrial Development, a body which takes decisions on incentives for investment. The Institute's Centre for Human Resources, however, had no representation. On an ad hoc basis it was sometimes asked for advice on the desirability of projects, but it was excluded from the regular decision-making

machinery which influences the investment pattern and thus also the employment situation.

    4.   This is not to argue that the project evaluator always needs information on labour demand to such a degree of detail.

Chapter 14

THE FUTURE WITH MICRO-ELECTRONICS

The intention in this final chapter is to open up our analysis
further and look into the future.1/ Judging from developments
in Japan, North America and Europe, there is little doubt that
the years ahead will be influenced in a major way by
micro-electronics based innovations. In fact, in the advanced
countries, most of the debate on technology and employment is
about the impact of micro-electronics. The microprocessor, or
computer on a chip, has become the symbol of new technology. No
other single invention since the steam engine can be expected
to have such a broad impact on all sectors of the economy. The
excitement about the new technical possibilities is, however,
more than tempered by the fear of a negative social impact,
particularly the displacement of labour. The new possibilities
for automation are so great that some of the early studies
predicted a rapid growth of Automatic Unemployment (Hines and
Searle 1979) and even the The Collapse of Work (Jenkins and
Sherman 1979). Indeed, the initial concern with the number of
jobs pushed discussions on the qualitative aspects of
employment into the background, but this has changed since.
This chapter deals - even though briefly - with both concerns.
The material one can draw upon relates primarily to the
advanced countries, but an attempt is made here to assess its
potential relevance for developing countries. In so doing, the
objective is not to provide a comprehensive literature review,
but to bring out the main issues.2/

NEW TECHNOLOGIES AND EMPLOYMENT

Mass unemployment has become a reality in the advanced
countries, but only part of it is due to technical change. The
European and North American countries are undergoing a severe
recession, which is responsible for the larger share of job
losses; but it is difficult to be more precise and say

what proportion of the unemployment is technological and what proportion is due to fiscal and monetary policies (not least because the crisis and the diffusion of automation technologies are interlinked).3/ While macro rates of technological unemployment are hard to give, examples of labour displacement caused directly or indirectly by the application of micro-electronics abound; such examples generally come from sector or firm specific studies.

For instance, employment in the telecommunications industry of Sweden and Britain dropped by 33 and 26 per cent respectively between 1975 and 1978, primarily due to micro-electronics related innovations. This is a trend which is expected to continue through the 1980s. The West German printing industry experienced a decline of 21 per cent in employment between 1970 and 1980 while productivity increased by 43 per cent (Hoffman 1982). In the office equipment and data processing industry of that country, employment fell by 20 per cent over 1970-79, whereas output grew by 74 per cent (Friedrichs 1982). In the Japanese television industry employment fell by 48 per cent between 1972 and 1976 despite an increase in output of 25 per cent (Jenkins and Sherman 1979). The labour displacement caused by the introduction of numerically controlled machine tools in Brazil is estimated to be in the order of 48 to 69 per cent (Tauile 1983). The introduction of computer aided design enabled British and American firms to realise, on average, gains in labour productivity of 3:1 or more over manual methods (Kaplinsky 1984). Ayres and Miller (1981-82) suggest that on a conservative count over 15 per cent of operative jobs in the US metal working industry could be performed by commercially available robots and over 40 per cent could be performed by (next generation) robots with sensing capabilities.

Such case material is essential to gain a feel for real or potential job losses. However, the net macro effect cannot be gauged from such sector or firm specific numbers (even if they could be added up). To start with, we must recall that the latter are themselves often speculative. More importantly, the new technology also has an employment creating effect. First, there is employment creation in the sector which produces the new technologies, particularly the electronic capital goods and components industry. Secondly, new jobs are created through the sales, installation and operation of new equipment. Thirdly, the advent of micro-electronics has not only brought about changes in capital goods and thus production processes, but also made possible a range of new consumer goods which require labour to produce them. A study of British industry, which tried to capture both the gains and losses arising from product and process applications (pre-1981), found that the 'estimated gain and loss represents less than a quarter of 1 per cent of total employment in manufacturing at the time of survey' (Northcott and Rogers 1982, p.60). A later survey confirmed a relatively small net decrease in jobs which was 'between 1981 and 1983 equivalent to...about 0.6 per cent of total employment in manufacturing' (Northcott and Rogers 1984 p.14). These studies must be treated with some caution (on methodological grounds), but even if one makes allowance for some unreliability of the figures, the results are sobering when compared with earlier predictions of mass technological unemployment. There is certainly some indication that, in spite of the revolutionary characteristics of the new technology, the <u>net</u> displacement effect may be more gradual and smaller than suggested earlier by 'a growing school of social catastrophists' (Cooper 1980b, p.2).

Surprisingly this seems to apply even to the tertiary sector, where the labour-saving applications of micro-electronics were feared to be the most dramatic. At least this is the gist of reports presented at a recent symposium on the social and economic implications of micro-electronics in Britain:

> As judged from case studies so far, there is reason to doubt whether the net labour-saving effects of electronic processes and procedures will displace labour at a great rate. So far net labour displacement in the tertiary sector as a consequence of micro-electronics has been small, though it is not possible to know how far a further rise has been held in check. (Williams 1983, p.10)

In conclusion, for both industry (which is our main concern) and services, caution is necessary in making pronouncements on technological unemployment at the macro level. Even for advanced countries it is still early to reach a verdict.

In developing countries, the diffusion of micro-electronics has been more limited; thus an assessment of their employment impact is even more precarious. However, it is not too soon to ask whether some fundamental differences can be expected between developing and advanced countries. Initially one may want to ask why firms operating in developing countries should want to automate at all when labour is relatively abundant and cheap. This is an old question in the debate on appropriate technology. In relation to micro-electronics based innovations the answer is that a decrease in labour costs is only one reason for automation, not always the most important. Others are higher efficiency, speed, flexibility and quality; in some cases the new technologies are also capital saving.[4]/ Where developing countries produce for external markets or where internal markets are internationalised, the pressures for micro-electronics based innovations may eventually become as strong as in advanced countries. The question is whether the overall employment effect would be similar.

We would suggest that the net effect is likely to be more negative in developing countries. Where the new technology is applied, the displacement of labour is probably similar to that in advanced countries, but the creation of jobs is likely to be much smaller.

Both arguments need some qualification. A difference in the severity of the displacement may occur if user firms in developing countries tend to use the new technologies only in an incremental process of automating parts of the labour process and if user firms in advanced countries tend to go for interlinking electronics based automation throughout the enterprise (which results in heavier job losses). This tendency may arise, but there is unlikely to be a clearcut division between the two groups of countries.

Perhaps the more important difference in this comparison lies in the question of where new employment opportunities arise. Here the developing countries are at a disadvantage because they tend to import the new technology, so the jobs created in its production remain outside their economies. Again, some qualifications are necessary. First, some of the more industrialised developing countries such as South Korea or Brazil are establishing their own electronic capital goods industry. For instance, Brazilian computer firms have successfully entered the market (protected from imports and local manufacture of multinationals); they now supply to local customers a wide range of licensed and locally designed products (Tigre 1983). Also numerically controlled machine tools are beginning to be produced in the country by foreign and national firms (Tauile 1982). Most developing countries are however barred from such industrial production and this is unlikely to change, given the fast pace and high cost of innovation in this field. Second, the production of certain electronic components is carried out in low wage developing countries. In the seventies, a good deal of the assembly of microchips, a labour-intensive operation, was moved to offshore sites in Asian countries. However, the production of microchips itself can now be automated and there are the first signs of it being relocated to the advanced countries (Ernst 1982; Rada 1982).

Thus, the developing countries are not entirely excluded from the sector which produces electronics based technology. The same applies to the production of software. But there is little doubt that the employment created in these industries is overwhelmingly concentrated in the advanced countries. In contrast, their products are likely to be applied in developing countries on a scale which may well become considerable. It is for these reasons that we believe that the balance between job displacement and creation arising from micro-electronics is likely to be more negative in developing countries than it is in the advanced countries. At the same time we have to recognise that there are other factors, all interlinked, which determine this balance; for example, the existence of a local capital goods industry incorporating electronics and of a local software capability, has implications for the diffusion of product and process innovations which in turn influence output growth and employment.

The overall negative impact of the new technologies for developing countries will probably be exacerbated by the effect on the competitiveness of their industries. Their comparative advantage lies above all in low wage costs. The new automation possibilities can undermine this advantage; there are already indications that this is hampering developing country exports and leading to relocation of production to the advanced countries (discussed in Hoffman 1982, 1984 and Kaplinksy 1982, 1984). In fact, there is a growing body of studies addressing this question, but the employment implications are rarely, if ever, followed through empirically. In any case, in the context of this study we cannot review the available evidence of the impact of micro-electronics on competitiveness, but we must note that the negative effect on job prospects in developing countries may become even more severe than that arising from the diffusion of micro-electronics in these countries.

From this excursion into the impact of new technologies on the number of jobs, we return to what has been the main concern of this book: the impact on the kind of labour required and the terms on which it is employed. More specifically, we focus on skill requirements and wages.

NEW TECHNOLOGIES AND SKILLS

The discussion on how micro-electronics affect skills is merely the latest round of a long-ranging debate, the history of which we reviewed in Part 1 of this book. Again there are conflicting assertions about the upgrading or de-skilling of labour. Given the 'newness' of the technology and the dearth of studies from developing countries, we have to rely mainly (though not exclusively) on material from the advanced countries.

Let us take up some of the conflicting scenarios. Senker et al. (1980) conclude their research on micro-electronics and skill requirements in the engineering industry as follows:

The principal message of this book is that the prime requirement for competitive success and for coping with micro-electronics is to have a highly educated, trained and skilled workforce at all levels. Those countries which recognise this and implement appropriate policies will be successful in the micro-electronics age. (p.176-7)

On the other hand, Shaiken (1980), in a study on the same industry, suggests that:

> The computerised factory contradicts a myth about automation that has received widespread acceptance: automation creates more new skills for workers than it destroys. Like many myths, there is an element of truth to this one. Some new skills are created and some existing jobs...are enlarged with new responsibilities. Many more jobs, however, are either eliminated entirely...or made to require fewer skills...(p.34)

Why are there such contrasting views (and the above are no isolated examples)? The differences probably reflect less the different realities than different approaches or questions on the part of the researchers. Most studies which are commissioned by training boards or private enterprise (and affiliated bodies) concentrate on where skill shortages are likely to arise. The fact that new skills are required which are in short supply (and without which the technologies would fail) is too often interpreted as the need to upgrade the workforce generally. In contrast, most research carried out on behalf of (or sympathetic to) workers' organisations focuses on the effects on existing workers and skills and therefore pinpoints above all the loss of skills or entire jobs. Concluding that the answer is 'somewhere in the middle' is of little help. The question is whether there are systematic differences (of skill losses or gains) in the various categories of labour.

Such systematic differences seem to exist in that micro-electronics have the potential of sharpening the polarisation in skill and know-how. The automation of batch metal cutting through numerically controlled (NC) machines is a good example.5/ An NC machine cuts metal in the same way as a conventional general purpose machine, using the same types of drills and cutters. A conventional machine is guided by the machinist himself, whose task it is to translate the information given on a drawing into a part - a skill requiring several years of training and practical experience. With NC, the movements of the machine are directed by pre-coded information. The machinist merely presses the start and stop buttons and loads and unloads the machine using standard fixtures; for most of the time he is a monitor rather than an active participant. Learning the trade becomes a matter of months rather than years.6/

The decision about how to produce a part that the machinist used to make is now made by a programmer. He prepares the tape which contains instructions on feeds and speeds. and proofs the programme out on the machine. Thus the skill has been taken away from the shop-floor and moved to the office. The knowledge to re-produce parts is captured on tapes; the knowledge to make new parts resides in the programmers, a (small) group of workers more akin to management through training and 'professional culture'.

The loss of skill on the shop-floor is, however, not a necessary outcome of technology. The latter merely opens a possibility which management can seize upon and often does. There is nothing inherent in NC technology which makes it necessary to assign programming and machine tending to different people. In fact, the introduction of NC machines has often been accompanied by battles between machinists and programmers over who can correct or change ('edit') the tapes.7/ Shaiken (1980) suggests that the tendency is for management to side with the programmers and to impose a strict division of labour so that planning and control of the work done on the shop-floor can be effectively carried out from a distance by the 'office'. So does Noble (1979), on the basis of research in America, but he also refers to a Norwegian experience where 'the operators routinely do all the editing'. Similarly, Sorge et al. (1983) found that German companies stressed the use of 'intelligence on the shop-floor' and the joint participation of planners, programmers, foremen and machine operators in programming related functions; in contrast they found that in Britain programming tends to be a specialised task, by-passing foremen and removed from the control of operators.8/

Interestingly, there is also evidence from Brazilian user firms that these considerations of taking the skill, know-how and control away from the shop-floor workers are a major reason for purchasing the equipment. What is more, 'manufacturers and salesmen seem to set an even higher value upon this feature, to the point of promising users, as a marketing resource, that they will rid themselves of their labour problems by adopting numerically controlled machine tools' (Tauile 1983, p.97).

Batch machining is one of the more prominent examples where micro-electronics based automation tends to lead to the de-skilling of blue-collar workers. The printing industry is a trade in which the new technology has had an even greater impact. Computerised type-setting and photo composition do not require apprentice trained craftsmen characteristic of the old technology (Zimbalist 1979; ILO 1981a). Many other instances of skill-degrading emerge from recent case studies. For example, Hugget (1980) suggests that in certain types of welding, new computer controlled systems will reduce the need for skilled welders (particularly in the heavy engineering area, involving bulky items and relatively long weld-cycle times). Automation in the garment industry still has a long way to go, but Hoffman and Rush (1982) indicate that the new technologies which have come on the market tend to lower workers' training times in the cutting, sewing and finishing stage of clothing production.

197

Buchanan and Boddy (1983) report on biscuit-making that with the introduction of computer controlled dough mixing semi-skilled 'mixing operators' replaced 'time served master bakers' (doughmen). In contrast the new technology complemented the skills and knowledge of the 'ovensman'. Indeed, it is worth reiterating that the new technology in itself is not skill-degrading. It tends to have this effect where management aims to increase its control over the labour process.9/

In assessing how the new technologies change skill requirements, we must pay equal attention to how they affect relatively unskilled or semi-skilled workers. They do so by substantially reducing their numbers. Paint-spraying robots are an example. So is robot welding:

> In the high-volume area of production, there is likely to be a reduction in demand which is likely to be heavily concentrated on the less-skilled end of the skill spectrum. New systems will use machinery to replace the less-skilled labour jobs involved in (a) the relatively simple tasks of manipulating welding devices through repetitive, standard routines - involving in some cases quite routine stop-start and basic monitoring functions, and in (b) the ancillary handling activities which have not yet been mechanised, but which are likely to be so. (Hugget 1980, p.46)

Assembly is probably the occupation which accounts for the highest number of low-skilled workers in industry. Most assembly work takes place in the production of electrical equipment, instruments and electronic devices and in motor vehicle manufacturing. While most of it continues to be done manually (even in the advanced countries), automated equipment is making substantial inroads. The most widely used (non-manual) method in large-scale assembly is fixed automation assembly machines. This is a set of simple machines (with stations) arranged along a transfer mechanism; each work station performs a simple operation on the product formerly carried out by low-skilled workers. Where electronic components need putting onto circuit boards, automatic insertion machines have reduced the need for assembly workers (for example, in the computer, office equipment, television and telecommunications industries). However, even when automatic insertion is used, certain components often need to be inserted manually because of awkward shapes or component variation (Senker 1980).

The continued existence of manual assembly work will depend largely on the progress made in programmable assembly automation. Intensive research and development is going on in the United States, Japan and Europe to produce economically viable, programmable assembly robots (as opposed to special purpose machines). The key to this technology lies in

198

continuous feedback of visual or sensory information, so that the machine can adjust as the need arises. Such robots are already in use, but there are still relatively few assembly robots, as compared with 'processing robots' which perform tasks such as welding, drilling or painting. Both types clearly can carry out work which is unpleasant in that it is monotonous and/or hazardous, and thus also reduce the un-/semi-skilled contingent of the industrial workforce.

The skill changes drawn out so far are accompanied by new skill requirements in essentially two areas: programming, or the production of software, and maintenance, or keeping the hardware functioning. We begin with the latter. There is little doubt that the traditional craft skills of maintenance personnel are inadequate to cope with the ever-increasing sophistication of automatic equipment. The question is whether this means an upgrading of skills across the board or in a few individuals only. Senker et al. (1980) in an early study on micro-electronics in the engineering industry incline towards the latter:

> Installation and maintenance are likely to be changed extensively by the advent of micro-electronics. Where micro-electronics equipment replaces electro mechanical equipment, there is substantial experience...to show that the number of people required in such functions is reduced sharply. However, it appears that there is a small though important demand for highly skilled installation and maintenance people...
>
> Manufacturers are conscious of the need to incorporate automatic diagnostic equipment in order to simplify maintenance...if they are successful, then the need for maintenance people highly skilled across several areas will be small...automatic diagnostic equipment may reduce the skill requirements, and even the numbers required, of less skilled maintenance people. This possibility of skill polarisation has many possibly severe consequences... (p.172-73)

In their own subsequent study on maintenance skills in the British engineering industry, however, Senker et al. (1981) found:

> no evidence that any de-skilled tasks which may be created - such as the replacement of electronic circuitboards - are being separated out into de-skilled jobs. Rather, the need for efficient and quick diagnosis and repair of faults in complex equipment demands that disparate skills be combined in one person. (p.34)

Overall they conclude:

> that the proportion of maintenance craftsmen to the total workforce is likely to rise; that these craftsmen are likely to require a wider range of skills in the future, particularly bridging the gap between mechanical and electrical/electronic skills; and that in the foreseeable future...the breadth of skill required of maintenance craftsmen is likely to increase rather than decrease. (p.33)

This is probably even more the case in developing countries. The reason lies in their distance from the suppliers of technologies. User firms in advanced countries can more readily rely on maintenance services provided by the supplier of the equipment or specialised repair firms; even if they use primarily their internal maintenance crew, outside maintenance provides an important fall-back position. In developing countries this is extremely difficult, especially with new electronics-based technology. Thus Tauile (1983) reports:

> The diffusion process of NCMTs (numerically controlled machine tools) in Brazil was negatively marked by the difficulty of ensuring efficient maintenance. On the one hand...there was a scarcity of qualified and skilled labour in user companies' staffs and in the labour market in general. On the other, the maintenance services provided by the suppliers of imported machines and of locally produced ones were rather deficient. The manufacturers of machines exported to Brazil were too far away to meet the users' need of support in a short time...there also were - and still are - legal and bureaucratic problems regarding the imports of parts and components. Maintenance services provided by local suppliers were inadequate owing to the manufacturers' own lack of experience in the local production of advanced technology. (p.102)

The situation is very similar in work on software - the design and detailed sequence of programming instructions. Originally 'programmer' was an all-inclusive term applied to those undertaking the entire range of activities required to instruct a computer. Today there are many subdivisions; above all the conceptual task of designing a programme is increasingly being separated from the mechanical task of writing down the detailed instructions. The former task lies with the 'systems analyst' and requires intimate knowledge of both software and hardware capacities. The latter can be given to a relatively less skilled specialist, requiring essentially the knowledge of the 'language' which the computer understands. Thus, while the increasing sophistication of hardware presents rapidly mounting challenges to the ingenuity of software specialists, this does not represent a general upgrading of computing skills. Instead 'software occupations are polarising ...programming has experienced a steady process of fragmentation and routinisation while programmers as a group have experienced a rapid de-skilling' (Kraft 1979, p.17; see also Duncan 1981).

This seemingly stark conclusion needs tempering in various ways, especially if one considers software skills in developing countries. First, programming is still very much an occupation in process where divisions of labour are rather fluid. Second, various forms of work fragmentation, such as 'structured programming', are only viable where large-scale programming needs arise. Third, the issue of de-skilling only arises if previously there was an existence of integrated skills (see chapter 11). Fourth, the trend towards skill polarisation is overshadowed by a shortage of programmers, especially but not only at the higher skill end.10/

The shortage of programmers is most easily overcome in applications programming (adapting standard programmes to specific jobs) and operating programmes for microcomputers. These are the tasks arising typically in the programming of robots and numerically controlled machines. More problematic are shortages in systems analysis/engineering. These tasks involve the design of new programmes, undertaking simultaneous changes in hard and software, or the computerised mating of different activities (for example, design and manufacture). In principle, individuals with the required skills could be hired from outside when the need arises. But as in maintenance problems, user firms in developing countries are often handicapped here. The geographical distance from technology suppliers tends to militate against reliance on external software skills. In general, there can be little doubt that computing and electronics are two areas in which skill shortages are, and will be, acute.

To sum up our assessment of the effect of the new technologies on skill requirements; while it is still early days to come to hard and fast conclusions, there can be little doubt that the advent of micro-electronics brings a Taylorist dream a step nearer to reality: the planning and control of production 'from the office'. More than ever before, management can determine the speed at which, and way in which, products are made from outside the shop-floor by feeding its instructions through a computer programme directly to the machine. In many cases this means that what used to be highly skilled jobs on the shop-floor can now be carried out by (fewer) workers with relatively short training. In other cases, tasks which had already been de-skilled are entirely abolished through automation. These changes are accompanied by an increase in new skills particularly in two areas: programming and electronic maintenance.

THE RELIABILITY WAGE

Let us now move on to the question of wages. Our case study of automated continuous flow production (chapter 5) and findings by other researchers led us to suggest the existence of a 'reliability wage'. To recall our earlier proposition (chapter 12), employers in such automated production seem to be prepared to pay high wages (and offer internal promotion prospects) in order to stabilise their workforce and achieve reliable performance. The rationale for this policy towards labour seems to lie above all in technological conditions. The costs of interruption are extremely high as is damage to machinery and equipment or the production of substandard products. This is what emerged from our analysis of automated plants which produce dimensional products such as chemical fibres, steel or cement. Micro-electronics has above all facilitated the automation of the manufacture of discrete products (for example, metal parts, cars, typewriters). The question is whether firms producing the latter adopt labour policies similar to those of the former.

As yet there is little material which addresses such questions, but there are some indications which seem to confirm our proposition. They come from various types of metal working where automation tends to reduce the skill requirements. In relation to skills therefore the selection of operators is relatively easy. Employers are however concerned with the responsibility of operators, as put vividly by a machine tool executive: 'If you have a $500,000 machining centre, you don't want some clown pressing the wrong button, even if the machine has all the fail-safe devices in the world built into it' (quoted from Shaiken 1980, p.17).

Indeed, the desire of management to reduce the involvement of the machinist, and the ability to do so, are not the same thing. Metal cutting is so varied a process, that even on the latest generation of NC equipment the operator has to monitor and intervene when something goes wrong. One need not necessarily think of the dramatic cases where the operator fails to stop a machine heading for a smash-up. The more common daily concern is to minimise the downtime on this expensive machinery. For this employers continue to rely on their workers (even though less so than on conventional machines). The point is made by Doring and Salling, two engineers, in an article, 'A Case for Wage Incentives in the NC Age':

> Under automation, it is argued, the machine basically controls the manufacturing cycle, and therefore the worker's role diminishes in importance. The fallacy in this reasoning is that if the operator malingers or fails to service the machine for a variety of reasons both

utilisation and subsequent return on investment suffer drastically.

Basic premises underlying the design and development of NC machines aim at providing the capability of machining configurations beyond the scope of conventional machines. Additionally, they 'de-skill' the operator. Surprisingly, however, the human element continues to be a major factor in the realisation of optimum utilisation or yield of these machines. This poses a continuing problem for management, because a maximum level of utilisation is necessary to assure a satisfactory return on investment. (Quoted from Noble 1980, p.44)

Whether employers adjust their policies towards labour accordingly is a different question. Tauile's (1983) study on the use of NC machines in Brazil suggests that they do. He noted:

a tendency towards the payment of higher wages to NCMT (numerically controlled machine tool) operators, either by granting them promotions or placing them on an average salary level above that paid for similar activities in the machining of parts in conventional equipments...despite the shorter training time required to enable workers to operate NCMTs...We believe that this wage differentiation essentially represents a remuneration for the trustworthiness of employees entrusted with the operation of such expensive and strategic equipment. (p.109-110)

Interestingly, he also found that these operators were generally recruited from within the firm and that labour turnover was low. Thus, what we seem to have is a confirmation of the pattern of labour utilisation found in continuous flow production. Of course, the evidence is still patchy, if not slight. Hopefully, this issue will be further explored in future studies, because as already noted (in chapter 12), the 'reliability wage' has theoretical and political implications which go beyond the narrow confines of technology related labour use.

THE FACTORY OF THE FUTURE

By way of concluding this chapter, we would like to raise a general question about the 'micro-electronics revolution'. Does it really, in its impact on labour, bring about a discontinuous kind of change? We have some doubts.

In this book we have reviewed and investigated the impact of various technologies, from the most rudimentary to the most sophisticated. A number of trends have emerged, particularly in workforce composition, skill profiles, labour turnover and wages (see previous chapters). In our assessment, the diffusion of micro-electronics based technologies means a continuation of already existing trends of technically induced changes in labour utilisation.11/ It may, however, accelerate these trends in the years to come.

This acceleration would depend on the speed and pattern of diffusion of micro-electronics. So far applications have generally meant that only parts of the labour process in user firms are affected. However, the full potential of the new automation technologies only comes to the fore when systems' economies are realised. Because of their common binary logic, electronic systems offer the possibility for mating various activities. The best known example is computer-aided-design/computer-aided-manufacture (CAD/CAM). Achieving systems gains to the full extent would require linking CAD and CAM further to electronics based internal accounting and marketing. Some Japanese, European and American firms are already striving for such 'factories of the future'; their obstacles are not so much technical but financial and political (Kaplinsky 1984). Even if they can be overcome, such factories are unlikely to become a widespread phenomenon in less developed countries before the year 2000.

NOTES

1. The title for this chapter is taken from one of the early forecasts of the effects of information technology on economy and society (Barron and Curnow 1979).

2. For a survey of the literature see Bessant et al. (1981) and Leppan (1983) and the collection of articles in Marstrand (1984).

3. Probably the most thorough analysis on the technology, the crisis and unemployment in the OECD countries is that being undertaken in the Science Policy Research Unit at the University of Sussex. Amongst the most important contributions emerging from this (ongoing) research programme are Freeman et al. (1982) and Soete and Freeman (1983).

4. See for example, some of the contributions in Hoffman (ed) (1984).

5. NC became important when electronic components much less powerful than microprocessors were available, but the latter have greatly contributed to the development of sophisticated and powerful NC machines.

6. Jacobson (1982) suggests that the operator of NC lathes requires a training time and practical experience of six (at the most 12) months. By contrast, for a qualified operator of a conventional lathe, five years' experience is necessary to acquire proficiency. Noble (1979) and Shaiken (1980) emphasise that on the early NC machines the de-skilling of operators did not take place as much as expected due to the unreliability of

machines. Contrary to advertisements, they did not always produce parts to tolerance without the repeated manual intervention of the operator.

7. The latest generation of NC machines come equipped with a mini computer attached to them (called computer numerical control or CNC). Thus the programme can be altered at the machine itself.

8. Such differences were more pronounced in large firms, whereas in smaller firms of both countries a great deal of flexibility was found in the handling of programming related functions.

9. In this context the work of Rosenbrock (1984) and co-researchers at the University of Manchester Institute of Science and Technology should be mentioned. Their aim is to show that economically viable automatic systems can be designed which enhance, rather than militate against, the skills and abilities of the worker.

10. One should add that the various forms of job fragmentation and work simplification have increased productivity in software, but advances in the production of hardware have been much faster. In fact the cost of software has considerably increased in relation to that of hardware (Willis 1983). This is also a factor which is likely to slow down the diffusion of micro-electronics based innovations, particularly in developing countries.

11. With regard to the impact of micro-electronics on outwork, the conclusion may be different. See Chapter 10.

ANNEX AND BIBLIOGRAPHY

ANNEX

Table A1: Specifications of the Product Studied

<u>Yarn</u> (warp and weft)	
Count (English, carded)	18
Twist coefficient	4.0
Turns per inch	17
Type of cotton	13/16"
Cloth	
Width (cm)	90
Threads per cm	20
Picks per cm	20
Total threads in warp	1880
Warp contraction (%)	7.3
Weft contraction (%)	7.3
Weight per linear metre (grammes)	
total	130
warp	66
weft	64
Weight per square metre (grammes)	144
Type of weave	Plain Weave

Table A2: Main Technological Characteristics of Spinning and Weaving Machinery in 1950 and 1960

Production stage	1950	1960
Opener & scutcher	Moving belt Vertical opener Single-process scutcher Dust collection room Output up to 180 kg an hour Lap roll up to 20 kg	Pneumatic delivery of cotton Shirley opener Single-process scutcher Dust removal by filter bags Output up to 200 kg an hour Lap roll up to 28 kg
Cards	Flexible wire Manual stripping 12" diameter cans Vibrating Comb Output up to 8 kg an hour	Rigid wire Stripping eliminated 16" diameter cans Vibrating comb Cross roll device Output up to 12 kg an hour
Drawing frame I	Drafting system 4 over 4 12" diameter cans Machine speed up to 160 feet per minute	Drafting system 3 over 4 or 4 over 5 14" diameter cans Machine speed up to 800 feet per minute Pneumatic dust removal

Drawing frame II	Drafting system 4 over 4 12" diameter cans Machine speed up to 160 feet per minute	Drafting system 3 over 4 or 4 over 5 14" diameter cans Machine speed up to 800 feet per minute Pneumatic dust removal
Roving frame	Slubber, 600 rpm Intermediate, 800 rpm Roving, 800 rpm 2-passage system for coarse counts Draft up to 12	2-passage system for time counts Slubber, 800 rpm Roving, 1,000 rpm 1-passage system for coarse counts 'Simplex', 1,000 rpm Draft up to 20
Spinning frame	High-draft system (4 cylinders or aprons) Lift up to 9" and ring diameter 2.1/4" Spindle speed up to 10,000 rpm Pneumafil	High-draft system, top-arm weighted or magnetic type Lift up to 11" and ring diameter 2.1/4" Spindle speed up to 13,000 rpm Pneumafil Traveller cleaners Controlled balloon
Cone winder	Grooved drum system Winding speed up to 600 yards per minute Slub catcher (blade or comb type)	Grooved drum system Winding speed up to 900 yards per minute Slub catcher (blade or comb type) Traveller cleaner

Table A2: cont.

Production stage	1950	1960
Pirn winder	Fixed-spindle type with reserve box Manual doffing Spindle speed up to 5,000 rpm	Semi-automatic type (manual supply magazine) Automatic doffing Spindle speed up to 8,000 rpm
Warper	Continuous warper, double creel Winding speed up to 600 yards per minute Mechanical yarn-break stop motion	Continuous warper, double creel Winding speed up to 900 yards per minute Electric yarn-break stop motion Magnetic brakes
Sizing machine	Hot-air type Working speed up to 100 yards per minute	Multi-cylinder or hot-air type Working speed up to 140 yards per minute Automatic temperature, humidity and size level controls
Loom	Automatic (pirn or shuttle changing system) Working speed 180 picks per minute, reed space 46"	Automatic, pirn-changing system Working speed 200 picks per minute, reed space 46"

Source: ECLA (1966).

Table A3: Main Technological Characteristics of Spinning and Weaving Machinery in 1970 and 1980

Production stage	1970	1980
Openers & scutchers	Continuous line for automatic bale opening, blending, cleaning, fibre conveying, and carding to produce 435 kg/hour of Ne. 0.12 card sliver comprising: 2 automatic opening lines (moving bales); 1 return opener; 2 cleaner/openers; 1 auto-blender; 2 fibre conveyors; 20 cotton cards with 24" x 28" cans, 40" wide, automatic exhaust, automatic stop motion and web purifier Doffer speed: 37 rev/min. NOTE: equipped with integrated automatic system for waste extraction and bagging	Continuous line for automatic bale opening, blending, cleaning, fibre conveying, carding, and first passage of drawing to product 465 kg/hour of Ne. 0.12 1st draw sliver to be used for producing open-end-spun yarn comprising: 2 automatic opening lines (stationary bales); 1 return opener; 2 cleaner/openers with micro-dust extraction; 1 auto-blender; 2 fibre conveyors; 20 cotton cards, 40" wide, automatic exhaust, automatic stop motion, web purifier, autoleveller & sliver reserve; 4 sliver conveyor lines with a fifth in reserve;

Table A3: cont.

Production stage	1970	1980
<u>First drawframe</u>	High-speed drafting system; 18" x 48" cans (double head); Speed: 1,000 feet/min; Automatic suction; Automatic can doffer	4 first-passage drawframes, with single delivery, automatic can doffing, 18" x 48" cans, and autolevelling Speed: 1,500 feet/min. NOTE: equipped with integrated automatic system for waste extraction and bagging
<u>Second drawframe</u>	High-speed drafting system 18" x 48" cans (double head) Speed: 1,000 feet/min; Automatic suction; Automatic can doffer	High-speed drafting system 12" x 36" cans (single delivery) Speed: 1,500 feet/min; Automatic suction; Automatic can doffer

Speedframes	Single passage system; Speed; 1,200 rpm; 7" x 14" bobbin; Pneumafil; Automatic photo-electric stop motion; Automatic preparation for doffing; Travelling blowers	Process eliminated
Spinning frames	High-draft system with spring or compressed air weighting; 260 mm lift and 54 mm rings; Spindle speed: 11,500 rpm; Pneumafil; Automatic preparation for doffing; Travelling blowers	Open-end with draft from 30 to 280; 125 x 300 mm packages; Rotor diameter: 55 mm; Rotor speed: 45,000 rpm; Clean-Cat (automatic rotor cleaner); Spin-Cat (automatic piecer); Automatic doffer
Cone winders	Electronic clearers; Yarn surface lubricator; Winding pressure controller; Automatic knotter; Package feeler; End breakage counter (meter) Carriage counter (meter); Travelling blowers	Process eliminated

Table A3: cont.

Production stage	1970	1980
<u>Pirn winder</u>	Automatic supply of pirns; Automatic doffing; Automatic dust extraction; Bunch length adjustment; Package length adjustment; Diameter control by disc; Tension control system; Automatic feeding of pirns into weft boxes; Speed up to 12,000 rpm;	Process eliminated
Beaming machines	System for controlling the distance between packages and tension devices, with tension devices to minimise variations of tension between yarns; Automatic electric stop motion for yarn breakages; Hydraulic pressure control; Hydraulic beam doffing; Pneumatic, electromagnetic, or hydraulic brake; 1 creel Speed: 600 metres/min.	System for controlling the distance between packages and tension devices, with tension devices to minimise variations of tension between yarns; Automatic electric stop motion for yarn breakages; Hydraulic pressure control; Hydraulic beam doffing; Pneumatic, electromagnetic, or hydraulic brake; Rails for displacement (2 creel system); 2 creels; Speed: 750 metres/min.

Sizing machines

Conventional beam braking by weights;	Automatic pneumatic or electro-magnetic beam braking;
Two roller immersion system to divide the warp into two sheets;	Two roller immersion system to divide the warp into two sheets;
Individual temperature control of cylinders by groups or collectively;	Automatic pressure control for the squeeze roller in the size box;
Instrumentation for detection of yarn stretching;	Individual temperature control of cylinders by groups or collectively;
Variable speed gear at various points and automatic tension controller;	Injection of air into the cylinders during stoppages to prevent excessive drying;
Hood over the size box and drying zone;	Drying cylinders with speed control gear or speed control clutch through the (yarn) sheet in case of (yarn) contraction (shrinkage);
Speed: 60 metres/min.	Pre-drying system;
	Storage (accumulator) system for yarns already sized;
	Instrumentation for detection of yarn stretching;
	Variable speed gear at various points and automatic tension controller;
	Hood over the size box and drying zone;
	Speed: 65 metres/min.

Table A3 cont.

Production stage	1970	1980
Looms	Shuttle loom; 1 warp beam producing two fabrics of 0.90 metres; Warp beam width: 2.06 metres; Automatic pirn changing; Cam-operated heald shafts; Weft insertion rate: 360 metres per minute.	Shuttleless loom (gripper-shuttle); 2 warp beams producing three fabrics of 0.90 metres; Warp beam width: 1.53 metres; equalizer; Cam-operated heald shafts; Low level of noise; Built-in oiling; Weft insertion rate: 900 metres per minute.

Source: CETIQT (1980).

Table A4: Production Plan and Machine Requirements of 1950 Spinning and Weaving Mill

Machine	Yarn count	Feed hank	Draft	Turns per inch	Speed of operation	Efficiency %	Production per machine hour	Production per day (23hr) Unit output (kg)
Opener/scutcher	0.0012	-	-	-	9.4 rpm	90	180 kg	4,140
Card	0.12	0.0012	100	-	14 rpm	90	8 kg	184
Drawing frame I	0.12	6/0.12	6	-	240 feet/min	85	18 kg	414
Drawing frame II	0.12	6/0.12	6	-	240 feet/min	85	18 kg	414
Roving frame	0.75	0.12	6.25	1	900 rpm	76	820 g	18,860
Ring spinning frame	18	0.75	24	17	9.100 rpm	90	24.1 g	0,554
Cone winder	18	18	-	-	400 yd/min	70	505 g	11,620
Pirn winder	18	18	-	-	310 yd/min	70	390 g	8,970
Warper	-	-	-	-	400 yd/min	50	168 kg	3,864
Sizing machine	-	-	-	-	48 yd/min	50	81 kg	1,863
Loom	-	-	-	-	180 picks/min	85	4.59 m	13.72

Table A4: cont.

Machine	Production per day(23h) Total output (kg)	Waste per day (23h) kg	Waste per day (23h) %	Number of production units Theoretical	Actual	Number of machines
Opener scutcher	8,280	436	5.0	2	2	Opening line
Card	7,783	497	6.0	42.3	44	44
Drawing frame I	7,744	39	0.5	18.7	20	5 with 4 deliveries
Drawing frame II	7,705	39	0.5	18.6	20	5 with 4 deliveries
Roving frame	7,667	38	0.5	406	420	5 with 84 spindles
Ring spinning frame	7,552	115	1.5	13,630	13,600	34 with 400 spindles
Cone winder	7,401	151	2.0	637	640	8 with 8 spindles
Pirn winder	3,594	33	1.0	400	416	13 with 32 spindles
Warper	3,736	38	1.0	1	1	1
Sizing Machine	3,700	36	1.0	2	2	2
Loom	7,294	-	-	531	534	534

Source: ECLA (1966).

Table A5: Production Plan and Machine Requirements of 1960 Spinning and Weaving Mill

Machine	Yarn count	Feed hank	Draft	Turns per inch	Speed of operation	Efficiency %	Production per machine hour	Production per day (23 hr) Unit output (kg)
Opener/scutcher	0.0012	–	–	–	11 rpm	95	210 kg	4,830
Card	0.12	0.0012	100	‥	21 rpm	90	12 kg	276
Drawing frame 1	0.12	6/0.12	6	–	700 feet/min	74	46.5 kg	1,070
Drawing frame II	0.12	6/0.12	6	–	700 feet/min	74	46.5 kg	1,070
Roving frame	0.75	0.12	6.25	1	1000 rpm	76	910 g	20,930
Ring spinning frame	18	0.75	24	17	9500 rpm	90	25.1 g	0.577
Cone winder	18	18	–	–	600yd/min	70	756 g	17,388
Pirn winder	18	18	–	–	800yd/min	80	1140 g	26,220
Warper	–	–	–	–	600yd/min	50	253 kg	5,820
Sizing machine	–	–	–	–	56yd/min	50	94 kg	2,162
Loom	–	–	–	–	200 picks/min	90	5.40m	16.1

Table A5: cont.

Machine	Production per day (23hr) Total output (kg)	Waste per day (23 hr) kg	%	Number of production units Theoretical	Actual	Number of machines
Opener/scutcher	9,660	508	5.0	2	2	Opening line
Card	9,080	580	6.0	32.9	14	34
Drawing frame I	9,035	45	0.5	8.4	10	5 with 2 deliveries
Drawing frame 2	8,990	45	0.5	8.4	10	5 with 2 deliveries
Roving frame	8,945	45	0.5	427	430	5 with 86 spindles
Ring spinning frame	8,811	134	1.5	15,270	15,200	38 with 400 spindles
Cone winder	8,635	176	2.0	497	500	5 with 100 spindles
Pirn winder	4,189	42	1.0	160	180	5 with 36 spindles
Warper	4,360	44	1.0	0.7	1	1
Sizing machine	4,317	43	1.0	2	2	2
Loom	8,506	-	-	527	530	530

Source: ECLA (1966).

Table A6: Production Plan and Machine Requirements of 1970 Spinning and Weaving Mill

Machine	Yarn count	Feed hank	Draft	Turns per inch	Speed of operation	Efficiency %	Production per machine hour	Production per day (23 hr) Unit output (kg)
Opener/scutcher	-	-	-	-	-	-	-	509
Card	0.12	-	-	-	37 rpm	94	22.11 kg	1,760
Drawing frame I	0.12	6/0.12	6	-	1,000feet/min	85	76.50 kg	1,760
Drawing frame II	0.12	6/0.12	6	-	1,000feet/min	85	76.50 kg	1,760
Roving frame	0.75	0.12	6.25	1	1,200 rpm	78	1,122 g	25,806
Ring spinning frame	18	0.75	24	17	11,500 rpm	93	31.4 g	0.722
Cone winder	18	18	-	-	1,145m/min	85	1914 g	44.02
Pirn winder	18	18	-	-	847m/min	85	1416 g	32.57
Warper	-	18	-	-	600m/min	50	316.8 kg	7,286
Sizing machine	-	-	-	-	60m/min	55	244 kg	5,612
Loom	-	-	-	-	200picks/min	91	10.92 m	32.7

Table A6: cont.

Machine	Production per day (23h) Total output (kg)	Waste per day (23h) kg	Waste per day (23h) %	Number of production units Theoretical	Actual	Number of machines
Opener/scutcher	10,450	550	5	-	-	opening line
Card	9,950	500	4.8	19.5	20	20
Drawing frame I	9,890	60	0.6	5.6	6	3 with 2
Drawing frame II	9,831	59	0.6	5.5	6	3 with 2
Roving frame	9,733	98	1	377	384	4 with 96 spindles
Ring spinning frame	9,538	195	2	13,210	13,300	35 with 380 "
Cone winder	9,347	191	2	212	220	22 with 10 "
Pirn winder	4,555	46	1	139	144	4 with 36 "
Warper	4,698	48	1	0.64	1	1
Sizing machine	4,651	47	1	0.83	1	1
Loom	9,114	92	1	278.7	279	280

Source: CETIQT (1980).

Table A7: Production Plan and Machine Requirements of 1980 Spinning and Weaving Mill

Machine	Yarn count	Feed hank	Draft	Turns per inch	Speed of operation	Efficiency %	Production per machine hour	Production per day (23 hr) Unit output (kg)
Opener/scutcher	-	-	-	-	-	-	-	-
Card	0.12	-	-	-	39 rpm	95	23.52 kg	541
Drawing Frame I	0.12	5/0.12	5	-	1,500feet/min	86	116.10 kg	2,670
Drawing frame II	0.12	6/0.12	6	-	1,550feet/min	96	133.90 kg	3,079
Open-end	18	0.12	150	20	45,000 rpm	98	110.25 kg	2.54
Warper	-	18	-	-	750m/min	65	540.7 kg	12,436
Sizing machine	-	-	-	1	65m/min	65	234.3 kg	5,389
Loom	-	-	-	-	290 picks/min	92	24.04 m	71.89

Table A7: cont.

Machine	Production per day (23h) Total output (kg)	Waste per day (23h) kg	%	Number of production units Theoretical	Actual	Number of machines
Opener/scutcher	-	-	-	-	-	Opening line
Card	10,716	564	5.0	19.8	20	20
Drawing frame 1	10,663	53	0.5	3.9	4	4 with 1
Drawing frame II	10,610	53	0.5	3.4	4	4 with 1
Open-end	1C,504	106	1.0	4,136	4,176	29 with 144 rotors
Warper	5,225	53	1.0	0.02	1	1 with 2
Sizing machine	5,173	52	1.0	0.96	1	1
Loom	10,295	104	1.0	143.2	144	144

Source: CETIQT (1980).

Table A8: Investment in Spinning and Weaving Machinery 1950-1980 (in US$ of 1980)

Equipment	1950	1960	1970	1980
Spinning	1,963,249	2,652,362	5,487,275	9,950,780
Openers/scutchers	133,200	148,700	705,400	806,000
Cards	381,000	551,000	1,584,000	1,680,000
Drawing frames I	32,000	49,800	141,300	177,000
Drawing frames II	32,000	49,800	141,300	180,700
Roving frames	143,600	219,600	251,500	-
Spinning machines	987,000	1,215,000	1,504,000	6,780,000
Cone winders	127,800	200,000	818,000	-
Auxiliary equipment and accessories	126,649	218,462	341,775	327,080
Weaving	2,190,795	3,222,358	5,717,413	10,197,440
Pirn winders	138,500	132,800	435,300	-
Warpers	20,400	27,460	91,200	98,200
Sizing machines	96,600	163,800	250,000	276,000
Looms	1,837,500	2,765,000	4,200,000	9,100,000
Auxiliary equipment and accessories	97,795	133,298	740,913	723,240
Total	4,154,044	5,874,720	11,204,688	20,148,220

Source: ECLA (1966), CETIQT (1980).

Annex

Table A9:   Labour Requirements of a Spinning and Weaving Mill by Occupation, Department and Shift, 1950-1980

Occupation	Code	1 9 5 0				
SPINNING DEPARTMENT		GS	1S	2S	3S	T
Superintendent	1	1	-	-	-	1
PRE-SPINNING						
Supervisor	1	1	-	-	-	1
Foreman	2	-	2	1	1	4
Opener tender	3	-	1	1	1	3
Picker tender	3	-	1	1	1	3
Operator of automatic blender	3	-	-	-	-	-
Card tender	3	-	2	2	2	6
Card helper	3	-	3	3	3	9
Operator of opening and carding unit	3	-	-	-	-	-
Operator of opening, carding and drawing unit	3	-	-	-	-	-
Drawing tender	3	-	5	5	5	15
Roving tender	3	-	3	3	3	9
Roving helper	3	-	2	2	2	6
Reserve operators	3	-	-	-	-	-
Roving transporter	4	-	-	-	-	-
Transporter of cans to open end	4	-	-	-	-	-
Sweeper	4	-	2	2	1	5
Oiler	5	-	2	1	-	3
Mechanic	5	-	2	2	2	6
SPINNING						
Supervisor	1	1	-	-	-	1
Foreman	2	-	1	1	1	3
Spinner	3	-	12	12	12	36
Doffer	4	-	6	6	6	18
Operator of open end	3	-	-	-	-	-
Open end helper	4	-	-	-	-	-
Creel loader	4	-	2	2	2	6
Roll picker	4	-	2	2	1	5
Steel roll cleaner	4	-	2	2	2	6
Traveller changer	4	-	1	1	-	2
Yarn hauler	4	-	1	1	1	3
Winder	3	-	32	32	32	96
Winding helper	4	-	-	-	-	-
Reserve operators	3	-	-	-	-	-
Sweeper	4	-	1	1	1	3
Oiler	5	-	-	-	-	-
Mechanic	5	-	1	1	1	3
Total of spinning department						253

228

	1 9 6 0					1 9 7 0					1 9 8 0			
GS	1S	2S	3S	T	GS	1S	2S	3S	T	GS	1S	2S	3S	T
1	–	–	–	1	1	–	–	–	1	1	–	–	–	1
1	–	–	–	1	1	–	–	–	1	1	–	–	–	1
–	2	1	1	4	–	1	1	1	3	–	1	1	1	3
–	1	1	1	3	–	–	–	–	–	–	–	–	–	–
–	1	1	1	3	–	–	–	–	–	–	–	–	–	–
–	–	–	–	–	–	1	1	1	3	–	1	1	1	3
–	1	1	1	3	–	–	–	–	–	–	–	–	–	–
–	2	2	2	6	–	–	–	–	–	–	–	–	–	–
–	–	–	–	–	–	1	1	1	3	–	–	–	–	–
–	–	–	–	–	–	–	–	–	–	–	1	1	1	3
–	2	2	2	6	–	1	1	1	3	–	–	–	–	–
–	2	2	2	6	–	2	2	2	6	–	–	–	–	–
–	1	1	1	3	–	–	–	–	–	–	–	–	–	–
–	–	–	–	–	–	2	2	2	6	–	1	1	1	3
–	–	–	–	–	–	1	1	1	3	–	–	–	–	–
–	–	–	–	–	–	–	–	–	–	–	1	1	1	3
–	1	1	1	3	–	–	–	–	–	–	–	–	–	–
–	1	1	–	2	1	–	–	–	1	1	–	–	–	1
–	2	1	1	4	–	1	1	1	3	–	1	1	1	3
1	–	–	–	1	1	–	–	–	1	1	–	–	–	1
–	1	1	1	3	–	1	1	1	3	–	1	1	1	3
–	8	8	8	24	–	5	5	5	15	–	–	–	–	–
–	4	4	4	12	–	3	3	3	9	–	–	–	–	–
–	–	–	–	–	–	–	–	–	–	–	4	4	4	12
–	–	–	–	–	–	–	–	–	–	–	1	1	1	3
–	1	1	1	3	–	–	–	–	–	–	–	–	–	–
–	1	1	1	3	1	–	–	–	1	–	–	–	–	–
–	–	–	–	–	–	–	–	–	–	–	–	–	–	–
–	1	–	–	1	1	–	–	–	1	–	–	–	–	–
–	1	1	1	3	–	1	1	1	3	–	1	1	1	3
–	12	12	12	36	–	3	3	3	9	–	–	–	–	–
–	–	–	–	–	–	1	1	1	3	–	–	–	–	–
–	–	–	–	–	–	1	1	1	3	–	1	1	1	3
–	1	1	1	3	–	1	1	–	2	1	–	–	–	1
–	–	–	–	–	1	–	–	–	1	1	–	–	–	1
–	1	1	–	2	–	2	2	1	5	–	1	1	1	3
				136					89					51

Table A9:   cont.

Occupation	Code	1950				
		GS	1S	2S	3S	T
WEAVING DEPARTMENT						
Superintendent	1	1	–	–	–	1
PRE-WEAVING						
Supervisor	1	1	–	–	–	1
Foreman	2	–	1	1	1	3
Pirn winder	3	–	13	13	13	39
Pirn winding helper	4	–	4	4	4	12
Warper tender	3	–	1	1	1	3
Assistant warper tender	3	–	1	1	1	3
Yarn hauler	4	–	1	1	1	3
Slasher tender (sizing)	3	–	2	2	2	6
Assistant slasher tender	3	–	4	4	4	12
Sizeman	3	–	1	1	1	3
Tying-in-hand	3	–	–	–	–	–
Drawing-in-hand	3	–	6	6	6	18
Sweeper and pirn stripper	4	–	4	4	4	12
Oiler	5	–	1	1	1	3
Mechanic	5	–	2	2	2	6
WEAVING						
Supervisor	1	1	–	–	–	1
Foreman	2	–	2	2	2	6
Weaver	3	–	26	26	26	78
Yarnhauler	4	–	4	4	4	12
Battery hand	4	–	14	14	14	42
Warp loader	4	–	4	4	4	12
Cloth inspector (on looms)	4	–	–	–	–	–
Cloth doffer	4	–	4	4	4	12
Reserve weaver	3	–	–	–	–	–
Sweeper and loom blower	4	–	4	4	4	12
Oiler	5	–	3	3	3	9
Mechanic	5	–	8	8	8	24
Total of weaving department						333

1960					1970					1980				
GS	1S	2S	3S	T	GS	1S	2S	3S	T	GS	1S	2S	3S	T
1	–	–	–	1	1	–	–	–	1	1	–	–	–	1
1	–	–	–	1	1	–	–	–	1	1	–	–	–	1
–	1	1	1	3	–	1	1	1	3	–	1	1	1	3
–	6	6	6	18	–	3	3	3	9	–	–	–	–	–
–	2	2	2	6	–	1	1	1	3	–	–	–	–	–
–	1	1	1	3	–	1	1	1	3	–	1	1	1	3
–	1	1	1	3	–	1	1	1	3	–	1	1	1	3
–	1	1	1	3	–	1	1	1	3	–	1	1	1	3
–	2	2	2	6	–	1	1	1	3	–	1	1	1	3
–	2	2	2	6	–	1	1	1	3	–	1	1	1	3
–	1	1	–	2	–	1	1	1	3	–	1	1	1	3
–	1	1	1	3	–	–	–	–	–	–	–	–	–	–
–	2	2	–	4	–	2	2	–	4	–	2	2	–	4
–	2	2	2	6	–	1	1	1	3	–	1	1	1	3
–	1	1	–	2	1	–	–	–	1	1	–	–	–	1
–	2	2	1	5	–	1	1	1	3	–	1	1	1	3
1	–	–	–	1	1	–	–	–	1	1	–	–	–	1
–	2	2	2	6	–	1	1	1	3	–	1	1	1	3
–	18	18	18	54	–	9	9	9	27	–	7	7	7	21
–	3	3	3	9	–	–	–	–	–	–	1	1	1	3
–	14	14	14	42	–	9	9	9	27	–	–	–	–	–
–	3	3	3	9	–	2	2	2	6	–	2	2	2	6
–	–	–	–	–	–	2	2	2	6	–	2	2	2	6
–	3	3	3	9	–	2	2	2	6	–	2	2	2	6
–	–	–	–	–	–	1	1	1	3	–	1	1	1	3
–	3	3	3	9	–	1	1	1	3	–	1	1	–	2
–	2	2	2	6	3	–	–	–	3	2	–	–	–	2
–	6	6	6	18	–	2	2	2	6	–	2	2	2	6
				235					137					93

Annex

Table A9: cont.

Occupation	Code	1 9 5 0				
MAINTENANCE DEPARTMENT		GS	1S	2S	3S	T
Superintendent	1	1	–	–	–	1
Supervisor mechanical maintenance	1	1	–	–	–	1
Supervisor electrical maintenance	1	–	–	–	–	–
Mechanics	5	7	–	–	–	7
Workshop hand	5	12	–	–	–	12
Air-conditioning mechanic	5	–	–	–	–	–
Welder	5	2	–	–	–	2
Caretaker of auxiliary installations (boilers etc.)	5	1	–	–	–	1
Carpenter	5	1	–	–	–	1
Electrician	5	1	–	–	–	1
Electronics serviceman	5	–	–	–	–	–
Instruments serviceman	5	–	–	–	–	–
Total of maintenance department						26
VARIOUS (including						
storage, quality control	1	6	–	–	–	6
training and	2	0	–	–	–	0
managerial & technical	3	1	–	–	–	1
staff not listed above)	4	24	–	–	–	24
Total various occupations						31
TOTAL						643

Note: Code of occupations
         1 = Managerial and technical staff
         2 = Foremen and instructors
         3 = Machine operators
         4 = Auxiliary workers
         5 = Maintenance workers
Source: ECLA (1966), CETIQT (1980).

	1 9 6 0					1 9 7 0					1 9 8 0			
GS	1S	2S	3S	T	GS	1S	2S	3S	T	GS	1S	2S	3S	T
1	–	–	–	1	1	–	–	–	1	1	–	–	–	1
1	–	–	–	1	1	–	–	–	1	1	–	–	–	1
–	–	–	–	–	1	–	–	–	1	1	–	–	–	1
7	–	–	–	7	4	–	–	–	4	4	–	–	–	4
9	–	–	–	9	8	–	–	–	8	6	–	–	–	6
1	–	–	–	1	1	1	1	1	4	1	1	1	1	4
2	–	–	–	2	2	–	–	–	2	1	–	–	–	1
1	–	–	–	1	–	1	1	–	2	–	1	1	–	2
1	–	–	–	1	1	–	–	–	1	1	–	–	–	1
1	–	–	–	1	1	1	1	1	4	1	1	1	1	4
–	–	–	–	–	1	–	–	–	1	3	–	–	–	3
–	–	–	–	–	1	–	–	–	1	2	–	–	–	2
				24					30					30
6	–	–	–	6	6	–	–	–	6	6	–	–	–	6
0	–	–	–	0	2	–	–	–	2	2	–	–	–	2
1	–	–	–	1	2	4	4	4	14	2	4	4	4	14
24	–	–	–	24	12	1	1	–	14	10	1	1	–	12
				31					36					34
				426					292					208

Shifts
GS = General shift
1S = First shift
2S = Second shift
3S = Third shift
T = Total

Table A10 : Job Descriptions of Maintenance Workers

---

1. Mechanic

    a) General purpose of job: carry out the mechanical activities associated with installing, maintaining or otherwise adjusting auxiliary plant and machinery as and when instructed by the Supervisor of Mechanical Maintenance or by the Maintenance Superintendent.

    b) Specific duties: carry out as instructed and according to working drawings the following activities: measuring; marking out; shearing, cutting and sawing, filing; chiselling, drilling and reaming, tapping and screwing; hand grinding; securing component parts; cutting and fitting keyways; extracting and fitting plain, ball or roller bearings; greasing or otherwise lubricating moving parts; assembling components and fixing machinery components, assembling and aligning driving and driven pulleys, chain sprockets, gears and other drive systems. Shearing metal with hand-held or power-driven shears, fold according to drawing and soldier joints. Carry out machinery duties on at least two of the following: lathe, shaper, milling machine, grinding machine and/or drilling machine.

2. Electrician

    a) General purpose of job: carry out the electrical activities associated with installing, maintaining or otherwise adjusting auxiliary and process plant and machinery as instructed by the Supervisor of Electrical Maintenance or the Maintenance Superintendent.

    b) Specific duties: carry out as instructed and according to work drawings and schematic networks, work on the following: electrical power plant equipment, transformers etc; wiring, conduits, switchboxes, cut-outs, power outlets; electric lighting; motors; rewinding, commutator repairs; alarm, signalling, call, and public address systems; private telephone systems; electrical equipment, e.g. hand tools, lathes etc; lightning protection devices; battery charging. Inspect and test each new installation or major alteration, and run routine inspections on established and electrical systems, to prove compliance with appropriate regulations and to ensure: all fuses and switches are correctly connected; insulation resistance is not less than the appropriate value laid down in regulations; continuity of circuits etc.

3. Electronics Servicemen

   a) General purpose of job: carry out the electronic activities associated with installing, maintaining or otherwise adjusting auxiliary and process plant and machinery as instructed by the Supervisor of Electrical Maintenance.

   b) Specific duties: carry out as instructed and according to working drawings and schematic networks, work on the following: electronic components, resistors, capacitors, chokes, coils, transistors, valves, cathode ray tubes etc.; logic circuits; sensors: position, temperature, light, and sound; servo-mechanisms and control loops; analogue and digital computers and other power controllers. Inspect and test each new installation or major alteration and run routine inspections on established plant.

4. Instrument Servicemen

   a) General purpose of job: carry out the repair and testing of gauges and instruments used throughout the site.

   b) Specific duties: carry out as instructed and according to work drawings, work on the following instrument categories: pressure measurement; level measurement, float, displacer, electrical and photo-electrical; flow measurement including differential pressure, magnetic, and variable temperature measurement, including bi-metal, resistance, thermister and optical radiation systems; timers; gas analysers; pH measurement; viscosity measurement. Carry out routine checks on the accuracy of such instruments.

Source: Shirley Institute, Manchester.

235

Table A11: Distribution of Machinery by Age in the Cotton Spinning and Weaving
Industry of the South-East and South in 1960

Machinery	Less than 10 years old	10-30 years old (percentage of total)	Over 30 years old	Total	Total number of machines
Preparation for spinning					
Scutchers	24.5	37.4	38.1	100.0	420
Cards	19.2	34.0	46.8	100.0	9,956
Waste cards	28.0	25.6	46.4	100.0	164
Drawing frames	27.0	32.0	41.0	100.0	11,233
Sliver lap machines	23.8	52.7	23.5	100.0	315
Ribbon lap machines	23.0	44.0	33.0	100.0	209
Combers	25.8	45.0	29.2	100.0	2,157
Roving frames	15.5	29.6	54.9	100.0	338,324
Spinning					
Ring spindles	25.1	35.3	39.6	100.0	2,892,292
Mule spindles	-	-	100.0	100.0	2,490

Preparation for weaving

Cheese winders				
(Cone winders)	32.4	51.5	16.1	100.0	107,639
Twisting frames	22.0	48.0	30.0	100.0	461,815
Reeling machines	11.9	51.9	36.2	100.0	32,521
Warp winders	33.7	40.8	25.5	100.0	1,277
Pirn winders	42.1	36.5	21.4	100.0	44,844
Slasher sizers	20.0	27.0	53.0	100.0	426

Weaving

Power looms	5.4	31.3	63.3	100.0	49,517
Plain looms	3.6	28.5	67.9	100.0	25,967
Check looms	7.4	37.0	55.6	100.0	10,245
Dobby looms	6.0	30.9	63.1	100.0	10,581
Jacquard looms	12.3	37.8	49.9	100.0	2,724
Automatic looms	49.6	39.7	10.7	100.0	21,496
Plain looms	49.8	39.0	11.2	100.0	15,442
Check looms	80.4	15.7	3.9	100.0	775
Dobby looms	44.4	45.3	10.3	100.0	5,173
Jacquard looms	35.9	64.1	-	100.0	106

Source: ECLA (1963).

Table A12: Distribution of Machinery by Age in the Cotton Spinning and Weaving Industry of the North-East in 1959

Machinery	Less than 14 years old	14 - 29 years old	Over 29 years old	Total number of machines
	(percentage of total)			
Scutchers	42.3	2.3	55.4	130
Cards	30.2	3.8	66.0	2,433
Combers	43.9	26.0	30.1	223
Drawing frames	32.4	-	67.6	4,073
Roving frames	18.2	7.1	74.7	99,355
Spindles	39.1	7.6	53.3	642,306
Cone winders	60.4	5.0	34.6	21,283
Pirn winders	63.6	11.7	24.7	7,990
Warp winders	33.2	4.7	62.2	193
Slasher sizers	29.3	7.1	63.6	140
Power looms	3.8	5.5	90.7	20,139
Automatic looms	96.4	3.6	-	2,337

Source: SUDENE 1961, Tables IV and VI.

BIBLIOGRAPHY

Abreu, A.R.P. (1980) 'O Trabalho Industrial a Domicílio na Indústria de Confecção', Doctoral thesis, University of São Paulo

Acero, L. (1980) 'Workers' Skill in Latin America: an Approach Towards Self-reliant Development', Development and Change, Vol.11, No.3, July

Acero, L. (1983) 'Technical Change, Skills and the Labour Process in a New Industrialising Country: a Study of Brazilian Firms and Workers' Perceptions in the Textile Sector', D. Phil thesis, University of Sussex

Allen, S. (1981) 'Invisible Threads', IDS Bulletin, Vol.12, No.3, July

Alonso, J.A. (1979) 'The Domestic Clothing Workers in the Mexican Metropolis and their Relation to Dependent Capitalism', paper presented to Latin American Studies Association, Pittsburgh, April, mimeo

Arnold, E., C. Huggett, P. Senker, N. Swords-Isherwood and C. Shannon (1982) 'Microelectronics and Women's Employment in Britain', based on a report for the Department of Employment and the Manpower Services Commission, SPRU Women and Technology Studies, SPRU Occasional Paper Series No.17, Science Policy Research Unit, University of Sussex

Arruda, M., H. de Souza and C. Afonso (1975) Multinationals and Brazil - The Impact of Multinational Corporations in Contemporary Brazil, Brazilian Studies, Latin American Research Unit, Toronto

Associação Brasileira de Produtores de Fibras Artificiais e Sintéticas (1978) A Indústria Brasileira de Fibras Químicas, São Paulo

Ayata, S. (1979) 'Capitalist Subordination of Household Production: the Carpet Industry of Turkey', paper presented to Urban Poverty Study Group of the British Sociological Association/Development Studies Association, London, mimeo

Ayres, R.U., and S. Miller (1981-82) 'Robotics, CAM, and Industrial Productivity', National Productivity Review (The Journal of Productivity Management) Vol.1, No.1, Winter

Bibliography

Babbage, C. (1832) On the Economy of Machinery and Manufacture, Charles Knight, Pall Mall East, London

Barron, I. and R. Curnow (1979) The Future with Microelectronics, Frances Pinter, London

Bell, R.M. (1972) Changing Technology and Manpower Requirements in the Engineering Industry, a report on a study of the Science Policy Research Unit, Sussex University Press in association with the Engineering Industry Training Board, Brighton

Bessant, J.R., J.A.E. Bowen, K.E.Dickson and J. Marsh (1981) The Impact of Microelectronics - a Review of the Literature, Frances Pinter, London

Beynon, H. (1973) Working for Ford, Penguin, Harmondsworth

Bhalla, A.S. (ed.) (1975) Technology and Employment in Industry: a Case Study Approach, International Labour Office, Geneva

Bienefeld, M., M. Godfrey and H. Schmitz (1977) 'Trade Unions and the "New" Internationalisation of Production', Development and Change, Vol.8, No.4, October

Blauner, R. (1964) Alienation and Freedom: The Factory Worker and his Industry, University of Chicago Press, Chicago and London

Borges, R.F. (1983) 'Transferência Tecnológica e Processo de Trabalho na Siderurgia Mineira - Um Estudo de Caso, Relatório de Pesquisa, Módulo II: Processo de Trabalho', CEDEPLAR, Universidade Federal de Minas Gerais, Belo Horizonte, mimeo

Bose, A.N. (1978) Calcutta and Rural Bengal: Small Sector Symbiosis, Minerva Associates, Calcutta

Bowles, S. (1978) 'Capitalist Development and Educational Structure', World Development, Vol.6, No.6, June

Brady, T., D. Scott-Kemmis and P.J. Senker (1982) The Implications of Technical Change for Skill Requirements in the Folding Carton Industry, Report of the Science Policy Research Unit, University of Sussex, Paper and Paper Products Industry Training Board, Potters Bar, Herts.

Braverman, H. (1974) Labor and Monopoly Capital, Monthly Review Press, New York and London

Bright, J. (1958) Automation and Management, Harvard University Graduate School of Business Administration, Boston

Bright, J. (1966) 'The Relationship of Increasing Automation to Skill Requirements', in National Commission on Technology, Automation and Economic Progress, The Employment Impact of Technological Change, Appendix Vol.II, Technology and the American Economy, U.S.Government Printing Office, Washington

Brighton Labour Process Group (1977) 'The Capitalist Labour Process', Capital and Class 1, Spring

Bruland, T. (1979) 'Industrial Conflict and Technical Innovation in the Textile Sector During British Industrialisation', M.A dissertation, University of Sussex

Bruland, T. (1982) 'Industrial Conflict as a Source of Innovation: Three Cases', Economy and Society, Vol.11, No.2, May

Buchanan, D.A. and D.Boddy (1983) 'Advanced Technology and the Quality of Working Life: the Effects of Computerised Controls on Biscuit Making Operators', Journal of Occupational Psychology 56

Business Week (1981) 'The New Industrial Relations', 11 May; and 'The Speedup in Automation', 31 August

Calsing, E.F. (1978) 'A Política Salarial no Brasil, Um Estudo do Salário Mínimo', Masters thesis, University Research Institute of Rio de Janeiro (IUPERJ)

Capelin Associados do Brasil (1977) 'Diagnóstico setorial da indústria de confecções', Pesquisa patrocinada pelo BNB, BNDE e SUDENE, São Paulo, mimeo

Catling, H. (1970) The Spinning Mule, David and Charles, Newton Abbot

Caulliraux, H.M. (1981) 'Estudo da Organização do Trabalho na Indústria do Vestuário', Masters thesis, Federal University of Rio de Janeiro (COPPE/UFRJ)

Centro de Tecnologia da Indústria Química e Têxtil (CETIQT) (1980) 'Efeitos dos Avanços Tecnológicos sobre o Emprego na Indústria Têxtil', SENAI, Rio de Janeiro, mimeo

Colclough, C. (1982) 'The Impact of Primary Schooling on Economic Development: a Review of the Evidence', World Development, Vol.10, No.3, March

241

Bibliography

Cooley, M. (1980) <u>Architect or Bee? The Human/Technology</u>
<u>Relationship</u>, Hand and Brain, Langley Technical Services,
Slough

Cooley, M. (1981) 'The Taylorisation of Intellectual Work', in
L. Levidow and B. Young (eds.), <u>Science, Technology and</u>
<u>the Labour Process</u>, Marxist Studies Vol.1, CSE Books,
London

Cooper, C. (1980a) 'Policy Interventions for Technological
Innovation in Developing Countries', <u>World Bank Staff</u>
<u>Working Paper</u> No. 441, Washington DC

Cooper, C. (1980b) 'Some Mistakes about Microprocessors'
(review of C. Jenkins and B. Sherman, 1979, op. cit.)
Science Policy Research Unit, University of Sussex, mimeo

Coriat, B. (1981) 'Transfert de Techniques, Division du Travail
et Politique de Main-d'oeuvre: une Etude de Cas dans
l'Industrie Brésilienne', <u>Critiques de l'Economie</u>
<u>Politique</u>, No.14, Ed. Maspero, Paris, Janvier-Mars

Cronberg, T. and I.L. Sangregorio (1981) 'More of the Same:
The Impact of Information Technology on Domestic Life in
Japan', <u>Development Dialogue 2.</u>

CSE Micro-electronics Group (1980) <u>Capitalist Technology and</u>
<u>the Working Class</u>, CSE Books, London

Davis, L.E. (1971a) 'The Coming Crisis for Production
Management: Technology and Organization', <u>International</u>
<u>Journal of Production Research</u>, Vol.9, No.4, reprinted in
Davis and Taylor (eds.) 1972, op. cit.

Davis, L.E. (1971b) 'Job Satisfaction Research: the
Post-industrial View', <u>Industrial Relations</u>, Vol.10,
reprinted in Davis and Taylor (eds.) 1972, op. cit.

Davis, L.E. and J.C. Taylor (eds.) (1972) <u>Design of Jobs</u>,
Penguin, Harmondsworth

Dobb, M. (1946) <u>Studies in the Development of Capitalism</u>,
Routledge and Kegan Paul, London and Henley

Doeringer, P. and M. Piore (1971) <u>Internal Labor Markets and</u>
<u>Manpower Analysis</u>, D.C.Heath, Lexington Books, Lexington,
Mass.

Dore, R. (1974) 'Late Development or Something Else? Industrial
Relations in Britain, Japan, Mexico, Sri Lanka, Senegal',
<u>IDS Discussion Paper</u> 61, University of Sussex, August

Dore, R. (1975) 'Some Reflections on the Late Development Hypothesis', IDS Bulletin, Vol.6, No.3, February

Dore, R. (1976) The Diploma Disease: Education, Qualification and Development, Allen and Unwin, London

Doring, M. and R. Salling (1971), 'A Case for Wage Incentives in the N.C. Age', Manufacturing, Engineering and Management, Vol.66, No.6

Duncan, M. (1981) 'Microelectronics: Five Areas of Subordination', in L. Levidow and B. Young (eds.) Science, Technology and the Labour Process, Marxist Studies, Vol.1, CSE Books, London

Economic Commission for Latin America (ECLA) (1963) The Textile Industry in Latin America, II Brazil, United Nations, New York

Economic Commission for Latin America (ECLA) (1966) Choice of Technologies in the Latin American Textile Industry, E.CN.12/746, United Nations, New York

Edwards, R. (1979) Contested Terrain - The Transformation of the Work Place in the Twentieth Century, Basic Books, New York

Elger, T. (1979) 'Valorisation and "Deskilling": a Critique of Braverman', Capital and Class, 7

Elson, D. and R. Pearson (1981) 'Nimble Fingers make Cheap Workers: an Analysis of Women's Employment in Third World Manufacturing', Feminist Review, 7

Ely, S.M.R. (1978) A Rotatividade da Mão-de-Obra na Indústria Metal-Mecânica de Porto Alegre - Implicações do Sistema do F.G.T.S., Programa de Pos-Graduação em Administração, Universidade Federal do Rio Grande do Sul, Porto Alegre

Erber, F., J.R. Tauile, L. Acero, M.V.J. Pena, P.V. da Cunha and V.M.C. Pereira (1981) 'O Estudo do Processo de Trabalho: Notas para Discussão', Literatura Econômica, Vol.3, No.2, IPEA/INPES, Rio de Janeiro

Ernst, D. (1982) Restructuring World Industry in a Period of Crisis - the Role of Innovation: an Analysis of Recent Developments in the Semi-conductor Industry, Global and Conceptual Studies Branch, Division of Industrial Studies, UNIDO, Vienna

Fei, J. and G. Ranis (1964) Development of the Labor Surplus Economy, Irwin, Homewood, Illinois

Fleury, A.C.C. (1978) 'Organização do Trabalho Industrial: Um Confronto entre Teoria e Realidade', Doctoral thesis, Polytechnic School, University of São Paulo

Ford, H. (1922) My Life and Work, Heinemann, London

Forslin, J. et al. (eds.) (1981) Automation and Industrial Workers, a Fifteen Nation Study, Vol. 1, Parts 1 and 2, European Coordination Centre for Research and Documentation in Social Sciences, Pergamon Press, Oxford

Fortune, (1981) 'Working Smarter', 15 June

Fransman, M. and K. King (eds.) (1984) Technological Capability in the Third World, Macmillan, London

Freeman, C., J.A. Clark and L. Soete (1982) Unemployment and Technical Innovation - a Study of Long Waves in Economic Development, Frances Pinter, London

Friedman, A. (1977), Industry and Labour: Class Struggle at Work and Monopoly Capitalism, Macmillan, London

Friedrichs, G. (1982) 'Microelectronics and Macroeconomics', in G. Friedrichs and A. Schaff (eds.) Microelectronics and Society - For Better or for Worse, A Report to the Club of Rome, Pergamon Press, Oxford and New York

Fröbel, F., J. Heinrichs, O. Kreye (1977) Die Neue Internationale Arbeitsteilung, Rowohlt, Reinbek bei Hamburg

Gerstenberger, F. (1975) 'Produktion und Qualifikation: Technisch-organisatorischer Wandel und die Veränderung der Qualifikationsanforderungen', Leviathan, June

Goddard, V. (1981) 'The Leather Trade in the Bassi of Naples', IDS Bulletin, Vol.12, No.3, July

Goldthorpe, J., D. Lockwood, F. Bechhofer and J. Platt (1969) The Affluent Worker in the Class Structure, Cambridge University Press, Cambridge

Goodman, D.E. and R. Cavalcanti de Albuquerque (1974) Incentivos à Industrialização e Desenvolvimento do Nordeste, Relatório de Pesquisa 20, IPEA/INPES, Rio de Janeiro

Harriss, J. (1982) 'Studies of Small-Scale Enterprise and Urban Labour in South India', Occasional Paper No.19, School of Development Studies, University of East Anglia, March

Harvey, D. (1982) The Limits to Capital, Basil Blackwell, Oxford

Heertje, A. (1973) Economics and Technical Change, Weidenfeld and Nicolson, London

Herzberg, F. (1966) Work and the Nature of Man, Harcourt, Brace and Jovanovich, London

Hines, C. and G. Searle (1979) Automatic Unemployment, Earth Resources Research, London

Hoffman, K. (1982) 'Microelectronics and Industry in the Third World: Policy Issues and Research Priorities', report prepared for the International Development Research Council, Canada, Science Policy Research Unit, University of Sussex, May, mimeo

Hoffman, K. (ed.) (1984) 'Microelectronics, International Competition and Industrial Strategies', Special Issue of World Development, forthcoming

Hoffman, K. and H. Rush (1980) 'Microelectronics, Industry and the Third World', Futures, Vol.12, No.4, August

Hoffman, K. and H. Rush (1982) 'Microelectronics and the Garment Industry: not yet a Perfect Fit', IDS Bulletin, Vol.13, No.2, March

Hope, E., M. Kennedy and A. de Winter (1976) 'Homeworkers in North London', in D. L. Barker and S. Allen, Dependence and Exploitation in Work and Marriage, Longman, London and New York

Hugget, C. (1980) 'Welding', in N. Swords-Isherwood and P. Senker (eds.) op. cit.

Humphrey, J. (1982) Capitalist Control and Workers' Struggle in the Brazilian Auto Industry, Princeton University Press, Princeton

Huws, U. (1984) The New Homeworkers: New Technology and the Changing Location of White Collar Work, Low Pay Unit, London

Bibliography

Instituto de Planejamento Econômico e Social (IPEA) Projeto de Planejamento de Recursos Humanos das Nações Unidas (PNUD) (1979) 'Proposta de Pesquisa sobre Tecnologia e Emprego na Indústria Têxtil', Brasília, mimeo

International Labour Office (1972) Employment, Incomes and Equality - A Strategy for Increasing Productive Employment in Kenya, ILO, Geneva

International Labour Office (1976) Wages and Working Conditions in Multinational Enterprises, ILO, Geneva

International Labour Office (1981a) Training and Retraining Needs in the Printing and Allied Trades (Report II) and Technological Developments and their Implications for Employment in the Printing and Allied Trades, with Particular Reference to Developing Countries (Report III), Second Tripartite Technical Meeting for the Printing and Allied Trades, ILO, Geneva

International Labour Office (1981b) Multinationals' Training Practices and Development, ILO, Geneva

Jacobsson, S. (1982) 'Electronics and the Technology Gap - the Case of Numerically Controlled Machine Tools', IDS Bulletin, Vol.13, No.2, March

Jenkins, C. and B. Sherman (1979) The Collapse of Work, Eyre Methuen, London

Joekes, S.P. (1982) 'Female-led Industrialisation: Women's Jobs in Third World Manufacturing: the Case of the Moroccan Clothing Industry' Research Report, Institute of Development Studies, University of Sussex

Kaplinsky, R. (1980) 'Microelectronics and the Third World', Radical Science Journal, No.10

Kaplinsky, R. (ed.) (1982) 'Comparative Advantage in an Automating World', IDS Bulletin, Vol.13, No.2, March

Kaplinsky, R. (1984) Automation - The Technology and Society, Longman, Harlow

Kraft, P. (1979) 'The Industrialisation of Computer Programming: from Programming to "Software Production"', in A. Zimbalist (ed.), op.cit.

Lenin, V.I. (1898) 'The Handicraft Census of 1894-95 in Perm Gubernia and General Problems of "Handicraft" Industry' (republished in) Collected Works Volume 2, Lawrence and Wishart, London (1977)

Lenin, V.I. (1899) The Development of Capitalism in Russia (republished) Collected Works Volume 3, Lawrence and Wishart, London (1977)

Leppan, E.D. (1983) 'A Literature Survey and Partially Annotated Bibliography on the Impact of Microelectronics on the "Third World", paper prepared for Meeting on the Impact of Microelectronics, Mexico City. Jointly sponsored by the Ministry of Industry, Government of Mexico, and the International Development Research Centre, Ottawa, December, mimeo

Lewis, A. (1954) 'Economic development with Unlimited Supplies of Labour', The Manchester School, reprinted in A. N. Agarwala and S. P. Singh (eds.) The Economics of Underdevelopment, Oxford University Press, New York (1963)

Mackintosh, M. (1975a) 'The Late Development Hypothesis versus the Evidence from Senegal', IDS Bulletin, Vol.6, No.3, February

Mackintosh, M. (1975b) 'Industrial Relations in the Republic of Senegal', IDS Discussion Paper No.81, University of Sussex, September

Mars, Z. (ed.) (1982) 'Women and Development', Development Research Digest, No.7, Institute of Development Studies, University of Sussex

Marshall, A. (1920) Principles of Economics, Macmillan, London,

Marstrand, P. (ed.) (1984) New Technology and the Future of Work and Skills, Frances Pinter, London

Marx, K. (1867) Capital Volume 1 (republished) Lawrence and Wishart, London 1970

Marx, K. (1886) Capital Volume 3 (republished) Lawrence and Wishart, London 1971

Marx, K. (1933) Resultate des unmittelbaren Produktionsprozesses (republished) Verlag Neue Kritik, Frankfurt, 1969

Mayo, E. (1933) The Human Problem of an Industrial Civilisation, Macmillan, London

Bibliography

McGregor, D. (1960) The Human Side of Enterprise, McGraw-Hill, New York

Meller, P. and A. Mizala (1982) 'US Multinationals and Latin American Manufacturing Employment Absorption', World Development, Vol.10, No.2

Mies, M. (1981) The Lacemakers of Narsapur: Indian Housewives in the World Market, (first published as Working Paper No.16, Rural Employment Policy Research Programme, World Employment Programme, ILO, Geneva, 1980) Zed Press, London

Moncrieff, R.W. (1970) Man-made Fibres, Heywood Books, London

Münster, A. (1980) 'Rationalisierung, Qualifikation, Verlagerung: Ein Fallbeispiel aus der Elektronik', in Starnberger Studien 4, Strukturveränderungen in der Kapitalistischen Weltwirtschaft, Suhrkamp Verlag, Frankfurt

Murray, F. (1983) 'The Decentralisation of Production – The Decline of the Mass-Collective Worker?', Capital and Class 19, Spring

National Economic Development Office (NEDO) (1971) Technology and the Garment Industry, HMSO, London

National Economic Development Office (NEDO) (1972) What the Girls Think! Summary of a Report on Employees' Attitudes and their Effect on Labour Turnover, Clothing EDC, NEDO, London

Nichols, T. and H. Beynon (1977) Living with Capitalism: Class-relations and the Modern Factory, Routledge and Kegan Paul, London

Nigam, S.B.L. and H.W. Singer (1974) 'Labour Turnover and Employment: Some Evidence from Kenya', International Labour Review, Vol.110, No.6, December

Nihei, Y. et al. (1979) 'Technology, Employment Practices and Workers - A Comparative Study of Ten Cotton Spinning Plants in Five Asian Countries', Occasional Papers and Monographs Series No. 29, Centre of Asian Studies, University of Hong Kong

Noble, D.F. (1979) 'Social Choice in Machine Design: the Case of Automatically Controlled Machine Tools', in A. Zimbalist (ed.) op. cit.

North American Congress on Latin America (1975) 'Hit and Run, US Runaway Shops on the Mexican Border', NACLA Report, Vol.IX, No.5, July-August

Northcott, J. and P. Rogers (1982) Microelectronics in Industry: What's Happening in Britain, Policy Studies Institute, London

Northcott, J. and P. Rogers (1984) Microelectronics in British Industry: the Pattern of Change, Policy Studies Institute, London

Nun J. (1969) 'Superpoblación Relativo, Ejército Industrial de Reserva y Masa Marginal', Revista Latino Americana de Sociologia 2

Oxenham, J. (ed.) (1980) 'Selection for Employment versus Education?', IDS Bulletin, Vol.11, No.2, May

Pacific Studies Centre (1978) 'Women's Place in the Integrated Circuit', Pacific Research, Vol.9, Nos.5-6

Pacific Studies Centre (1980) 'Delicate Bonds: the Global Semi-conductor Industry', Pacific Research, Vol.11, No.1

Pereira, V.M.C. (1979) O Coração da Fábrica - Estudo de Caso entre Operários Têxteis, Editora Campus, Rio de Janeiro

Politics and Society (1978) 'The Labour Process and the Working Class', Special Double Issue, Vol.8, Nos.3-4,

Quijano, A. (1974) 'The Marginal Pole of the Economy and the Marginalised Labour Force', Economy and Society, Vol.3, No.4, November

Rada, J.F. (1981) 'The Microelectronics Revolution: Implications for the Third World', Development Dialogue 2, Upsala

Rada, J.F. (1982) 'Structure and Behaviour of the Semiconductor Industry', Report prepared for the United Nations Centre on Transnational Corporations, New York

Reichmuth, M. (1978) 'Dualism in Peru: an Investigation into the Interrelationships between Lima's Informal Clothing Industry and the Formal Sector', B. Litt. thesis, University of Oxford

Rios, J.A. e Associados (no date, probably 1962) Artesanato e Desenvolvimento, O Caso Cearense, Serviço Social da Indústria/Confederação Nacional da Indústria

Bibliography

Rocha, J.B.V. (1979a) 'Manufatura de Redes-de-Dormir, Um Estudo de Caso sobre a Evolução das Relações de Produção Capitalistas no Nordeste', Masters thesis, University of Brasília

Rocha, J.B.V. (1979b) 'Setor Informal na Paraíba, A Indústria de Fabricação de Redes-de-Dormir de São Bento', Volume II of Pequenas Empresas Não Agricolas Polonordeste, PDRI - Vale do Piranhas, Núcleo de Assistência Industrial, Paraíba

Rosenberg, N. (1976) 'The Direction of Technological Change: Inducement Mechanisms and Focusing Devices', in N. Rosenberg, Perspectives of Technology, Cambridge University Press, Cambridge, first published in Economic Development and Cultural Change, October 1969

Rosenbrock, H.H. (1984) 'Designing Automated Systems: Need Skills be Lost?', in P.Marstrand (ed.) op. cit.

Rothwell, R. (1976a) 'Innovation in Textile Machinery: Some Significant Factors in Success and Failure', Occasional Paper Series No. 2, Science Policy Research Unit, University of Sussex, June

Rothwell, R. (1976b) 'Picanol Weefautomaten: a Case Study of a Successful Textile Machinery Builder', Textile Institute and Industry, March

Rothwell, R. and W. Zegveld (1979) Technical Change and Employment, Frances Pinter, London

Sanchez Padron, M. (1975) 'Recruitment and Promotion in Some Mexican Firms', IDS Bulletin, Vol.6, No.3, February

Sandmeyer, U. (1976) Wahl der Industriellen Technologie in Entwicklungsländern - Theoretische Grundlagen und Darstellung am Beispiel des Nordostens Brasiliens, Institut für Lateinamerikaforschung und Entwicklungszusammenarbeit an der Hochschule St. Gallen, Band 10, Verlag Ruegger, Diessenhofen

Santos, M. (1975) L'espace Partagé, les Deux Circuits de l'Economie Urbaine des Pays Sous-Developpés, Editions Genin, Paris

Schmitz, H. (1978) 'Emprego Formal e Informal no Setor de Confecções de Roupas no Brasil 1950-1970', UNDP/ILO Human Resources Planning Project, Brasília, mimeo

Schmitz, H. (1979a) 'Divergências nas Estatísticas Sobre Emprego na Indústria Têxtil do Nordeste', UNDP/ILO Human Resources Planning Project, Brasília, mimeo

Schmitz, H. (1979b) 'Factory and Domestic Employment in Brazil: a Study of the Hammock Industry and its Implications for Employment Theory and Policy',IDS Discussion Paper No.146, University of Sussex

Schmitz, H. (1982) Manufacturing in the Backyard - Case Studies on Accumulation and Employment in Small-scale Brazilian Industry, Frances Pinter, London

Schmukler, B. (1977) 'Relaciones Actuales de Producción en Industrias Tradicionales Argentinas, Evolución de las Relaciones no Capitalistas', Centro de Estudios de Estado y Sociedad (CEDES), Estudios Sociales No.6, Buenos Aires

Senker, P. (1980) 'Assembly', in N. Swords-Isherwood and P. Senker (eds.) op. cit.

Senker, P., N. Swords-Isherwood and E. Arnold (1980) 'Conclusions: Skill Requirements Arising from Microelectronics', in N. Swords-Isherwood and P. Senker (eds.) op. cit.

Senker, P., N. Swords-Isherwood, T. Brady and C. Hugget (1981) Maintenance Skills in the Engineering Industry: The Influence of Technological Change, Engineering Industry Training Board, Watford

Sethuraman, S.V. (1976) 'The Urban Informal Sector: Concept, Measurement and Policy', International Labour Review, Vol.114, No.1, July-August

Shaiken, H. (1980) 'Computer Technology and the Relations of Power in the Workplace', Discussion Paper IIVG/dp/80-217, International Institute for Comparative Research, Berlin, October

Shinohara, M. (1968) 'A Survey of the Japanese Literature on Small Industry' in B.F. Hoselitz, The Role of Small Industry in the Process of Economic Growth, Mouton, The Hague and Paris

Sit, V.F.S., S.L. Wong and T.S. Kiang (1979) 'Small Scale Industry in a Laissez-Faire Economy, a Hong Kong Case Study', Occasional Papers and Monographs 30, Centre of Asian Studies, University of Hong Kong

Smith, A. (1776) <u>The Wealth of Nations</u> Books 1-3, (republished) Penguin, Harmondsworth (1976)

Soete, L. and C. Freeman (1983) 'New Technologies, Investment and Employment Growth', paper prepared for Intergovernmental Conference on Employment in the Context of Structural Change, Directorate for Social Affairs, Manpower and Education, OECD, Paris

Sorge, A., G. Hartmann, M. Warner and I. Nicholas (1983) <u>Microelectronics and Manpower in Manufacturing</u>, Gower, Aldershot

Spindel, C.R. (1981) 'A Mulher na Indústria do Vestuário', Fundação Carlos Chagas, São Paulo, mimeo

Stewart, F. (1978) <u>Technology and Underdevelopment</u>, Macmillan, London

Stewart, M. (1963) <u>Why Train? A Summary of a Report on Training in the Clothing Industry</u> (an investigation carried out by E. Belbin and R. Sergeant) Twentieth Century Press, London

Stone, K. (1975) 'The Origins of Job Structures in the Steel Industry', in R.C. Edwards, M. Reich and D. Gordon (eds.) <u>Labor Market Segmentation</u>, D.C. Heath, Lexington-Toronto-London

Superintendência do Desenvolvimento Econômico do Nordeste (SUDENE) (1961) 'Sumário do Programa de Reequipamento da Indústria Têxtil', Recife, mimeo

Superintendência do Desenvolvimento Econômico do Nordeste (SUDENE) (1971) <u>Pesquisa sobre a Indústria Têxtil do Nordeste</u>, SUDENE, Recife

Swords-Isherwood, N. and P. Senker (eds.) (1980) <u>Microelectronics and the Engineering Industry - The Need for Skills</u>, Frances Pinter, London

Tauile, J.R. (1982) 'A Difusão de Maquinas Ferramenta com Controle Numérico no Brasil', paper presented to the Seminario Internacional sobre Inovação e Desenvolvimento no Setor Industrial, UNICAMP, Campinas, August, mimeo

Tauile, J. R. (1983) 'Numerically Controlled Machine Tools in Brazil: Effects on Labour and the Organisation of Production', Institute of Industrial Economics, Federal University of Rio de Janeiro, mimeo

Tavares de Araujo Jr., J., and V.M.C. Pereira (1976) 'Teares Sem Lançadeira na Indústria Têxtil', in Difusão de Inovações na Indústria Brasileria: Três Estudos de Caso, Monografia 24, IPEA/INPES, Rio de Janeiro

Taylor, F.W. (1903) Shop Management, New York, reprinted in F.W. Taylor, Scientific Management, Harper and Brothers, New York (1947)

Taylor, F.W. (1911) The Principles of Scientific Management, New York, reprinted in F.W. Taylor, Scientific Management, Harper and Brothers, New York (1947)

Tigre, P. (1983) Technology and Competition in the Brazilian Computer Industry, Frances Pinter, London

Tokman, V. (1978) 'An Exploration into the Nature of Informal-formal Sector Relationships', World Development, Vol.6, Nos.9 and 10

Touraine, A. (1962) 'An Historical Theory of the Evolution of Industrial Skills', in C.R. Walker (ed.), Modern Technology and Civilization, McGraw Hill, reprinted in Davis and Taylor (eds.) 1972, op.cit.

United Nations Industrial Development Organisation (UNIDO) (1973) 'Reorientation of the Traditional Textile Industry in Brazil', Ref. 123.3/G 446/04/8, UNIDO Project SIS 70/900, July

Ure, A. (1835) The Philosophy of Manufactures, first edition London, reprinted by Frank Cass, London (1967)

Vaitsos, C.V. (1974) Intercountry Income Distribution and Transnational Enterprises, Oxford University Press, Oxford

Vargas, N. (1979) 'Organização do Trabalho e Capital - Um Estudo da Construção Habitacional', Masters thesis, Federal University of Rio de Janeiro (COPPE)

Versiani, F.R. (1971) 'Technical Change, Equipment Replacement and Labor Absorption: The Case of the Brazilian Textile Industry', Ph.D. thesis, Vanderbilt University, Nashville

Visão (1977) Quem é Quem na Economia Brasileira, Editora Visão, São Paulo

Walker, C.R. and R.H. Guest (1952) The Man on the Assembly Line, Harvard University Press, Cambridge, Mass.

Bibliography

Watanabe, S. (1971) 'Subcontracting, Industrialization and Employment Creation', International Labour Review, Vol.104, Nos. 1-2, July-August

Watanabe, S. (1978) 'Technological Linkages Between Formal and Informal Sectors of Manufacturing Industry', Technology and Employment Programme, WEP 2-22, Working Paper 34, ILO Geneva, March

Watanabe, S. (1983) 'Market Structure, Industrial Organisation and Technological Development: the Case of the Japanese Electronics Based NC-Machine Tool Industry', Working Paper 111, WEP 2-22, ILO, Geneva, February

Whiston, T., P. Senker and P. Macdonald (1980) An Annotated Bibliography on the Relationship Between Technological Change and Educational Development, International Institute for Educational Planning, UNESCO, Paris

White, L.J. (1978) 'The Evidence on Appropriate Factor Proportions for Manufacturing in Less Developed Countries: a Survey', Economic Development and Cultural Change, Vol.27, No.1, October

Wilkinson, B. (1983) The Shopfloor Politics of New Technology, Heinemann, London

Williams, B. (1983) 'Micro-processors and Employment', SSRC Newsletter 49, London, June

Willis, R.M. (1983) 'Software Policies for the Developing World', a report for the International Development Research Centre, Ottawa, September, mimeo

Woodword, J. (1965) Industrial Organization - Theory and Practice, Oxford University Press

Zimbalist, A. (ed.) (1979) Case Studies on the Labour Process, Monthly Review Press, New York and London